"These nineteenth- and early-twentieth-century biographies, now republished by Chelsea House, reveal an unsuspected significance. Not only are a good many of them substantively valuable (and by no means entirely superseded), but they also evoke a sense of the period, an intimacy with the attitudes and assumptions of their times."

—Professor Daniel Aaron

William Cullen Bryant

Other titles in this Chelsea House series:

WILLIAM CULLEN BRYANT

JOHN BIGELOW

INTRODUCTION BY
JOHN HOLLANDER

American Men and Women of Letters Series

GENERAL EDITOR
PROFESSOR DANIEL AARON
HARVARD UNIVERSITY

CHELSEA HOUSE
NEW YORK, LONDON
1980

Cover design by Zimmerman Foyster Design

Library of Congress Cataloging in Publication Data

Bigelow, John, 1817-1911.
   William Cullen Bryant.

   (American men and women of letters)
   Reprint of the 1890 ed. published by Houghton,
Mifflin, Boston, issued in series: American men
of letters.
   1. Bryant, William Cullen, 1794-1878.
2. Poets, American--19th century--Biography.
I. Title.   II. Series.   III. Series: American
men of letters.
PS1181.B5 1980   811'.3 [B]   80-19850
ISBN 0-87754-160-4   92
                        BRY

Chelsea House Publishers
Harold Steinberg, Chairman & Publisher
Andrew E. Norman, President
Susan Lusk, Vice President
A Division of Chelsea House Educational Communications, Inc.
70 West 40 Street, New York 10018

CONTENTS

General Introduction

THE VISITABLE PAST
Daniel Aaron

THE TWENTY-FIVE BIOGRAPHIES of American worthies reissued in this Chelsea House series restore an all but forgotten chapter in the annals of American literary culture. Some of the authors of these volumes—journalists, scholars, writers, professional men—would be considered amateurs by today's standards, but they enjoyed certain advantages not open to their modern counterparts. In some cases they were blood relations or old friends of the men and women they wrote about, or at least near enough to them in time to catch the contemporary essence often missing in the more carefully researched and authoritative later studies of the same figures. Their leisurely, impressionistic accounts—sometimes as interesting for what is omitted as for what is emphasized—reveal a good deal about late Victorian assumptions, cultural and social, and about the vicissitudes of literary reputation.

Each volume in the series is introduced by a recognized scholar who was encouraged to write an idiosyncratic appraisal of the biographer and his work. The introductions vary in emphasis and point of view, for the biographies are not of equal quality, nor are the writers memorialized equally appealing. Yet a kind of consensus is discernible in these random assessments: surprise at the insights still to be found in ostensibly unscientific and old-fashioned works; in some instances admiration for the solidity and liveliness of the biographer's prose and quality of mind; respect for the pioneer historians among them who made excellent use of the limited material at their disposal.

The volumes in this American Men and Women of Letters series contain none of the startling "private" and "personal" episodes modern readers have come to expect in biography, but they illuminate what Henry James called the "visitable past." As such, they are of particular value to all students of American cultural and intellectual history.

Cambridge, Massachusetts
Spring, 1980

INTRODUCTION
TO THE
CHELSEA HOUSE EDITION

John Hollander

The figures of William Cullen Bryant and Thomas Cole stand over a gorge in the Catskills, the "Kindred Spirits" of their friend Asher B. Durand's painting of that name. Cole is expounding, his long painter's brush at rest against his palette, pointing out for the viewer of the painting the rock formation across the gorge—the kind, indeed, that it was Cole's delight to paint. Bryant stands deep in meditation. But in a deeper sense, poet, painter and the scene that surrounds them are all engaged in another sort of mutual interpretation: the spirits of language and art both half-perceive and half-create the vision of the natural sublime before them. They also present us with a parable of American romanticism.

Bryant is our first poet of nature, recapitulating even in the earliest years of his work the movement from the passive speculations of a

poetic derived from the later eighteenth-century
poets of sensibility, to a meditative mode in
which the mind is more actively engaged in intercourse with the natural emblems and figures
of itself. Though lacking the mighty poetic intellect and cataclysmic originating power of an
Emerson, Bryant nonetheless preceded him in
transplanting imaginative seeds that would not
fall on barren ground. "He's a Cowper condensed, with no craziness bitten, / And the advantage that Wordsworth before him had written," jingled James Russell Lowell: and yet to
have responded to a reading of Wordsworth—as
the testimony of the successive drafts of
"Thanatopsis" assures us he did—was as crucial
for its moment in the history of American
poetry as the responses of Wyatt, and particularly Surrey, to Petrarch were for the literature
of England, or as Hawthorne's to Spenser
would be later on.

Thomas Cole's presence in Durand's painting
is also of significance for the American imagination. Cole had encountered the romantic tab-
leaux of John Martin (and, after going abroad,
German romantic painting as well), but produced a major oeuvre of his own kind of myth-
ological landscape. In groups of paintings like
The Voyage of Life, Past and Present and *The
Course of Empire* he had imprinted upon Eu-

ropean conventions of landscape painting new
versions of the picturesque and the sublime. He
gave meaning to American scenery by means of
a poetic narrative of cyclic fable and moral
journey. But it was Cole's romantic landscapes
that allowed followers like Durand, Cropsey,
Kensett—and even Albert Bierstadt and Frederick Church later on—to naturalize the narrative
scenes and patterns, and reinvest with meta-
phoric significance the structures of uninhabit-
ed natural scene. In this way, Cole not only
kept—as Bryant urged him to do in a sonnet
written for the painter's departure on a voyage
to Europe—"that wilder [i.e., American] image
bright" but, indeed, first illuminated it.

Bryant's own vision of nature is more immediately like that of the later Hudson River
School painters than like Cole's. And yet the
Spenserian stanzas of his Harvard Phi Beta
Kappa poem of 1821, "The Ages," suggest the
mode of poetic history revealed in Cole's *The
Course of Empire* sequence. Stanzas 28-29 contemplate a bright bay full of the sails of commercial shipping, observing that there, once,
"The savage urged his skiff like wild bird on
the wing." The next two stanzas move through
ironies going far beyond any eighteenth-century
vision of the nobility of savagery, even as they
avoid the entrepreneurial self-satisfaction of

manifest destiny, erasing historical knowledge
and perhaps sentimentalizing relics:

> There stood the Indian hamlet, there the lake
> Spread its blue sheet that flashed with many an oar,
> Where the brown otter plunged him from the brake,
> And the deer drank; as the light gale flew o'er,
> The twinkling maize-field rustled on the shore;
> And while that spot, so wild, so lone, so fair,
> A look of glad and guiltless beauty wore,
> And peace was on the earth and in the air,
> The warrior lit the pile, and bound his captive there.
>
> Not unavenged—the foeman from the wood
> Beheld the deed, and when midnight shade
> Was stillest, gorged his battle-axe with blood;
> All died—the wailing babe—the shrinking maid—
> And in the flood of fire that scaled the glade,
> The roofs went down; but deep the silence grew,
> When on the dewy woods the day-beam played;
> No more the cabin-smokes rose wreathed and blue,
> And ever, by their lake, lay moored the bark canoe.

All of "The Ages" is not up to this; and indeed, the difference is generally great between
Bryant's best poetry and the indifferent verse
of his later years. While a student at Dartmouth,
reading law in Massachusetts and then practic-
ing it with limited success and satisfaction, he
conceived his best work. After he moved to
New York City in 1825 to function there as a
Man of Letters, and particularly after he became editor of the important *New York Post* in
1829, Bryant's power as a true poet fell off. We

can be more grateful for his 1844 editorial pro-
posing that "a tract of beautiful woodland" at
that time "on the road to Harlem" be set aside
for a public park "to match Regent's Park or
the Prater" (the eventual Central Park) than
we can for most of what he wrote in verse after
the 1830s (an exception is "A Rain-Dream" of
1854). Of a severely pruned list of his truly
fine poems, the first five were published in a
collection by 1821. I should say that the following represent the oeuvre that, the remarkable felicities of Freneau and the passionate
purity of Bradstreet aside, makes Bryant our
first true poet: "Thanatopsis"; "To a Waterfowl"; "Inscription for the Entrance to a
Wood"; "Green River"; "The Ages"; "A Winter
Piece"; the wonderful "Summer Wind"; "Autumn Woods"; "A Forest Hymn"; "June"; "To
the Fringed Gentian"; the sonnet to Cole; "A
Scene on the Banks of the Hudson"; "The Con-
jugation of Venus and Jupiter"; "The Prairies";
"Earth"; "The Snow-Shower"; and "A Rain-
Dream."

The blank-verse translation of Homer to
which Bryant devoted many of his later mornings is somewhat flat, possessing some of the
more dubious virtues of "readability," but its
projection evidences traces of its author's
somewhat surprising lifelong admiration of

Pope (even if its execution owes more to Cowper). No wit appears in Bryant's verse (save for one juvenile effort), although his generally libertarian—but by no means prematurely abolitionist—*Post* editorials can be quite sharp at times. Bryant was ideologically unadventurous and intellectually unenterprising. Lowell's *Fable for Critics* depicts him in his early fifties, shortly before the time of Durand's painting, as being cold and somewhat distant ("There's no doubt that he stands in complete iceolation"). But it never seems to have been the life of the mind to which Bryant had retreated. Indeed, the inability to build further on his earlier vision, with that power of poetic intellect which interprets the very grounds on which previous intuitions have been received, is what finally limits him as an American poet, when compared with the giants of his century—Emerson, Whitman, Dickinson.

But as a craftsman he explored a host of forms and took poetic structure very seriously, writing as early as 1819 an essay on trisyllabic feet in iambic verse, partly, perhaps, to justify his own neo-accentual leanings, which produced the lovely "Green River":

> "As if the bright fringe of herbs on its brink
> Had given their stain to the waves they drink;
> And they, whose meadows it murmurs through,
> Have named the stream from its own fair hue."

(The stream sounds like a tributary to Robert Frost's "West-Running Brook.") His invention of the quatrain form of "To a Waterfowl"—a poem Matthew Arnold and Hartley Coleridge once agreed was the best short poem in English —broke the tetrameter quatrain into a new species of lyric strophe that Horace never knew, but that seemed somehow always to have existed. And yet it is no mere ingenuity of verse, but a creation of poetry. The opening and closing lines, contrasting with the middle lines in length as well as in the way by which they coincide or not with syntactic units, constantly remind us of the poem's set tropes of flight, paths, distance and ultimately significant journeying. The opening question—

> Whither, midst falling dew,
> While glow the heavens with the last steps of day
> Far, through their rosy depths, dost thou pursue
> Thy solitary way?

—and the closing lesson read from the emblem of contemplating the bird's flight—

> He who, from zone to zone,
> Guides through the boundless sky thy certain flight,
> In the long way that I must tread alone
> Will lead my steps aright.

interpret the form of their utterance even as they give meaning to the object of the invocation.* Bryant never wrote better than he did in early poems like this one, and we might apply to him—*mutatis mutandis* to himself and his life of letters and journalism in New York—the rest of the caveat he urged on Cole's imagination, not to become too Europeanized as he encountered

> everywhere the race of men.
> Paths, homes, graves, ruins, from the lowest glen
> To where life shrinks from the fierce Alpine air.
> Gaze on them, till the tears shall dim thy sight,
> But keep that earlier, wilder image bright.

Bryant's biographer, friend and longtime colleague John Bigelow (1817-1911) was also a lawyer. In 1848 he became joint owner and co-editor with Bryant of the *New York Post*, serving until 1861, when he did diplomatic service in France. Bigelow edited Benjamin Franklin's *Autobiography* and wrote his own biography of Franklin in 1868, and one of Samuel J. Tilden (he became the latter's Secretary of State for New York) in 1895. His life of Bryant is particularly valuable for the light it casts on the poet's work as journalist and editor during a turbulent period in the nation's social and

---

*Whitman understood this when he revised both the form and the poetics of emblem in "Eidolons."

political—and New York's cultural—history.
Bigelow is, moreover, more sophisticated in his
literary observations than might be expected,
realizing as he does the importance of Bryant's
reading of Cowper, Thomson and, particularly,
Wordsworth—the poets who, Bryant himself
said, "fostered this taste in me." Like many a
nineteenth-century man of letters, Bigelow relies on his memory and misquotes occasionally,
and not unamusingly: thus "I cannot forget
with such tender devotion," the first line of a
strangely self-revelatory set of verses in the
meter of Moore, and the matter of Wordsworth,
becomes "fervid devotion" for Bigelow, who
thus imports his commentary on the poem's
second line into his quotation. He also reveals,
in his use of the phrase "the visible churches"
in a discussion of Bryant's rather broad piety,
his own Swedenborgian background.

Given that Bigelow cannot distinguish between the true romantic power of Bryant's
early poems and the respectable, high, versified
diction of most of what he wrote in New York,
his judgment of the poet's work is no worse
than all of their contemporaries'. He quotes
copiously from the prose writings, although it
is unfortunate that he ignores the oration of
Thomas Cole—indeed he seems totally unaware

of, or uninterested in, the friendship of Cole, Asher B. Durand and Bryant at an important moment in the relations between poetry and painting in America—while drawing liberally and with ill-considered approval from Bryant's even more ill-considered attack on Darwin. But all in all, this is a lively and refreshing work.

New Haven, Connecticut
June, 1980

AUTHOR'S PREFACE
TO THE
1890 EDITION

—◆—

IF there is any excuse for this publication, it must be found in the fact that I was associated with Mr. Bryant for many years in the management of "The Evening Post" newspaper, my connection with it commencing at about the same period of life as his; in the fact that we there contracted personal relations which he was pleased late in life to crown by naming me one of the executors of his will; and finally in the hope I entertain that a compendious and comparatively inexpensive sketch of his instructive career may reach a class, not inconsiderable in numbers, who have neither the leisure nor opportunities for perusing the elaborate and scholarly biography by Mr. Godwin.

Whatever may be the imperfections of this work, — and no one is likely to be more sensible of them than I am, — I permit myself to indulge the hope that in quarters where the nature and importance of Bryant's life-work are little known or imperfectly appreciated, it may assist to awaken a curiosity which will not be satisfied until the name of Bryant has become a household word, and his example the very lowest standard of public and private morals in any American family.

THE SQUIRRELS, *February* 3, 1890.

WILLIAM CULLEN BRYANT.

CHAPTER I.

ANCESTRY.

EARLY in the summer of 1817, a package of manuscript poems was left at the office of the "North American Review"[1] without their author's name or any intimation of their real parentage. In due time they found their way into the hands of Mr. William Phillips, one of the editors of the "Review," to whom they were addressed.

No sooner had he finished their perusal — such is the tradition — than he seized his hat and set out in hot haste for Cambridge, to submit them to his editorial colleagues, Richard H. Dana and Edward T. Channing, who with Mr. Phillips constituted the Editorial Trinity to whom the management of the "Review" was then confided.

They listened while the manuscript was read, and what little was known of its history was recapitulated to them. "Ah, Phillips," said Dana at last, his face breaking the while into a skeptical

[1] This *Review* was published in Boston, and at this time was but two years old.

smile, " you have been imposed upon. No one on this side of the Atlantic is capable of writing such verse." Mr. Dana's view seemed to have so many presumptions in its favor that he set out at once to Boston to investigate the subject, with the aid of such clues as the package itself afforded. The final result of his inquiries was that Phillips, though under an erroneous impression as to the author, had not been imposed upon as to its American genesis.

The verses which had produced such a fluttering among the presiding justices of our highest literary tribunal in those days were not an imported article, still less the work of any American literary notability of the period, but of a country lad of only seventeen years, residing at Cummington, in the western part of Massachusetts, who had never been out of his native county in his life. One of the poems was entitled "Thanatopsis." It appeared in the September number of the "North American Review" for 1817, and proved to be not only the finest poem which had yet been produced on this continent, but one of the most remarkable poems ever produced at such an early age, and a poem which would have added to the fame of almost any poet of any age, while it would have detracted from the fame of none.

From the day this poem appeared, the name of its author, which till then had scarcely been heard farther from home than the range of the human voice, was classed among the most cherished literary assets of the nation. Like the mythic Hermes, who before the sun had reached its zenith on the day of his birth had stolen and slaughtered the cattle of Apollo, young William Cullen Bryant, with scarcely less startling precocity, before he was out of his teens had possessed himself of Apollo's lyre, and established himself as the undisputed laureate of America.

One of the wisest of Spanish proverbs says,[1] "There is little curiosity about the pedigree of a good man."

There certainly is no higher patent of nobility than goodness, and yet the biographer cannot help dwelling with satisfaction upon the fact that the gifted bard whose career is to be the theme of the following pages was descended through both his parents from passengers in the Mayflower, the oldest and noblest pedigree of which our republican heralds take any note. One of these ancestors, Josiah Snell, married Anna Alden, the granddaughter of Captain John Alden of the Mayflower party and Priscilla Mullins, whose story is so sweetly told by Longfellow.[2]

The first of the name in this country and founder of the family, Stephen Bryant, was also one of the Mayflower party. The poet's great

---

[1] Al hombre bueno no le busquen abolengo.

[2] "I cannot refer to this poem," says Mr. Godwin, "without remarking how much it adds to our interest in John and Priscilla to know that our two earliest and most eminent poets, Bryant and Longfellow, were descended from them." — Godwin's *Life*, i. 50.

grandfather, Ichabod Bryant, was noted for his gigantic size and strength. His grandfather, Dr. Philip Bryant, who was a physician, lived to the age of eighty-five, and visited his patients till within a fortnight of his death. It is related of the poet's uncle, Ebenezer Snell, Jr., that while at work in his father's cornfield, hearing unusual sounds he put his ear to the ground and recognized the thundering roar of distant cannon. It was the memorable battle of Bunker Hill. He enlisted at once as a volunteer, and later had the distinguished privilege of witnessing the surrender of Burgoyne at Saratoga.

Dr. Peter Bryant, the father of William Cullen, in defiance of obstacles and privations in early life to which a feeble nature must have succumbed, attained an honorable rank as a physician and surgeon, was fond of books, was well read in his profession according to the standard of the time, had a more than elementary acquaintance with some of the ancient and modern tongues, delighted in poetry and music, played the violin, and was sufficiently handy with tools to make for himself a bass-viol, upon which he also learned to play.

His son has described him as a man of a mild and indulgent temper, somewhat silent, though not hesitating in conversation, not thrifty in a worldly sense, his patients usually paying him whatever they pleased. He was careful, however, and scrupulously neat in his attire, and "had a certain metropolitan air." In figure he was square built, with muscular arms and legs, and in " his prime was possessed of great strength." He took a lively interest in politics, and belonged to the party called Federalists, who at that time were strong in Massachusetts, but in the Union at large in a minority. He represented Cummington for several successive years in both branches of the Massachusetts legislature.

Of his mother, Sarah Snell, the daughter of Ebenezer Snell, of Cummington, the poet has left the following graphic portrait : —

" She was born in North Bridgewater, and was brought by her father when a little child to Cummington. She was tall, of an erect figure, and until rather late in life of an uncommonly youthful appearance. She was a person of excellent practical sense, of a quick and sensitive moral judgment, and had no patience with any form of deceit or duplicity. Her prompt condemnation of injustice, even in those instances in which it is tolerated by the world, made a strong impression upon me in early life, and if in the discussion of public questions I have in my riper age endeavored to keep in view the great rule of right without much regard to persons, it has been owing in a great degree to the force of her example, which taught me never to countenance a wrong because others did. My mother was a careful economist, which the circumstances of her family compelled her to be, and by which she made some amends for my father's want of attention to the main chance. She had a habit of keeping a diary, in which the simple occupations of the day and the occurrences in which the family or the neighborhood had an interest were noted down."

Having been taken to a new settlement when she was only six years old, Mrs. Bryant had enjoyed few of the advantages of a school-taught education. She had managed, nevertheless, to acquire a creditable mastery of the rudimentary branches of learning. As a wife and mother she did most of the household work. She spun and wove, cut and made most of the clothing of her large family, wove her own carpets, made her own candles, taught her children to read and write, and was one of the first at the bedside of the sick and afflicted of her neighborhood. She took a lively interest in public affairs, both state and national, and exerted no inconsiderable influence in promoting township and neighborhood improvements. She was, in fact, a housewife fashioned on the old Hebrew model : —

"The heart of her husband doth safely trust in her. She will do him good and not evil all the days of her life.

"She seeketh wool, and flax, and worketh willingly with her hands.

"She riseth also while it is yet night, and giveth meat to her household, and a portion to her maidens.

"She layeth her hands to the spindle, and her hands hold the distaff.

"She stretcheth out her hand to the poor; yea, she reacheth forth her hands to the needy.

"Strength and honor are her clothing; and she shall rejoice in time to come.

"She openeth her mouth with wisdom; and in her tongue is the law of kindness.

"She looketh well to the ways of her household, and eateth not the bread of idleness.

"Her children rise up, and call her blessed; her husband also, and he praiseth her." [1]

[1] Proverbs xxxi.

CHAPTER II.

SCHOOL-DAYS.

1794-1810.

WILLIAM CULLEN BRYANT, the second of seven children of Dr. Peter and Sarah Snell Bryant, was born at Cummington,[1] in the county of Hampshire,

[1] In the *Massachusetts Historical Society Collection*, vol. **xx**. p. 41, may be found the following account of Cummington as it was in 1820: —

" Name derived from Col. Cummings (John) of Concord, who purchased this town of the General Court June 2d, 1762.

" Situated on a ridge of mountains and owing to the abrupt declivities of the hills, the pastures and woods may be viewed as a picture.

" Westfield River, a considerable stream, rising in Windsor runs through this town in a southeast direction, and empties into the Connecticut at Westfield.

" The inhabitants have a library of 72 volumes. The largest private library belongs to Peter Bryant, Esq., and contains about 700 volumes.

" Hon. Peter Bryant, member of Massachusetts Medical Society, died of pulmonary consumption at his residence March 19, 1820, in the 53d year of his age. Born at Bridgewater August 12, 1767. Studied physic and surgery at Norton with Dr. Prilete, a French practitioner. When about twenty-two years of age came to Cummington, where he settled and acquired a very extensive and lucrative practice and a reputation truly enviable. He was also in the habit of instructing students in medicine. These were attracted from different parts of the country

in the State of Massachusetts, on the third day of
the month of November, 1794. Our republic, consisting then of only fifteen States, was not quite ten
years old; the second term of our first President
had not expired; Washington, Jefferson, Hamilton, Adams, Gallatin, and Madison were foremost
among the statesmen to whom the nation had confided its political destinies; they were also the models
it commended to the young men of that and succeeding generations. Europe was convulsed by the
new idea of human rights which for the first time
received national sanction and guaranties from
her wronged and exiled offspring on this side the
Atlantic, while Kant, Goethe, Schiller, and Burns
were in an unconscious way doing what in them lay
to reconcile her people to greater social and political
changes which were impending.

William Cullen was thought to be a precocious
child. On his first birthday there is a record that
" he could go alone, and when but a few days more
than sixteen months old, that he knew all the letters of the alphabet."

by his well-selected library, his extensive practice, and his general
reputation. The advantages enjoyed at this school are thought
to have been superior to any in the western part of the State.

" In 1806 Williams College conferred on him the degree of Master of Arts, University of Cambridge that of Doctor of Physic
1818.

According to the Census of 1820 population of Cummington
1060."

Cummington was incorporated June 23, 1779. The first town
meeting was held December 20th, same year. At this meeting
Ebenezer Snell among others was elected one of the selectmen
and assessors.

Though apt to learn, he is reported to have been "puny and very delicate in body, and of a painfully delicate nervous temperament."

Before he had completed his fourth year he was sent to the district school, " but not with much regularity."

"I have no recollection," he has told us, "of irksomeness in studying my lessons or in the discipline of the school. I only recollect gathering spearmint by the brooks in company with my fellow scholars, taking off my hat at their bidding in a light summer shower that the rain might fall on my hair and make it grow, and that I once awoke from a sound nap to find myself in the lap of the schoolmistress, and was vexed to be thus treated like a baby."

In the spring of 1799, Dr. Bryant went to live at the homestead of his wife's father, Ebenezer Snell, a property which is still in the family. While there William went with his elder brother Austin to a district school kept in a little house which then stood near by on the bank of the rivulet which flows by the dwelling. The instruction which he received there was of the most elementary character, stopping at grammar, unless we include theology as learned from the Westminster Catechism, which was one of the Saturday exercises.

" I was an excellent, almost an infallible speller," he tells us, " and ready in geography; but in the Catechism, not understanding the abstract terms, I made but little progress." He was also one of the fleetest runners in the school, and not inexpert at playing ball, though his frame was too light for distinction in some of the rougher games.

In the year 1808, and in the twelfth year of his age, it having been decided that he was worth a collegiate education, he was sent to live with his uncle, the Rev. Thomas Snell, at North Brookfield, to perfect himself in Latin. In eight months he had mastered all the language then required for admission to the Sophomore class at Williams College, and on the 9th of August, 1809, he was transferred to the care of the Rev. Moses Halleck, in the neighboring township of Plainfield, to be equipped with the requisite knowledge of Greek. He always thought himself most fortunate in his instructors, especially in the moral influence which they exerted upon him at that tender age.

"My Uncle Snell," he tells us, "was a man of fine personal appearance and great dignity of character and manner, the slightest expression of whose wish had the force of command. He was a rigid moralist, who never held parley with wrong in any form, and was an enemy of every kind of equivocation. As a theologian, he was trained in the school of Dr. Hopkins, which then, I think, included most of the country ministers of the Congregational Church in Massachusetts. The Rev. Moses Halleck was somewhat famous for preparing youths for college, and his house was called by some the Bread and Milk College, for the reason that bread and milk was a frequent dish at the good man's table. And a good man he really was, kind and gentle and of the most scrupulous conscientiousness. 'I value Mr. Halleck,' my grandfather used to say, 'his life is so exemplary.' He was paid a dollar a week for my board and instruction. 'I can afford it for that,' he was in the habit of saying, 'and it would not be honest to take more.' "

With such guides and under such influences young Bryant made marvelous proficiency. He went through the Colloquies of Corderius, the Æneid, Eclogues, and Georgics of Virgil, and a volume of the Select Orations of Cicero with his uncle Snell in eight months, and in two months with the Rev. Mr. Halleck, " knew the Greek Testament as if it had been English." He then returned to his father's house to perfect his preparations for admission to college by himself, with the exception of two months in the following spring spent with Mr. Halleck in the study of mathematics.

Bryant began to rhyme at almost as early a period of life as a chicken begins to scratch, and when scarce ten years old received a ninepenny coin from his grandfather for a rhymed version of the first chapter of the book of Job. The same year he wrote and declaimed a rhymed description of the school he attended, which was thought worthy of a place in the columns of the county paper. Though these early verses gave no particular poetical promise, they were remarkable for two characteristics by which all his poetry was destined to be distinguished: the correctness both of the measure and the rhyme.

At this early age he had already conceived the hope and was inflamed by the ambition to be a poet. There seemed to him to be no other kind of success in life so desirable. He greedily devoured whatever poetry fell in his way, and even made the favors of the muse one of the subjects of his daily devotions.

"In a community so religious," he relates, "I naturally acquired habits of devotion. My mother and grandmother had taught me, as soon as I could speak, the Lord's Prayer and other little petitions suited to childhood, and I may be said to have been nurtured on Watts' devout poems composed for children. The prayer of the publican in the New Testament was often in my mouth, and I heard every variety of prayer at the Sunday evening services conducted by laymen in private houses. But I varied in my private devotions from these models in one respect, namely, in supplicating, as I often did, that I might receive the gift of poetic genius and write verses that might endure. I presented this petition in those early years with great fervor, but after a time I discontinued the practice, I can hardly say why. As a general rule, whatever I might innocently wish I did not see why I should not ask, and I was a firm believer in the efficacy of prayer. The Calvinistic system of divinity I adopted, of course, as I heard nothing else taught from the pulpit, and supposed it to be the accepted belief of the religious world."

Bryant has recorded the delight with which in those early days he and his brothers welcomed the translation of the Iliad by Pope, when it was added to their household library. He thought them the finest verses that had ever been written, not a very surprising estimate for a lad whose poetical diet had consisted mainly of the hymns of Dr. Watts. Already, too, his peculiar susceptibility to the poetical aspects of the varied phenomena of nature was fully devoloped.

"I was always," he says, "from my earliest years, a delighted observer of external nature, — the splendors of a winter daybreak over the wide wastes of snow seen from our windows, the glories of the autumnal woods, the gloomy approaches of the thunderstorm and its departure amid sunshine and rainbows, the return of the spring with its flowers, and the first snow-fall of winter. The poets fostered this taste in me, and though at that time I rarely heard such things spoken of, it was none the less cherished in my secret mind."

The embargo laid upon all the ports of the republic at the suggestion of President Jefferson proved disastrous to many private interests in New England, and rendered the President and his party extremely unpopular in that section of the Union. Dr. Bryant was a zealous Federalist, and as he represented that party in the legislature for many years, a good deal of political reading of an inflammatory character naturally found its way into the Bryant household, and made all the boys more or less ardent partisans.

It had already become so much the habit of William Cullen to reduce to verse whatever interested him deeply, that it was probably without surprise that his father learned his son had found relaxation from the study of Virgil and Cicero in inditing a satire against democracy and its accredited chieftain.

The tone of his verses harmonized so completely with the temper of the Federalists of Massachusetts in those days, that his father encouraged him to extend them until they numbered some five hundred lines, which the proud father took to Boston and had published in a little pamphlet, partly no doubt to indulge his zeal as a politician, but more to indulge his fatherly pride.[1]

Some disparaging lines about President Jefferson, concluding with a recommendation to him to resign his office, have given to this poem a notoriety which it never would have acquired but for the fact that Mr. Bryant lived to become one of

---

[1] This poem appeared in a thin pamphlet under the title of *The Embargo, or Sketches of the Times.* A Satire by a Youth of Thirteen. Boston. Printed for the purchasers, 1808. It sold promptly, and received enough praise from the press to have turned a lighter head than Bryant's.

The prompt sale of this satire encouraged the father to publish a second edition the following year, with the addition of some half-dozen shorter poems, and the author's name on the title-page. In his mature years Bryant declined any responsibility for these juvenilia.

the most influential champions of the so-called
Jeffersonian democracy, and for the lack of more
effective weapons, it delighted the Federal press
occasionally to quote these lines about Jefferson,
omitting the fact that they were written when the
author was a schoolboy in roundabouts.

" And thou the scorn of every patriot's name
     Thy country's ruin and thy council's shame!
 Poor servile thing! derision of the brave!
 Who erst from Tarleton fled to Carter's Cave;
 Thou who when menaced by perfidious Gaul,
 Did'st prostrate to her whisker'd minion fall;
 And when our cash her empty bags supplied
 Did'st meanly strive the foul disgrace to hide;
 Go, wretch, resign the Presidential chair,
 Disclose thy secret measures, foul or fair.
 Go search with curious eye for horrid frogs
 Mid the wild wastes of Louisianian bogs;
 Or where Ohio rolls his turbid stream,
 Dig for huge bones, thy glory and thy theme.
 Go scan, Philosophist, thy Sally's charms,
 And sink supinely in her sable arms;
 But quit to abler hands the helm of State."

Not discouraged by Jefferson's neglect to resign
the presidency at his bidding, the young poet is
next found disciplining Napoleon, who also had incurred the censure of the good people of Hampshire County. The genius of Columbia is invoked,
and ten stanzas only are required to bring " the
Eastern despot's dire career" to an ignominious
close.

While neither the embargo nor any of the forty
or fifty smaller pieces of verse which date from his
school-days were thought by their author to be wor-

thy of appearing in any collection of his writings, they were justly regarded by his contemporaries as " the flowering laurel on his brow." Though but " surface indications " of vernal fertility, they were conspicuous for their correctness both in measure and rhyme, about which he was always singularly conscientious. Nor had his time been lost upon them, for they had given him an uncommon dexterity in handling the tools of the poet. Had he not acquired this dexterity early in life and before he was thrown upon his own resources for a livelihood, it may be doubted if he would now be most widely known to the world as a poet.

Bryant entered the sophomore class at Williams College on the 9th of October, 1810. " He was well advanced in his sixteenth year," says one of his classmates, "tall and slender in his physical structure, and having a prolific growth of dark brown hair." He was quick and dexterous in his movements, and his younger brother used to brag to other boys about his " stout brother," but afterwards learned that his strength was not so remarkable as his skill and alertness in the use of it. He passed also for being comely in his appearance.

Dr. Fitch was President of Williams College when Bryant entered, and was the sole instructor of the senior class. Professor Chester Dewey taught the junior class, and two recent graduates superintended the recitations of the two lower classes. As these four gentlemen represented the entire educational force of this seat of learning at that time, we are not surprised to learn from the poet himself " that the standard of scholarship was so low that many graduates of those days would be no more than prepared for admission as freshmen now." [1]

Before the close of his first year he asked from the college an honorable dismission. His purpose then was to enter Yale at the commencement of the next collegiate year. [2] The reason assigned for this step was the example of his room-mate, to whom he was greatly attached, and who had formed the purpose of going to Yale at the same time. From some verses, however, which he delivered before one of the college societies, the existence of motives less complimentary to the college were disclosed. They show that he was satisfied neither with the climate, town, college, nor its authorities. The strength of his feeling upon the subject may be inferred from the following extract : —

> " Why should I sing these reverend domes
> Where Science rests in grave repose ?

[1] 1874–1875.

[2] In a note addressed to the Rev. H. W. Powers, written only a few months before his death, in 1878, Mr. Bryant said : —

" I entered Williams College a year in advance, that is to say, I was matriculated as sophomore, never having been a freshman. I remained there two terms only, but I pursued my studies with the intent to become a student at Yale, for which I prepared myself, intending to enter the junior class there. My father, however, was not able, as he told me, to bear the expense. I had received an honorable dismission from Williams College, and was much disappointed at being obliged to end my college course in that way."

> Ah me! their terrors and their glooms
> Only the wretched inmate knows.
> Where through the horror breathing hall
> The pale-faced moping students crawl
> Like spectral monuments of woe:
> Or, drooping, seek the unwholesome cell
> Where shade and dust and cobwebs dwell,
> Dark, dirty, dank and low."

The facts were that the college was poor, the students were generally poor, the instruction in the main must have been poor, and, to a person brought up as Bryant had been, the diet and domestic accommodations seemed and doubtless were poor.

" When the time drew near that I should apply for admission at Yale," says Bryant, " my father told me that his means did not allow him to maintain me at New Haven, and that I must give up the idea of a full course of education. I have always thought this unfortunate for me, since it left me but superficially acquainted with several branches of education which a college course would have enabled me to master and would have given me greater readiness in their application."

We only feel the want of what we have not, commonly overlooking what Providence may have substituted in its place, and it was natural for Bryant to regret his ignorance of what he might have learned in the two succeeding years at Yale; but I have little doubt that he passed that time far more profitably than he was likely to have passed it in any American college of that period, or, indeed, perhaps of any period. He was at home, and surrounded, as he would not have been at college, with the choicest domestic influences, and was as diligent a student as he could or should have been anywhere. If he lacked some advantages, he secured others of equal or greater value, among which the employments of the farm and an active open-air life were to him of prime importance.[1]

He carefully explored his father's medical library, and read so much in it and with such profit that he narrowly escaped being a physician. By the aid of experiments performed in his father's laboratory and such text-books as he found at hand, he acquired more than a smattering of chemistry. From some books in which the Linnæan system was explained and illustrated, he made himself quite an accomplished botanist. He devoured, besides, all the poetry he could lay his hands on; enlarged his acquaintance with the literature of antiquity, of which he had before only possessed himself partially of the languages; made extensive translations from Lucian's Dialogues of the Dead

[1] The quality of his daily life at this period may be gathered from the following lines written in 1812. They also show that he was not quite reconciled to the "peasant's toil" which filled each "long laborious day," in this respect not differing from most other boys: —

> "The time has been when fresh as air
> I loved at morn the hills to climb.
> With dew drenched feet and bosom bare
> And ponder on the artless rhyme;
> And through the long laborious day
> (For mine has been the peasant's toil),
> I hummed the meditated lay
> While the slow oxen turned the soil."

in prose, and from Anacreon, Bion, and Sophocles in verse, and became thoroughly imbued with what was least perishable in the writings of Burns, Cowper, Thompson, Wordsworth, and Southey, and later of Henry Kirke White, whose poetry had for him at that time a peculiar fascination.

" The melancholy tone which prevails in them," he says, " deepened the interest with which I read them, for about that time I had, as young poets are apt to have, a liking for poetry of a querulous cast."

" Enterprising poverty," says Horace, " made me a poet." [1] The restrictions, privations, and depressing associations which are the heritage of the youthful poor always lead them, at the age when the imagination is yet more active than the judgment, to make a world for themselves which is abundantly equipped with what their real life most lacks. To perpetuate these dreams in verse is as natural for them as to fly to shelter from a storm, or to seek food when hungry.

The measure of poverty which recalled Bryant from college, which shut out from his gaze the great world and the expanded life about which he had read in his books, which condemned him to the " peasant's toil " on his father's farm, and the sequestered life of his native village drove him early —

---

[1] Decisis humilem pennis, inopemque paterni
Et laris et fundi, *paupertas* impulit *audax*
Ut versus facerem.

Epist. II. 2. 50.

> " To quiet valley and shaded glen
>   And forest and meadow and slope of hill,"

where his teeming fancy constructed a world more to his taste, a world which expanded with his years, and in which he was destined to pass the happiest and by far the largest portion of his life. Let the aspiring lad who drags the chain of poverty, and who sighs for the opportunities which wealth alone confers, consider that those who have such opportunities pretty uniformly dwell in houses made with hands, and know nothing of the cloud-capped towers and gorgeous palaces which the imagination provides so generously for the gifted poor. Hence perhaps it is, that great poets are so scarce who in their early years have been swathed in purple and fine linen and fared sumptuously every day.

CHAPTER III.

1811–1814.

IF his parents could not allow William Cullen the means of completing his course of study at college, William Cullen was not the sort of boy to allow himself to settle down at home in permanent dependence upon them. With four brothers, each more robust than himself, his services on the farm were superfluous. Where and how was he to provide for himself was the question which intruded upon him perpetually from the moment he became aware that his academic hopes were extinguished. He did not think seriously of literature for a livelihood, though all his tastes allured him in that direction. He had as yet no assurance of his ability to attain any prominence among the men of letters of his generation, and, had he measured his forces less modestly, no one knew better than he that literature in those days was anything but a bread-winning profession.

It had been taken for granted almost from his birth that he was to follow the calling to which his paternal ancestors for three successive generations had been trained; but the hardships of that calling had proved so trying, and its rewards so scanty, that Dr. Bryant was indisposed to entail it upon any of his descendants. Perhaps, too, by the time this crisis occurred in the young man's fortune, Dr. Bryant had reached the conclusion at which most intelligent physicians sooner or later arrive, that they are more dependent for their livelihood upon the credulity and ignorance of their patients than upon their own skill, and he did not care to introduce his son to a profession in which he might prove too conscientious to succeed.

The lively interest in the politics of the country which William Cullen had exhibited from his earliest youth, and the success with which in his verses he had on several occasions interpreted popular emotions, suggested for him a public career. To that, the profession of the law was then the most if not the only remunerative avenue. The art of entering public life penniless and in a few years blooming into a millionaire was the discovery of a considerably later stage of republican evolution.

The law was not precisely the calling to which he could consecrate himself with his whole heart, and he was not without misgivings that his shy and sensitive nature unfitted him for the life of conflict by which the votaries of Themis have to win their laurels. Still it offered him the readiest means then in sight of earning his bread by his brains and a final exemption from the detested "peasant toil." These considerations, strength-

ened, as he thought, by a perusal of the " Life of
Sir William Jones," [1] "kicked the beam," and in
December of the year he quit college, and in the
seventeenth year of his age he entered the law
office of a Mr. Howe, of Worthington, a quiet
little village some four or five miles from Cummington.

A young man's first year's study of the law
commonly affects him like his first cigar, or his
first experience " before the mast." Such appears
to have been Bryant's experience. His new work,
which he was too conscientious to neglect, was not
"peasant's toil," but it was scarcely less irksome
to him. He sighed for the companionship and
studies of his old classmates. Worthington he
described to one of them in one of his moments
of dejection as consisting of "a blacksmith's shop
and a cow stable," where his only congenial entertainment was derived from the pages of Irving's
" Knickerbocker."

---

[1] "One day," says Bryant in his autobiographic sketch, "my
uncle brought home a quarto volume, the *Life of Sir William
Jones,* by Lord Teignmouth, which he had borrowed, as I imagine, expressly for my reading. I read it with great interest, and
was much impressed with the extensive scholarship and other
literary accomplishments of Sir William. I am pretty sure that
his example made me afterward more diligent in my studies, and
I think also that it inclined me to the profession of the law, which
in due time I embraced. I recollect that a clergyman from a
neighboring parish who came to exchange pulpits with my uncle
observing me occupied with the book kindly said to me: 'You
have only to be as diligent in your studies as that great man was,
and, in time, you may write as fine verses as he did.' "

He was too shy to enjoy the little society that was accessible to him, and incurred a rebuke from Mr. Howe for giving to Wordsworth's "Lyrical Ballads" time that belonged to Blackstone and Chitty. Then, too, he appears about this time to have experienced an affection of the heart to which all young men of his age are subject, especially if their time is not fully or pleasantly occupied. Nothing came of it, however, except verses. Even the name of their inspiration has not been preserved. She had "blue eyes," . . . "of timid look and soft retiring mien," . . . "moist lip and airy grace of frame." So much we learn from his tell-tale muse. For two summers the young poet seems to have worn the colors of this mysterious maid. Then misgivings began to disturb the current of his passion, which soon terminated in an explosion and a declaration of independence. His fair one seems to have tried to impose terms upon her thrall which his pride resented, and he took his leave of her and of Love in terms which showed that his disenchantment was complete.

> "I knew thee fair — I deemed thee free
>   From fraud and guile and faithless art;
>   Yet had I seen as now I see
>   Thine image ne'er had stained my heart.
>
> "Trust not too far thy beauty's charms.
>   Though fair the hand that wove my chain
>   I will not stoop with fettered arms,
>   To do the homage I disdain.

"Yes, Love has lost his power to wound;
    I gave the treacherous homicide,
With bow unstrung and pinions bound,
    A captive to the hand of pride."

This heroic termination of his first love affair was
naturally the prelude to other changes. Worthington was too small a place, and its literary and
social horizon too circumscribed, to long content a
young man who already felt the expansive forces
of genius. He pined for the privilege of pursu-
ing his studies in Boston. His father replied to
his appeals that they could not be indulged except
at an expense which would work injustice to the
other members of the family. They compromised,
and he went to Bridgewater, a somewhat larger
town than Worthington and the residence of his
grandfather, Dr. Philip Bryant, with whom he was
to reside. He there entered the law office of Mr.
William Baylies, a cultivated gentleman and a
jurist of considerable repute.

Young Bryant found the association congenial
in every way, and at once concentrated upon the
studies of his profession all the devotion he had
been accustomed to waste upon "blue eyes" and
"moist lips" during his residence at Worthington.

This change of state is faithfully noted in some
lines addressed about this time "to a friend on his
marriage," and published a few years later in the
"North American Review."

"O'er Coke's black letter
Trimming the lamp at eve, 't is mine to pore,
Well pleased to see the venerable sage

> Unlock his treasured wealth of legal lore;
> And I that loved to trace the woods before,
> And climb the hills a playmate of the breeze,
> Have vowed to tune the rural lay no more,
> Have bid my useless classics sleep at ease,
> And left the race of Bards to scribble, starve, and freeze."

Bryant a little overstated the measure of his loyalty to " Coke's black letter," for within a month after his installation at Bridgewater he appears in the role of " the poet " at a Fourth of July celebration in the village, and, while deploring in some indifferent verses the folly of war, rejoiced over the downfall of Napoleon, upon whose movements he still kept a pretty sharp eye, and to heaven and England ascribed all the honor and glory of delivering the world from a scourge.

> "To thee the mighty plan we owe
>   That bade the world be free;
> The thanks of nations, Queen of Isles,
>   Are poured to heaven and thee.
> Yes, hadst not thou with fearless arm
>   Stayed the descending scourge,
> These strains, that chant a nation's birth,
>   Had haply hymned its dirge."

This poem, however, deserves to be regarded rather as the discharge of a civic duty than an infidelity to Coke, and certain it is that the written evidences that survive of his assiduity as a law student at this period are abundant and conclusive.

The best possible proof of his diligence may be found in the relations the young student early established with Mr. Baylies, who during his ab-

sence at the seat of government [1] appears by their
correspondence to have left his home business, political as well as professional, mainly in Bryant's
hands. His constituents were wont to repair to
Bryant to learn what their representative at Washington thought and was doing, and Baylies studied Bryant's letters to know the views of his
constituents. The war of 1812 was very unpopular in Bridgewater. Mr. Madison was known as
" His Imbecility " in the young patriot's correspondence, and " His Imbecility " was warned if he
imposed any more taxes the people would revolt.
Nay, this predestined editor of the New York
" Evening Post," and one of the most eloquent
and uncompromising of all the American Ciceros
in denouncing the Catilines of disunion a half century later, did not hesitate, in one of his ecstasies
of youthful enthusiasm, to advise an open defiance
of the Federal government if it persisted in the
war. He even solicited a commission in the army,
not for the defense of the United States, but for
the defense of his native State against the United
States, and the letter in which he opened his purpose to his father in October, 1814, was as full of
treason as the Southern Confederate manifesto of
1860.

" I have a question for you," he wrote, " whether
it would be proper for me to have anything to do
with the army which is to be raised by voluntary

---

[1] Mr. Baylies was a member of Congress almost uninter-
ruptedly from 1809 to 1817, and again for the years 1833–34–35.

enlistment for the defense of the State. Attached
as you are to your native soil, to its rights and
safety, you could not surely be unwilling that your
son should proffer his best exertions and even his
life to preserve them from violation. The force
now to be organized *may not be altogether employed against a foreign enemy; it may become
necessary to wield it against an intestine foe* in
the defense of dearer rights than those which are
endangered in a contest with Great Britain. *If we
create a standing army of our own — if we take
into our own hands the public revenue* (for these
things are contemplated in the answer to the
Governor's message) *we so far throw off all our
allegiance to the general government; we disclaim
its control and revert to an independent empire.*
The posture therefore which is now taken by the
State Legislature, if followed up by correspondent
measures, is not without hazard. If we proceed
in the manner we have begun and escape a civil
war, it will probably be *because the Administration is awed by our strength from attempting our
subjection.* By increasing that strength, therefore,
we shall lessen the probability of bloodshed. Every
individual who helps forward the work of collect-
ing this army takes the most efficient means in his
power to bring the present state of things to a
happy conclusion. . . . It is not probable that the
struggle in which we are to be engaged will be a
long one. The war with Britain certainly will not.
The people cannot exist under it, and *if the gov-*

ernment will not make peace Massachusetts must.
Whether there may be an intestine contest or not
admits of doubt; and if there should be, the entire
hopelessness of the Southern States succeeding
against us will probably terminate it after the first
paroxysm of anger and malignity is over."

It is curious and instructive to see how precisely
the arguments used by this hyper-patriotic young
enthusiast correspond with those by which the
Southern States of our Union, less than a half
century later, were beguiled into open rebellion
against the same national government. He rec-
ommends "a standing army of our own," to be
officered "not by the President" but "by our Governor," and "the taking into our own hands the
public revenue," the very step that compelled the
military occupation of Fort Sumter by Federal
troops. These, like similar measures in 1860,
were expected "to awe the administration at
Washington from attempting our subjection"
and to be followed, as proposed in 1861, by an
alliance with England and the final reduction of
the Southern States, either by the superior force
of these Northern Confederates, or by despair, as
later the Northern States were confidently expected to yield to the assumed physical or moral
superiority of the Southern Confederates.

Not long after the letter to his father just cited
was written, Bryant wrote another to Mr. Baylies,
in the course of which he said : —

" We hear that you legislators have got through

with the Conscription bill and it is presented to the
President to receive his sanction. God forgive the
poor perjured wretch ['His Imbecility,' Mr. Madison, is the unfortunate party here referred to] if
he dare sign it. If the people of New England
acquiesce in this law I will forswear Federalism." [1]

Bryant proved as good as his word. The people
of New England did acquiesce, and he did forswear Federalism.

If the people of South Carolina, when they fired
upon Fort Sumter to prevent the collection of the
Federal revenues in the port of Charleston, in
1861, had been able to quote this letter, which its
author had, no doubt, forgotten, his unfaltering
sense of justice would possibly have constrained him
to deal more charitably with at least that portion of
the insurgent population that was under twenty-
one years of age than he did, or than the public
opinion of the North was then prepared to tolerate.

The family seem to have done nothing to dis-
courage William Cullen's military aspirations, for
in the year following, in July, 1816, a commission
as adjutant in the Massachusetts militia was sent
to him.[2] Meantime, however, the treaty of peace

[1] This threat was "the last ditch" in embryo.

[2] The following letter, dated Cummington, November 16,
1814, has recently been discovered in the Massachusetts State
Archives. The Hartford Convention met on the 15th of December following : —

*To his Excellency Caleb Strong, Governor and Commander-in-chief
    of the Commonwealth of Massachusetts:*

Humbly represents that William C. Bryant, of Cummington,
in the County of Hampshire, your petitioner, being desirous to

had been negotiated at Ghent, and the Federalists were so delighted with the result that Bryant concluded to throw up his commission and to give the government at Washington another trial.

It is a curious fact that the army which has furnished the inspiration of so much good poetry can hardly be said to have given to the world a single great poet, and yet the most eminent English and the most eminent American poet were both at one time on the point of embracing the profession of arms.[1] Had they done so, it is doubtful if either would ever have been heard of again as a bard.

In August of the year in which the war with England was brought to a close, Bryant came of age and was admitted to the bar. With his license in his pocket he took leave of Bridgewater on the 15th of the month, and returned to his family in Cummington, to take counsel in regard to the future, towards which he had thus far been walking by faith rather than by sight.

enter the service of the State, in the present struggle with a powerful enemy, respectfully solicits your Excellency for a lieutenancy in the army about to be raised for the protection and defense of Massachusetts. Your petitioner presumes not to choose his station, but were he permitted to express a preference, he would request the place of first lieutenant in the First Regiment of Infantry, but in this, as becomes him in all things, he is willing to rest on your Excellency's decision. Should your Excellency be induced to favor his wishes in this respect, he hopes to be faithful and assiduous in the discharge of his duty. And your petitioner shall ever pray, etc. WILLIAM C. BRYANT.

[1] Phillips tells us that it was in contemplation at one time to make his uncle, John Milton, adjutant-general in Sir William Waller's army.

CHAPTER IV.

THE BARRISTER.

1815–1822.

WHERE young Bryant was to pursue his profession was now as embarrassing a problem in the Bryant household as the choice of a profession to pursue had been four years before. He yearned to go to Boston; but how was an unknown and morbidly shy young man like him to subsist in that comparatively expensive city while its inhabitants were discovering his professional merits? Northampton, New Bedford, and other places were in turn discussed, but for one reason or another rejected, and finally, taking counsel of the family exchequer, he decided " to settle " at Plainfield, a modest village in full view of Cummington, though four or five miles distant, where, though his legal skill might not be in great demand, his expenses would be proportionately light. Plainfield is still a village of less than five hundred inhabitants. Seventy years ago, when the sign of " William Cullen Bryant, Attorney-at-Law " decorated its principal street, it had less than one fourth its present population. Time has vindicated the conclusion

which soon forced itself upon him, that there was
no future for a lawyer in Plainfield, and that the
earliest opportunity of taking his professional accomplishments to a better market was not to be
neglected. He had been there but about eight
months when he was invited to enter into partnership with a young lawyer of Great Barrington,
whose practice was then worth about $1200 a year.
Bryant accepted the proposal with alacrity, and
early in the month of October, 1816, set out for
his new field of labor on the banks of the Housatonic. Of this change of base, Bryant has left the
following account: —

"I had attempted the practice of the law in a
neighborhood where there was little employment
for one of my profession, and, after a twelve
months' trial, I transferred my residence to Great
Barrington, near the birthplace and summer residence of Miss Sedgwick, in the pleasant county of
Berkshire. It was on the 3d of October that I
made the journey thither from Cummington. The
woods were in all the glory of autumn, and [in
1871] I well remember as I passed through Stockbridge how much I was struck by the beauty of
the smooth green meadows on the banks of that
lovely river which winds near the Sedgwick family mansion; the Housatonic, whose gently flowing waters seemed tinged with the gold and crimson of the trees that overhung them. I admired
no less the contrast between this soft scene and the
steep, craggy hills that overlooked it, clothed with

their many-colored forests. I had never before seen the southern part of Berkshire, and congratulated myself on becoming an inhabitant of so picturesque a region."

It is too characteristic of Bryant to escape notice, that the things which absorbed his attention and commended this new home to his affections were the smooth green meadow, the gently flowing waters of the Housatonic ; the craggy hills, the many-colored forests, while not a thought is given apparently to the indications of social, industrial, and commercial activities of the country around him, out of which as a lawyer he might hope to get a livelihood. His eye was more intent upon the material his new home would afford him for making verses than for making briefs.

Before the first year of his partnership had rolled around he purchased his partner's interest " for a mere trifle," and from that time until his retirement from the profession prosecuted it alone.

Though now as comfortably established as the average country lawyer, Bryant did not " accept the situation" cheerfully. Writing to his old teacher and friend, Mr. Baylies, he says :—

" You ask whether I am pleased with my profession. Alas, sir, the muse was my first love, and the remains of that passion which is not cooled out nor chilled into extinction will always, I fear, cause me to look coldly on the severe beauties of Themis. Yet I tame myself to its labors as well as I can, and have endeavored to discharge with punctuality and attention such of the duties of my profession as I am capable of performing."

While he had a partner the trial and argument of causes fell mostly to him, but when they separated he had to resume the duties of the barrister. Speaking of this change he wrote to Mr. Baylies :

" I am trying my hand at it again. . . . Upon the whole I have every cause to be satisfied with my situation. Place a man where you will, it is an easy thing for him to dream out a more eligible mode of life than the one which falls to his lot. While I have too much of the *mauvaise honte* to seek opportunities of this nature, I have whipped myself up to a desperate determination not to avoid them."

There is something in the tone of this letter which shows that the dove from young Bryant's ark had not yet found its resting-place. *Audax paupertas* was doing, but had not yet done for him its perfect work. It had effectively thus far prevented his becoming content with the opportunities and alliances then within his reach. It was still his best friend. It had better work and on a larger theatre in reserve for him than the *invisa negotia* of settling the disputes of country villagers. The Fates were spinning for him the thread out of which quite a different destiny was to be woven than was yet in sight.[1]

[1] In a lengthy notice of Bryant which appeared in the *Berkshire Eagle* shortly after his death, June 20, 1878, some facts relating to his professional career are given which seem too char-

In June of 1817 Bryant received a letter from his father, then in Boston, informing him that Mr. Willard Phillips, an old Hampshire friend, had in-

acteristic to be overlooked in any sketch of the events which shaped the ends of the maturing poet and journalist.

"In the old times there were three grades of lawyers in Massachusetts: Attorneys of the Common Pleas, entitled to practice in that court, Attorneys of the Supreme Court, entitled to manage cases in that tribunal, and Counselors of the Supreme Court, who alone had the right to argue cases before the full bench. Mr. Bryant's admission at Plymouth was to the Common Pleas: at the September term, 1817, he was admitted an attorney of the Supreme Court, and at the same term in 1819 as counselor; Calvin Martin, Esq., of this town, and Charles A., afterwards Judge, Dewey, taking these legal degrees at the same time. Mr. Bryant was an active, learned, and rather fiery young lawyer. His name appears four or five times in the reports of the Supreme Court, which would indicate a practice somewhat greater than the majority of lawyers obtained in those days at his age. He was not particularly distinguished as a lawyer, but might have become so could he have overcome his disgust with a profession in which — then, even more than at present — law was not synonymous with justice. Finally he struck upon an experience which, if the well supported tradition of the bar is to be trusted, was so intolerable that he relinquished practice altogether. The case, that of Grotius Bloss *vs.* Augustus Tobey, of Alford, is reported in the second volume of Massachusetts Reports.

"Mr. Bryant had obtained for Bloss a verdict of $500 for slander by Tobey, who appealed, having E. H. Mills, General Whiting, and Henry W. Dwight as counsel. At the law term of the Supreme Court, in 1824, — Mr. Bryant having submitted a plain, common-sense argument in writing during the vacation, — the case was decided against him, by an opinion which is thus summarized in the Reports:

"'Simply to burn one's store is not unlawful, and the words, *"He burnt his store"* or *"there is no doubt in my mind that he burned his own store, he would not have got his goods insured if he had not meant to burn it,"* or a general allegation that the defendant charged the plaintiff with having willfully and maliciously

timated to him a desire that William Cullen would
contribute to the " North American Review," then
only two years old, of which Phillips was an associate editor.   In communicating this invitation to
his son, the doctor advised him to avail himself of
it as a means of making himself favorably known
at the state capital, "for those who contribute,"
he added, "are generally known to the *literati* in
and about Boston."   While William Cullen had
Mr. Phillips's request under consideration his decision was curiously anticipated.   Doctor Bryant
having occasion one day to look through the draw-
ers in his son's desk, which he had left behind him
at Cummington, his eyes fell upon some manuscript
verses, one of which proved to be the poem to

burnt his own store, will not sustain an action for slander without
a colloquium or averment setting forth such circumstances as would
render such burning unlawful, and that the words were spoken
of such circumstances; and the want of such colloquium will
not be cured by an innuendo.'

"Thus, for a technical omission which did not in the least obscure
the meaning of Mr. Bryant's declaration, his client's just rights
were denied.   That his claim to damage *was just* the court admitted practically, Chief Justice Parsons prefacing its opinion, by
remarking: 'It is with great regret, and not without much labor
and research, to avoid this result, that we are obliged to arrest
judgment.'

"Mr. Bryant's just indignation against an administration of the
law which compelled its servants to do acknowledged wrong to
those who sought justice in its highest state tribunal led him to
be ready to relinquish his profession at the first opportunity; his
feeling being probably intensified by an angry quarrel with General Whiting concerning the costs, in which the disputants became so heated that it is remembered to this day by those who
witnessed it.

which he had given the name of "Thanatopsis" (a
View of Death), and the other "An Inscription
upon the Entrance to a Wood." He read them, and
was so impressed by them that he hurried off at
once to the house of a lady friend residing in the
neighborhood, and thrusting the verses into her
hand exclaimed, while tears ran down his cheeks,
" Read them, they are Cullen's."

Without communicating his intention to his son,
the good doctor with as little delay as possible set
out for Boston with these poems to show them to
his friend Phillips. The result of his visit has
already been recited.

"Thanatopsis" appeared in the September number of the "North American Review" for 1817.
It was written by Bryant, Mr. Godwin tells us,

"shortly after he was withdrawn from college, while residing with his parents at Cummington in the summer of
1811, and before he had attained his eighteenth year.

"There was no mistaking the quality of these verses.
The stamp of genius was upon every line. No such
verses had been made in America before. They soon
found their way into the school books of the country.
They were quoted from the pulpit and upon the hustings.
Their gifted author had a national fame before he had
a vote, and in due time 'Thanatopsis' took the place
which it still retains among the masterpieces of English
didactic poetry."

The poem which accompanied "Thanatopsis"
and appeared in the same number of the "Review"
under the title of "Fragment" is now known as

"An Inscription for the Entrance to a Wood."[1] Though not sufficient, perhaps, to confer a reputation, it contributed largely to confirm and strengthen one already made. With two such poems as "Thanatopsis" and "The Fragment" sleeping in his desk, it may be assumed that during the six succeeding years, in which we have followed the young poet in his efforts to solve the more practical problems of life, he had not left his poetical talent wrapped in a napkin. On the contrary, his muse was his comforter, counselor, and friend, with whom he uniformly took refuge from the perplexities, doubts, and discouragements of his professional life. She always sent him back to his daily task resigned, if not contented. The tone of his life at this period is reflected as in a mirror from his verses. The closing passage of his poem on "Green River" no doubt presents the state of feelings which was habitual with him, while, like Samson grinding in the prison house of the Philistines, he felt himself inexorably condemned for life to obscurity and "low thoughted care."

> "Though forced to drudge for the dregs of men,
>   And scrawl strange words with the barbarous pen,
>   And mingle among the jostling crowd
> Where the sons of strife are subtle and loud,
> I often come to this quiet place
> To breathe the airs that ruffle my face,
> And gaze upon thee in silent dream;
> For in thy lonely and lovely stream
> An image of that calm life appears
> That won my heart in my greener years."

[1] The first title was doubtless given it by the editors, the latter was subsequently given it by its author.

When he journeyed on foot over the hills to Plainfield on the 15th of December, 1816, to see what inducements it offered him to commence there the practice of the profession to which he had just been licensed, he says in one of his letters that he felt "very forlorn and desolate." The world seemed to grow bigger and darker as he ascended, and his future more uncertain and desperate. The sun had already set, leaving behind it one of those brilliant seas of chrysolite and opal which often flood the New England skies, and, while pausing to contemplate the rosy splendor, with rapt admiration, a solitary bird made its winged way along the illuminated horizon. He watched the lone wanderer until it was lost in the distance. He then went on with new strength and courage. When he reached the house where he was to stop for the night he immediately sat down and wrote the lines "To a Waterfowl," the concluding verse of which will perpetuate to future ages the lesson in faith which the scene had impressed upon him.

> " He who, from zone to zone,
> Guides through the boundless sky thy certain flight,
> In the long way that I must tread alone,
> Will lead my steps aright." [1]

Bryant was only twenty-one years of age when he wrote this poem, which by many is thought to be the one they would choose to preserve, if all but one of his poems were condemned to destruction.[2]

[1] Godwin's *Life of Bryant*, vol. i. p. 144.
[2] I have from Mr. Parke Godwin an incident which belongs to

There is something strangely pathetic in the following lines written in 1815, and while still a student at home.

"I cannot forget with what tender devotion
    I worshiped the visions of verse and of fame;
  Each gaze at the glories of earth, sky, and ocean,
    To my kindled emotions was wind over flame.

"And deep were my musings in life's early blossom,
    Mid the twilight of mountain groves wandering long,
  How thrilled my young veins, and how throbbed my full bosom,
    When o'er me descended the Spirit of Song.

  .   .   .   .

"Bright Visions! I mixed with the world and ye faded.
    No longer your pure rural worshiper now;
  In the haunts your continued presence pervaded
    Ye shrink from the signet of care on my brow.

the history of this poem. In a note to me dated Roslyn, November 6, 1889, he says : —

"Once when the late Matthew Arnold, with his family, was visiting the ever-hospitable country home of Mr. Charles Butler, I happened to spend an evening there. In the course of it Mr. Arnold took up a volume of Mr. Bryant's poems from the table, and turning to me said, ' This is *the* American poet, *facile princeps;*' and after a pause he continued: 'When I first heard of him, Hartley Coleridge (we were both lads then) came into my father's house one afternoon considerably excited and exclaimed, "Matt, do you want to hear the best short poem in the English language?" "Faith, Hartley, I do," was my reply. He then read a poem "To a Waterfowl" in his best manner. And he was a good reader. As soon as he had done he asked, "What do you think of that?" "I am not sure but you are right, Hartley; is that your father's?" was my reply. "No," he rejoined, "father has written nothing like that." Some days after he might be heard muttering to himself,

        "'"The desert and illimitable air,
            Lone wandering, but not lost."'"

"In the old mossy groves on the breast of the mountains,
   In deep lonely glens where the waters complain,
   By the shade of the rock, by the gush of the fountain,
   I seek your loved footsteps, but seek them in vain.

"Oh leave not forlorn and forever forsaken
   Your pupil and victim, to life and its tears;
   But sometimes return, and in mercy awaken
   The glories ye showed to his earlier years."

It is by no means the least singular thing about
all these exquisite verses that they should have
slept several years in their author's portfolio,
neither read, seen, nor even heard of by any other
living soul.   His early "prentice" verses he was
wont to read to his father and to other members of
the family, but when "the Spirit of Song" descended upon him he became as shy as a maiden
who first feels, not yet comprehending, the mysteries of love.   He no longer showed his verses even
to his father, and but for the accident that betrayed his secret no one can confidently say when,
if ever, any of those verses would have seen the
light.   "Thanatopsis" was already six years old
when it was printed; "The Fragment," two years;
"To a Waterfowl," three years; and "I cannot forget with what fervid devotion," eleven years.

Such "patient waiting" is very rare, with young
writers at least, but Bryant even then had no ambition to be a mere newspaper poet.   Whatever
may have been his own estimate of his verses, he
knew that time could not deprive them of any of
their value.   Whether they were vein ore or only
washings he evidently had not fully settled in his

own mind when his father took some specimens to Boston to be subjected to the assay of public opinion.

The reception of "Thanatopsis" in 1817 and of "To a Waterfowl" in 1818 removed whatever doubts lingered in his own or the public mind in regard either to the dignity or fertility of his muse, one of the immediate fruits of which was an invitation from Mr. Phillips [1] to enlist among the regular contributors to the "Review," — an invitation of which he was only too happy to avail himself, for to his provincial vision it seemed the only gate through which he might at last find his way to that great world of which, like Rasselas, he had dreamed so much, but knew so little.

A collection of American poetry by Solyman Browne was suggested to him for review. After much difficulty in finding a copy of this long for-

[1] In a letter to Dana from Cummington, in September, 1873, Bryant wrote: —

"I thank you for telling me so much about the last days of our friend Phillips. He lived when a lad and a youth for some time in a house which I see from my door here, on a somewhat distant hillside, and while studying for college came to this house to take lessons from one of my father's medical pupils. The publication of the poems which you mention, through his agency, was properly my introduction to the literary world, and led to my coming out with a little volume which you and Channing and he encouraged me to publish, and which he so kindly reviewed in the *North American*. To me he was particularly kind — unconsciously so as it seemed; it was apparently a kindness that he could not help. I am glad to learn that his last years were so tranquil and his death so easy, dropping like fruit, as Milton says, into his mother's lap."

gotten book, which in a letter to his father he described as "poor stuff," he made it the basis of an essay on American poetry. It appeared in the "North American Review" for July, 1818. In it he passes in review all the writers of verse on this side of the Atlantic who had yet ventured into print, save some "whose passage to that oblivion, towards which, to the honor of our country they were hastening," he did not wish to interrupt. Those whose passage to oblivion he thought worthy of being interrupted, though at this day it is not so easy to see why, were the Rev. John Adams, whose verses showed "the dawning of an ambition of correctness and elegance;" Joseph Green, whose poetical writings "have been admired for their humor and the playful ease of their composition;" Francis Hopkinson, "whose humorous ballad entitled 'The Battle of the Kegs' is in most of our memories;" Dr. Church, whose "keen and forcible invectives are still recollected by his contemporaries;" Philip Freneau, "whose occasional productions, distinguished by a coarse strength of sarcasm and abounding with allusions to passing events, which are perhaps their greatest merit;" the Connecticut poets, Trumbull, Dwight, Barlow, Humphreys, and Hopkins, in all whose productions "there is a pervading spirit of nationality and patriotism: a desire to reflect credit on the country to which they belonged, which seems, as much as individual ambition, to have prompted their efforts, and which at times gives a certain glow

and interest to their manner." Trumbull's Mc-
Fingal is "a tolerably successful imitation of the
great work of Butler," though the reviewer thinks
"The Progress of Dullness" the more pleasing
poem. He asks to be excused from feeling any high
admiration for the poetry of Dr. Dwight, which is
"modeled upon a manner altogether too artificial
and mechanical." "Barlow's ' Hasty Pudding ' is
a good specimen of mock heroic verse." "The plan
of 'The Columbiad' is utterly destitute of interest, and that which was at first sufficiently
wearisome has become doubly so by being drawn
out to its length." Humphreys's poems are in
better taste than those of Barlow and Dwight, but
"most happy when he aims at nothing beyond
an elegant mediocrity." " Dr. Lemuel Hopkins's
smaller poems have been praised for their wit.
There is a coarseness, a want of polish in his style ;
and his imagination, daring and original but unre-
strained by a correct judgment, often wanders into
absurdities and extravagances. Still if he had all
the madness, he must be allowed to have possessed
some of the inspiration of poetry."

There is none of our American poetry on which
the reviewer dwells with more pleasure than the
charming remains of William Clifton, who died at
the early age of twenty-seven. "His diction is refined to an unusual degree of purity, and through
this lucid medium the creations of his elegant fancy
appear with nothing to obscure their loveliness."

The posthumous works of St. John Honeywood "contain many polished and nervous lines." Robert Treat Paine "must be allowed to have possessed an active and fertile fancy. Yet more instances of the false sublime might, perhaps, be selected from the writings of this poet than from those of any other of equal talents who lived in the same period. The brilliancy of Paine's poetry is like the brilliancy of frostwork, cold and fantastic. Who can point out the passage in his works in which he speaks to the heart in its own language? He was a fine but misguided genius."

After this charitable not to say generous estimate of his brother bards in America, he proceeds to denounce " the style of poetry then prevalent, as in too many instances tinged with a sickly and affected imitation of the peculiar manner of the late popular poets of England," and the servile habit of copying, which adopts the vocabulary of some favorite author, and apes the fashion of his sentences, and cramps and forces the ideas into a shape which they could not naturally have taken, and of which the only recommendation is not that it is most elegant or most striking, but that it bears some resemblance to the manner of him who is proposed as a model. " This way of writing," he continues, " has an air of poverty and meanness. It seems to indicate a paucity of reading as well as a perversion of taste, and it ever has been and ever will be the resort of those who are sensible

that their works need some factitious recommendation to give them even a temporary popularity."
"On the whole," he concludes, "there seems to be
more good taste among those who read than among
those who write poetry in our country."

I have dwelt upon this paper longer than the
present interest of the theme might seem to warrant because it exhibits many of the moral and intellectual habits which made its author for more
than half a century the most conspicuous man of
letters in the country, among which were a mastery
of his subject, temperance in judgment, moderation
in statement, a patriotic interest in the adoption
of sound standards of poetical merit, and withal a
profound sense of responsibility for what he ventured to put in print.

It is not much to say that no one now questions
the substantial correctness of the opinions so modestly set forth in this paper. It is much, however,
to say that no one had ventured to make himself
responsible to the public for these opinions before.
The editors of the "Review" highly approved of
the tone of the article, and so encouraged him by
their epistolary commendations that he now allowed
himself to be relied upon as one of their favorite
contributors.

Nor does his professional character seem to
have suffered in the eyes of his fellow-citizens by
these infidelities, for only a few months after
"To a Waterfowl" and the paper on early American poetry appeared in the "North American

Review," he was chosen one of the tithing-men of the town[1] and soon afterwards town clerk.[2] He held this office for five years, and until he left Great Barrington. If his duties bore any proportion to his salary, they could not have been very engrossing, for he discharged them all for the sum of just five dollars per annum.

To these civic dignities the Governor of the State also added that of Justice of the Peace.

Though few men who wrote so well have ever written so much on the political problems of his time as Mr. Bryant, or did more by his professional and personal example to give dignity to political strife, these were the only public offices he ever filled. He had his eyes already fixed upon a crown even then slowly settling upon his head, to which official distinctions could add no lustre.

About this time Bryant was called upon to submit to the greatest trial that had ever yet befallen him, in the death of his father,[3] who had been to him from his earliest youth, in the largest accepta-

[1] March 9, 1819.

[2] "One may still see his records at Great Barrington, where they form an object of considerable curiosity to summer visitors. Written in a neat flexible hand, it is remarked that almost the only blot is where he registered his own marriage, and the only interlineation, where in giving the birth of his first child he had left out the name of the mother." — Godwin's *Life,* i. 159.

[3] Dr. Bryant died on the 20th of March, 1820, at the comparatively early age of fifty-three. He inherited weak lungs, which could not endure any longer the wear and tear of a country physician's life in the bleak and hilly region where Providence had fixed his home.

tion of the words, his counselor and friend. For this loss, however, Providence sent him what was destined to constitute as far as possible a compensation. Soon after his settlement in Great Barrington, he met a Miss Fairchild, who chanced to be visiting in the neighborhood. She left upon his heart at once an impression that proved to be durable. Death had recently deprived her of both her parents, and she was at this time the guest of one of her married sisters. She proved during the period of their courtship the inspiration of a good many poems, of which "Oh! fairest of the rural maids " is the only one which for one reason or another the author has cared to print. They were married on the 11th of June, 1821, at the residence of Mrs. Henderson, the bride's sister. In announcing this event to his mother, he wrote: "I have not ' played the fool and married the Ethiop for the jewel in her ear.' I looked only for goodness of heart, an ingenuous and affectionate disposition, a good understanding, etc., and the character of my wife is too frank and single-hearted to suffer me to fear that I may be disappointed. I do myself wrong. I did not look for these nor any other qualities, but they trapped me before I was aware, and now I am married in spite of myself." [1]

[1] The following prayer, prepared for this occasion, was happily found among Bryant's papers. Why their union was so remarkably blessed finds in it at least a partial explanation : —

"May Almighty God mercifully take care of our happiness

In the following year, Bryant accepted an invitation to deliver the usual poetic address before the Phi Beta Kappa Society of Harvard College. It was for this occasion he wrote the poem of " The Ages," which was not only a very remarkable poem to be written by any young man of twenty-eight years, but which was conceded by those who heard it to be " the finest that had ever been spoken before the Phi Beta Kappa Society." So highly was it esteemed that nothing would do but he must consent to its publication, with whatever else he had done in a poetical way. The result was a *volumette* of forty-four pages, containing "The Ages," "To a Waterfowl," "Fragment from Simonides," "The Inscription for the Entrance to a Wood," "The Yellow Violet," "The Song," "Green River," and "Thanatopsis." These eight poems

here and hereafter. May we ever continue constant to each other, mindful of our mutual promises of attachment and troth. In due time, if it be the will of Providence, may we become more nearly connected with each other, and together may we lead a long, happy, and innocent life, without any diminution of affection till we die. May there never be any jealousy, distrust, coldness, or dissatisfaction between us, nor occasion for any, nothing but kindness, forbearance, mutual confidence, and attention to each other's happiness. And that we may be less unworthy of so great a blessing, may we be assisted to cultivate all the benign and charitable affections and offices not only toward each other, but toward our neighbors, the human race, and all the creatures of God. And in all things wherein we have done ill, may we properly repent our error, and may God forgive us and dispose us to do better. When at last we are called to render back the life we have received, may our deaths be peaceful, and may God take us to his bosom.

"All which may He grant for the sake of the Messiah."

furnished forth the first "collection" of Bryant's poems, and though the volume was small and the poems few in number, they were enough, had he never written another line, to secure for him a permanent place among the poets of America.

His visit to Boston and Cambridge did not contribute much to make Bryant and his profession more cordial friends. He had been suddenly thrown into a society of the most distinguished and cultivated people of the period, — a society which conceded to him a reputation which required him to call none of them "master." Nor was there any one at that already famous literary centre so distinguished that he could afford to be indifferent to the young poet's acquaintance. The law had yielded him no such rewards. He was doubtless right in thinking it had none such in store for him. At all events, he acted upon that conviction.

CHAPTER V.

1823–1829.

Soon after his father's death, an appeal was made to Bryant on behalf of the Unitarian Society of Massachusetts through Miss Catherine M. Sedgwick, of Stockbridge, to whom he was only known by reputation, to contribute to a collection of hymns that society had projected. Miss Sedgwick, in giving an account of her mission to her brother Robert in New York, said, "He has a charming countenance, modest, but not bashful manners. I made him promise to come and see us shortly. He seemed gratified; and if Mr. Sewall has reason to be obliged to me (which I certainly think he has), I am doubly obliged by the opportunity of securing the acquaintance of so interesting a man."

The acquaintance thus casually formed was destined to exercise a curious influence upon Bryant's future career. At the time of his arrival in Great Barrington, he tells us in his Memoirs, "I had no acquaintance with the Sedgwick family. The youngest of them, Charles Sedgwick, a man of most genial and engaging manners and agreeable conversation as well as of great benevolence and worth, was a member of the Berkshire bar, and by him, a year or two afterwards, I was introduced to the others, who, from the first, seemed to take pleasure in being kind to me."

At the instance of this amiable and accomplished family, Bryant was led seriously to consider the expediency of directing his steps toward New York rather than Boston, as his Land of Promise. Mr. Henry Sedgwick, Miss Sedgwick's elder brother, and one of the more prominent members of the New York bar, had been so impressed by what he had seen of Bryant's writings that he did not hesitate to recommend him to try his fortune as a man of letters in our commercial capital. "The time," he wrote, "is peculiarly propitious; the Athenæum, just instituted, is exciting a sort of literary rage, and it is proposed to set up a journal in connection with it. Besides, 'The Atlantic Magazine,' which has pined till recently, is beginning to revive in the hands of Henry J. Anderson, who has a taste or whim for editorship, and he unquestionably needs assistance. Bliss & White, his publishers, are liberal gentlemen; they pay him five hundred dollars a year, and authorize an expenditure of five hundred dollars more." "Any deficiencies of salary, moreover," Mr. Sedgwick adds, "may be eked out by teaching foreigners, of whom there are many in New York, eager to learn our language and literature. In short, it would

be strange if you could not succeed where everybody and everything succeeds."

This would scarcely seem a very tempting proposal to a young man nowadays to quit the profession to which he had been trained and the seat
of whatever family and personal influence he possessed ; but Bryant's aversion to the law had increased as his literary talents were more widely
recognized, and he readily persuaded himself to
make a prospecting tour to New York in the spring
of 1824. His reception was seductive. He notes
in his letters to his wife that he " dined at Robert
Sedgwick's in company with Cooper, the novelist,
Halleck, the author of 'Fanny,' Sands, author of
'Yamoyden,' Johnson, the reporter of the Court of
Appeals, and some other literary gentlemen ; " that
one Sunday he heard "two sermons from Parson
Ware, and very good ones, too," and on Tuesday
had Sparks, who had succeeded to the editorship of
the " North American Review," to dine with him.
The Sedgwicks did all they could, and that meant
a great deal, to make New York inviting to him.
The result of his visit is easy to anticipate. Though
upon his return he did not at once abandon his
profession, his mind had evidently received during
his absence such impressions as were sure to put
an end to a prolonged residence at Great Barrington. This was apparent in the earnestness
with which he now devoted himself to literary
work.   " The United States Literary Gazette "
had been then recently established in Boston under

the editorial management of Theophilus Parsons, a young lawyer of promise, afterward eminent as a writer and as a jurist. He solicited Bryant's aid. The application came at a propitious moment; and during the first three years of the " Gazette's " existence, Bryant contributed to its pages from twenty to thirty poems, several of which rank among his best.[1] Of these pieces there was one which Mr. Godwin tells us had a deep and tender personal meaning. It is the " Sonnet to ――," his sister, the beloved companion of his earlier years, but then in the last stages of the disease of which their father had died a few years before. She is remembered as a person of rare endowments and of the loveliest disposition. It was but natural he wrote that

> " death should come
> Gently to one of gentle mould like thee,
> As light winds wandering through groves of bloom
> Detach the delicate blossoms from the tree."

She died in the twenty-second year of her age, and thereafter the old familiar places wore a gloom for him which, perhaps, inclined him more willingly to the change of residence to which influ-

[1] These were " The Massacre of Scio," " Rizpah," " The Rivulet," " March," " The Old Man's Funeral," " Sonnet to ――," " An Indian Story," " Summer Wind," " An Indian at the Burial Place of his Fathers," the song called " The Lovers' Lessons," " Monument Mountain," the " Hymn of the Waldenses," " After a Tempest," " Autumn Woods," " Mutation," " November," " Song of the Greek Amazon," " To a Cloud," " The Murdered Traveler," " Hymn to the North Star," " The Lapse of Time," " The Song of the Stars," and the " Forest Hymn."

ences from every quarter seemed to be entreating
him. To this cherished companion of his childhood he erected one of the noblest monuments with
which the memory of any American has yet been
honored, in his lines on "The Death of the Flowers." No one is to be envied who can read the
closing stanzas to-day without emotion.

"The melancholy days are come, the saddest of the year,
 Of wailing winds, and naked woods, and meadows brown and sere.
 Heaped in the hollows of the grove, the autumn leaves lie dead;
 They rustle to the eddying gust, and to the rabbit's tread.
 The robin and the wren are flown, and from the shrubs the jay;
 And from the wood-tops calls the crow through all the gloomy
   day.

"Where are the flowers, the fair young flowers, that lately sprang
   and stood,
 In brighter light and softer airs, a beauteous sisterhood?
 Alas! they all are in their graves; the gentle race of flowers
 Are lying in their lowly beds, with the fair and good of ours.
 The rain is falling where they lie; but the cold November rain
 Calls not from out the gloomy earth the lovely ones again.

"The wind-flower and the violet, they perished long ago;
 And the brier-rose and the orchis died amid the summer glow;
 But on the hills the golden-rod, and the aster in the wood,
 And the yellow sun-flower by the brook in autumn beauty stood,
 Till fell the frost from the clear, cold heaven, as falls the plague
   on men,
 And the brightness of their smile was gone from upland, glade,
   and glen.

"And now, when comes the calm, mild day, as still such days will
   come,
 To call the squirrel and the bee from out their winter home;
 When the sound of dropping nuts is heard, though all the trees
   are still,
 And twinkle in the smoky light the waters of the rill, —

The south-wind searches for the flowers whose fragrance late he
  bore,
And sighs to find them in the wood and by the stream no more.

"And then I think of one who in her youthful beauty died,
  The fair, meek blossom that grew up and faded by my side:
  In the cold, moist earth we laid her when the forests cast the
    leaf,
  And we wept that one so lovely should have a life so brief;
  Yet not unmeet it was that one, like that young friend of ours,
  So gentle and so beautiful, should perish with the flowers."

In "The Past," which at the time it was written
he was inclined to think the best poem he had
written, there occurs also a touching allusion to
both his then recent bereavements.

  "All that of good and fair
  Has gone into thy womb from earliest time
    Shall then come forth to wear
  The glory and the beauty of its prime.

  "They have not perished, — no!
  Kind words, remembered voices once so sweet,
    Smiles, radiant long ago,
  And features, the great soul's apparent seat.

  "All shall come back; each tie
  Of pure affection shall be knit again;
    Alone shall Evil die,
  And Sorrow dwell a prisoner in thy reign.

  "And then shall I behold
  Him by whose kind paternal side I sprang,
    And her who, still and cold,
  Fills the next grave, — the beautiful, the young."

When asked what compensation he expected for
these poems, Bryant named two dollars for each,
with which remuneration he was "abundantly sat-

isfied." Fifty years later, any publisher in the land would gladly have paid him a hundred times that sum for them, — a pleasing evidence of the rapid growth both of the literary taste and wealth of the country. His publishers, with a juster sense of the value of his contributions than his modesty permitted him to entertain, had the grace to offer him two hundred dollars a year for an average of one hundred lines a month, with an expression of their " profound regret that they were unable to offer a compensation more adequate." Small as this compensation seems to us, it had its influence in determining him to take all the risks and to trust to his pen for a livelihood. Accordingly in January of the year 1825, he revisited New York, where, in the course of the ensuing month, he undertook in connection with Henry J. Anderson the editorship of a monthly periodical, entitled the " New York Review and Athenæum Magazine," the first number of which was announced to appear in June.

Mr. Bryant did not abandon his profession — if the law can fairly be said to have ever been his profession — hastily or inconsiderately; nor did he trust himself to the precarious resources of his pen with any chimerical expectations. No one knew better than he how limited was the market at that time for such literary work as he was willing and able to execute. He was animated solely by a desire to exchange an uncongenial employment for a congenial one. The meanest livelihood achieved by his pen in the metropolis was more agreeable to him than affluence as a village attorney.

"I have given up my profession, which was a shabby one," he wrote about this time to his lifelong friend Dana, "and I am not altogether certain that I have got into a better. Bliss & White, however, the publishers of the 'New York Review,' employ me, which at present will be a livelihood, and a livelihood is all I got from the law." In another letter to Dana, written a few weeks later, he adds, "I do not know how long my connection with this work will continue. My salary is one thousand dollars; no great sum, to be sure, but it is twice what I got by my practice in the country. Besides, my dislike for my profession was augmenting daily, and my residence in Great Barrington, in consequence of innumerable quarrels and factions which were springing up every day among an extremely excitable and not very enlightened population, had become quite disagreeable to me. It cost me more pain and perplexity than it was worth to live on friendly terms with my neighbors; and, not having, as I flatter myself, any great taste for contention, I made up my mind to get out of it as soon as I could and come to this great city, where, if it was my lot to starve, I might starve peaceably and quietly. The business of sitting in judgment on books as they come out is not the literary employment most to my taste, nor that for which I am best fitted, but it affords me, for the present, a certain compensation."

In the latter part of June, he gives a yet more emphatic expression to his feelings in a letter to Mrs. Bryant, whom, in this experimental stage of his career, he had not ventured to expose to the heats of summer in New York: "Notwithstanding the heat, the noise, and the unpleasant odors of the city, I think that if you and Frances were with me I should pass my time here much more pleasantly than at Great Barrington. I am obliged to be pretty industrious, it is true, but that is well enough. In the mean time I am not plagued with the disagreeable, disgusting drudgery of the law; and, what is still better, am aloof from those miserable feuds and wranglings that make Great Barrington an unpleasant residence, even to him who tries every method in his power to avoid them."

It is apparent from these letters that Bryant's quarrel was not so much with the profession of the law as with the conditions under which he had been required to pursue it. Had not Providence given him wings with which to fly to more congenial spheres of activity, there is no reason to doubt that he would have risen to eminence in some department of that profession. He had every faculty, both moral and intellectual, for acquiring and deserving the confidence of clients. Like the poet Cowper, with whom he had more points of resemblance than with any other English poet, the shyness and delicacy of his nature disinclined him to the duties of a barrister; but, unlike Cowper, his shyness was not so morbid, while his courage and conscientiousness would have sustained him in the discharge of any duty which his profession might impose. Then there are departments of the profession in which his great talents and virtues would have proved most effective without doing any violence to his singularly acute and refined sensibilities; not perhaps in Great Barrington, nor indeed in any other country village, for no country village could have long detained such a lawyer as Bryant would have made. Had his father's means permitted him to study and practice his profession in Boston, he probably would have adhered to it for life, and now be known, and only known, to us as having once been a leading member of the Massachusetts bar. Here again the *audax paupertas* providentially intervened and said, "No, not a lawyer. There are a plenty of men who can become leading members of the Massachusetts bar, but I have work for you in another sphere for which there is no one else at present equally fitted."

As Bryant had staked everything upon his New York venture, he led an anxious as well as laborious life for the next few years. But he had youth and its inexhaustible faith to sustain him; he had congenial if not very remunerative employment; and in Cooper and Verplanck and Anderson and Sands and William Ware he had the society of friends, whose devotion to him only terminated

with their lives. Though his share of work on the
" Review " was quite enough for him, it did not
prevent his availing himself of every opportunity
of putting down new roots in the community to
which he had been transferred. In the autumn of
1825 he accepted an invitation from the Athenæum
Society to deliver some lectures on English poetry.
Though elementary in their scope and prepared
for a temporary forum, these lectures, four in
number, are still worth reading. While delivering these discourses, Bryant was appointed a professor in one of the schools organized under the
auspices of the National Academy of the Arts of
Design, then recently established. He read to his
classes five lectures on the subject of Mythology,
in December, 1827, which proved so acceptable
that he was called upon to repeat them in each of
the three or four succeeding years. To the " Review " he was also the principal contributor both
in prose and verse, and among his poetical contributions, " The Song of Pitcairn's Island," " Lines
on Revisiting the Country," " I cannot forget,"
" The Death of the Flowers," and " Hymns to
Death," are now as much read, perhaps, as any
verses he ever wrote. Halleck's " Marco Bozzaris,"
" Burns," " Wyoming," and " Connecticut," the
poems to which he owed his fame, also first appeared in the " Review." But in spite of these
and all its other attractions it did not thrive, and
Bryant's prospects at the close of his first year's
experience as "a literary adventurer," as he

styled himself, were anything but encouraging. Various expedients were resorted to, but in vain, to revive the drooping fortunes of the " Review." In March, 1826, it and " The New York Literary Gazette " were united under the name of " The New York Literary Gazette or American Athenæum." In July following this conglomerate was united with the " United States Gazette " of Boston, taking the title of the " United States Review and Literary Gazette," under the joint editorship of James G. Carter in Boston and Bryant in New York. Bryant was allowed a quarter ownership, five hundred dollars a year salary, and a prospective increase contingent upon the increase of subscribers. But these changes were only changes in name; the subscribers did not increase, and the divided editorial control proved anything but an advantage. The horizon seemed to be shutting in with darkness all around him. He was a young man; he had a wife and child dependent upon him; he had embarked in a new profession among strangers in a strange city. Like a castaway in the wide ocean, the more he exerted himself the more rapidly he exhausted his strength, with no evidence apparent that his prospects of succor were improving. His confidence in the sustaining power of his pen was so shaken that he applied for and obtained a license to practice law in the courts of New York, in anticipation of being again obliged

"to drudge for the dregs of men,
And scrawl strange words with the barbarous pen,

> And mingle among the jostling crowd
> Where the sons of strife are subtle and loud.''

Whatever Bryant strongly felt was pretty sure, sooner or later, to find expression in verse, and it was under the depressing influences about him that he wrote the following lines, which he entitled "The Journey of Life."

> " Beneath the waning moon I walk at night,
>   And muse on human life — for all around
> Are dim uncertain shapes that cheat the sight,
>   And pitfalls lurk in shade along the ground,
> And broken gleams of brightness here and there
> Glance through, and leave unwarmed, the death-like air.

> " The trampled earth returns a sound of fear —
>   A hollow sound, as if I walked on tombs;
> And lights, that tell of cheerful homes, appear
>   Far off, and die like hope amid the glooms.
> A mournful wind across the landscape flies,
> And the white atmosphere is full of sighs.

> " And I, with faltering footsteps, journey on,
>   Watching the stars that roll the hours away,
> Till the faint light that guides me now is gone,
>   And, *like another life, the glorious day*
> *Shall open o'er me from the empyreal height,*
> *With warmth and certainty and boundless light.*''

When read by the light of the circumstances in which they were written, these lines are very affecting, and yet more than with their pathos one is impressed with the unfaltering faith with which they are eloquent. There is no repining, no attempt to shield his self-love by holding Providence responsible for his hardships; still less do we find there any sign of surrender or of despair, but the same pious trust in the Divine guidance which a dozen years before had sustained him at another crisis in his career, and which found such lofty expression in the lines "To a Waterfowl." In perusing these verses, the classical student can hardly fail to be reminded of the Gentile but not unchristian faith revealed in the following lines of the great lyric poet of pagan Rome: —

> "Ut tuto ab atris corpore viperis
> Dormirem et ursis; ut premerer sacra
> Lauroque collataque myrto,
> Non sine Dis animosus infans." [1]

Bryant's trust in Providence was happily justified, as it always is to those who "hold out to the end." When his situation seemed most desperate, he was invited to assist in the editorship of the "New York Evening Post." This paper, then owned by William Coleman and Michael Burnham, had already acquired the commanding position in the country which it still maintains, and was a valuable property. Bryant's engagement at first was temporary. The place had been offered to his friend Dana, from whom, however, no answer had been received. Dana ultimately declined. This gave Bryant for the first time in his life a tolerably firm footing in an employment infinitely more

---

[1] Horace, Lib. III. Carmen IV. Thus rendered by Dean Milman: —

> "From the black viper safe and prowling bear,
> Sweet slept I, strewn with sacred leaves
> And myrtle twigs — bold child
> Not of the Gods unwatched."

congenial than that which he had abandoned, and
fairly remunerative.

While serving what may be termed his appren-
ticeship as a journalist, Bryant continued his labors
on the "Review" until it paid the debt of nature,
if no other.[1]   He then joined his friends Verplanck
and Sands in editing an annual called the "Talisman."   The first one appeared in 1828.   It was
succeeded by another in 1829, and a third in 1830,
when it was abandoned by its editors for more engrossing and profitable employment.[2]

With permanence of position Bryant was also
wise and fortunate enough to acquire an interest
in the property of the "Evening Post."

---

[1] Bryant's poetical contributions to the *Review* were, "October,"
"The Damsel of Pem," "The African Chief," "Spring in
Town," "The Gladness of Nature," "The Greek Partisan,"
"The Two Graves," and "The Conjunction of Jupiter and
Venus."

[2] Bryant's poetical contributions to the *Talisman* were, "A
Scene on the Banks of the Hudson," "The Hurricane," "Wil-
liam Tell," "Innocent Child and Snow-white Flower," "The
Close of Autumn," "To the Past," "The Hunter's Serenade,"
"The Greek Boy," "To the Evening Wind," "Love and Folly,"
"The Siesta," "Romero," "To the River Arve," 'To the Painter
Cole," and "Eva," including "The Alcayde of Molina," and
"The Death of Aliatar."   It is a proof how little the *Review*
had been known that two or three of these were republished from
it without detection.   His prose pieces were, "An Adventure in
the East Indies," "The Cascade of Melsingah," "Recollections
of the South of Spain," "Moriscan Romances," "Story of the
Island of Cuba," "The Indian Spring," "The Whirlwind,"
"Early Spanish Poetry," "Phanette des Gautelmes," "The
Marriage Blunder," and parts of the "Devil's Pulpit" and
"Reminiscences of New York."

Writing to Dana in February, 1829, he said, " I am a small proprietor in the establishment, and am a gainer by the arrangement. It will afford me a comfortable livelihood after I have paid for the eighth part, which is the amount of my share. I do not like politics any better than you do; but they get only my mornings, and you know politics and a bellyful are better than poetry and starvation."

Only five months after this letter was written Mr. Coleman, the editor-in-chief and proprietor, died, and Bryant was immediately promoted to his seat. With this promotion, also, he acquired an additional interest in the property,[1] of which he continued the proprietor during the remainder of his life, about half a century.

[1] For this purpose I am told that Henry Sedgwick lent him two thousand dollars.

CHAPTER VI.

THE JOURNALIST.

WHEN Bryant entered the office of the " Evening Post," he embarked in a profession which was destined to absorb his best energies for the remaining years of a long life. For more than half of our national existence he was the directing mind of that journal. During all this long period he contracted no other business engagements, he was never officially engaged in the administration of any other financial or industrial enterprise, nor did he ever accept any political office. And yet I do not recall the name of any other American, save Dr. Franklin, who for as long a period was so unremittingly and effectively occupied in shaping public opinion, nor one who ever gave so many hours of conscientious thought to questions involving so exclusively the interests and welfare of mankind. Nowhere else in our literature, I believe, can be found such a continuous, complete, and satisfactory record of the growth and expansion of political thought in the United States as in the columns of the " Evening Post " during the first fifty years of Bryant's connection with it. It would be difficult to name any subject of general concern that fell properly within the domain of secular journalism during that period that he did not deal with, and in a way to deserve, and usually to command, the respectful attention even of those who were not prepared to accept all his conclusions.

Journalism when Bryant entered the profession was as little like the journalism of 1889 as Jason's fifty-oared craft " Argo" was like a modern steam packet. The commercial value of news merely as news to the daily press was as much undervalued as anthracite coal for fuel, or electricity for light. The newspaper was usually established in the interest of some prominent party leader, who fought his battles in its columns. The editor was more or less his party's mouthpiece, and the readers consulted its columns mainly for its political indications. The modern reporter was yet in the chrysalis stage of existence, while the "interviewer" was as one of those remote stars, the light of which had not yet reached our planet. A weekly packet with the news in a file of London papers, condensed into a few paragraphs, supplied all the information from the outside world for which there seemed to be any demand, while local news was limited pretty much to such items as friends of the editor or interested parties might take the trouble to communicate. The evolution or transformation of our journalism from its stage of organism to the newspaper proper was of a later date, and was due to the absence rather than to the presence of qualities from which success could then

have been predicated. Lacking the literary training and accomplishment of an effective writer, the
late James Gordon Bennett had the sagacity to find
in news and gossip a cheap substitute for brilliant
leaders. These features of the "Herald" newspaper, which he founded, attracted readers from the
larger class who had only a secondary interest in
politics, and placed his journal upon an independent financial footing which delivered it from the
thrall of scheming politicians. It was, I believe,
the first politically independent secular journal
published in the United States. In proportion as
the daily prints, following the example of the
"Herald," have become in fact as well as in name
newspapers, have they become representatives of
the whole people, instead of being merely the representatives of political parties and factions.

For the first twenty years of his connection with
the "Evening Post," Bryant had but one permanent assistant in his office, a scanty report of the
shipping and financial intelligence being supplied
to the "Evening Post" in common with some
other papers, each bearing its proportion of the
expense. The attraction and influence of the paper depended mainly upon its editorials, which
rarely occupied more than a column.

As the "Evening Post" was published in the
afternoon, the work on it had to begin at an early
hour of the morning. During the first forty years
of his editorial life, it was a rare thing for Mr.
Bryant, if in town, not to be found at his desk

before eight o'clock in the morning. He was not a fluent nor a very prolific writer. Beside his natural fastidiousness, he had a literary reputation to sustain, with which he never allowed himself to trifle. His manuscripts, as well as his proofs, were commonly so disfigured by corrections as to be read with difficulty even by those familiar with his script.

Good poets have usually been masters of a superior prose style. Bryant was no exception. Though he neither sought nor expected fame from his prose, he was careful to print nothing that could in any way compromise his reputation as a poet. As a consequence, in all his contributions to his paper, I doubt if as many erroneous or defective forms of expression can be found as in the first ten numbers of the "Spectator." He never allowed slang or affectations of expression of any kind a place in its columns, nor would he allow the clients of the "Evening Post" ever to be described or recognized as "patrons." In a letter to a young man who had asked his opinion of an article he had written, he has given the following brief exposition of what he regarded as the rudimentary principles of good writing for the periodical press : —

"I observe that you have used several French expressions in your letter. I think if you will study the English language, that you will find it capable of expressing all the ideas you may have. I have always found it so, and in all that I have written I do not recall an instance where I was tempted to use a foreign word but that, on searching, I have found a better one in my own language.

"Be simple, unaffected ; be honest in your speaking and writing. Never use a long word where a short one will do as well.

"Call a spade by its name, not a well-known oblong instrument of manual labor ; let a home be a home, and not a residence ; a place, not a locality, and so on of the rest. When a short word will do, you will always lose by a long one ; you lose in clearness, you lose in honest expression of meaning, and, in the estimation of all men who are capable of judging, you lose in reputation for ability.

"The only true way to shine, even in this false world, is to be modest and unassuming. Falsehood may be a thick crust, but in the course of time Truth will find a place to break through. Elegance of language may not be in the power of us all, but simplicity and straightforwardness are."

He rarely quoted, in support of his own opinions, or for a more effective statement of them ; and, as a rule, he never quoted in a foreign tongue. If he did by chance, it was apt to be with an apology.

Bryant's prose, like his poetry, was always clear. No one could mistake his meaning, nor have the least difficulty in gathering it from his language. Nor did he ever try to leave a different impression from that which his words strictly imported. Though master of a genial humor as well as of a refined irony, he never trifled with serious matters, nor with his readers. He never made sport of the calamities or afflictions even of the most depraved, taught both by what nature discloses and by what she conceals,

> "Never to blend our pleasure or our pride
> With sorrow of the meanest thing that feels."

He rigorously eschewed the discussion of religious topics, especially those of a controverted character. He never could be beguiled into personal controversy, insisting that every line of a newspaper belonged to the public that paid for it, and could not honestly be perverted to the gratification of the vanity or spite or self-sufficiency of its editors. How much Bryant's example has had to do with the marvelous improvements in the literary quality and moral tone which distinguishes the journalism of to-day from that which prevailed during the first quarter of the century is only known to those who have been witnesses of the change, and they will soon have all passed away. The number of such as are disposed to disinter the genius and professional virtues which are sepulchred in the files of an old newspaper is very limited. Nor would Bryant have had it otherwise, for he had no desire to be remembered as a "journalist," profoundly as he was interested in all he sought to accomplish as such for human society.

Bryant had one peculiarity which would hardly have been so conspicuous in any other profession. He rarely if ever gave advice, and, unless in his

domestic circle, of which I cannot speak, never un-
asked. Even the juniors in his office, the "'prentice hands" of his staff, had to study their profession from his example, not from his precepts. His
reasons for this can only be conjectured. He may
have felt with Shaftesbury that "that which we
call 'giving advice' was properly taking an occasion to show our wisdom at another's expense." A
gentleman who was associated with him many years
in the management of the "Evening Post," commenting upon this peculiarity, remarked: —

"When I entered the office I had had some little practice as a writer for magazines, such as is common to most
young men of strong literary tastes, but I had had no experience in journalism proper. As a matter of course I
was continually doing things I ought not to have done,
and leaving undone things I ought to have done. Bryant
never rebuked me; he never criticised me. In looking
over my proofs he would occasionally say, 'Had not this
word better be changed for that or the other? Does that
phrase express all or more than you mean, or as clearly
as you wish it to?' Even this mode of correction was
very rare. As I became more familiar with my duties,
and compared my own work with his, I realized how often
I must have offended; how much I must have written that
he would not have written; how many canons of the
master I must have violated, and in my hours of solitary meditation often wondered what could be the secret
of his silence and forbearance. My heart once almost
ceased to beat when the suspicion crossed my mind that
he thought criticism and instruction would be wasted
upon me. But just in proportion to his tolerance was my

vigilance in searching for the difference between his work and mine, and as far and as fast as possible were my efforts to diminish their number. Before long I became sensible that he had pursued the wiser course, and that I improved much faster by being driven for guidance to his example, which, like the shadow of St. Peter, exerted a healing influence upon whomsoever it fell, than if he had begun with me by pointing out my errors and deficiencies, which would probably have had the effect either of making me timid and of discouraging me, or of leaving me to suppose that all he did not censure was satisfactory. Of course all his literary standards were at least as much higher than mine as he was my senior. He knew, therefore, that he could not impose them successfully upon me then, but that I must, as far as in me lay, grow to them, as the acorn grows to be an oak, and that the attempt would only result either in rebellion or in converting me into a machine. The respect I thus acquired for his example, not only as a journalist, but for his standards in every relation in life, grew upon me steadily while our professional association lasted, so that, for years after it ceased, when in perplexing situations and in doubt about what it was becoming and proper for me to do or to leave undone, I found myself instinctively and habitually asking myself, 'What would Bryant do in my situation?' And it almost invariably happened that when subjected to this test all my doubts promptly vanished. I had no hesitation in doing what I should not have been surprised to see him do, while I shrank from anything which would have surprised me if done by him. I have known many wise and excellent men in my life, but no one whose example pursued me so faithfully or with any such results. And I trust I have learned from him to have a more just appreciation of the relative importance of example and advice."

Though he had been trained in the strictest principles of New England Federalism, Bryant found, when he came to be clothed with the responsibilities of a leader and guide, that his controlling sympathies and instincts were with the Democratic party. Jackson was President. His battle with nullification in the South, and with the Bank of the United States, and his vetoes of road, river, and harbor bills, as being special or local instead of national in their bearing, commanded his cordial approval. He early embraced the conviction which lies at the foundation of the Democratic polity, not that that government is best that governs least, but that that government is best which shall limit its functions most completely to those of an effective police in keeping every man's hand off of every other man, and off of his property. Whenever government transcended these functions, he thought it required close watching, with all the presumptions against it. This conviction led him early to question the wisdom of granting special charters to banks; to denounce the inspection, conspiracy, and usury laws; to favor the removal of all legislative restrictions upon commerce, and to provide for the expenses of government by a strictly revenue tariff. He assented to and effectively supported the tariff of 1846, framed upon the principle enunciated by Governor Silas Wright, — a tariff for revenue, with incidental protection. The formula would have pleased him better with the "incidental protection" left out.

Whenever he had occasion to speak of slavery, he never was its apologist, nor did he ever neglect an opportunity of rendering any practical assistance to the cause of emancipation ; and when the question of extending the territory afflicted with slavery arose, no journal in the country labored more or suffered more in resisting such extension. He never advocated the abolition of slavery by the federal government until it became justifiable and expedient as a war measure. The courts and the laws, if not the Constitution, had placed slavery within the States under the protection of the Constitution in the judgment of the leading statesmen of all parties. Mr. Bryant acquiesced in this judgment as he acquiesced in many other national abuses which he saw no means of remedying. But when the census of 1860 revealed to the country the fact that the political ascendency of the slaveholding States had departed, and that the nonslaveholding States had a majority in both houses of Congress; and when, for the purpose of restoring such ascendency, they endeavored to carry slavery into all the vast unsettled territories of the Northwest, the "Evening Post" did not hesitate to take the attitude of unhesitating and uncompromising opposition, preferring that the question should be settled by the dread arbitrament of war to any responsibility for the surrender of one more inch of American soil to be tilled by the hands of bondmen. War ensued, and while supporting the government in its prosecution with all the vigor of his pen and the weight of his character, true to his Democratic instincts, he denounced the financial policy of the government by which its paper promises were made a lawful tender in discharge of its pecuniary obligations.

When Mr. Lincoln, in January, 1863, issued his proclamation of freedom to the slaves in certain States which persisted in their insurrection against the government, Bryant, while disposed to accept it with gratitude as a step in the right direction, found it less comprehensive and definite in its terms than he thought the occasion called for. He did not believe in gradual emancipation as a measure suited to the emergencies of flagrant war. In a speech which he made at a meeting held in behalf of the loyalists of Missouri who were calling upon the nation to protect them, he portrayed the follies of gradual emancipation in terms as nearly approaching to genuine eloquence, probably, as he ever reached.

" Gradual emancipation ! " he exclaimed. " Have we not suffered enough from slavery without keeping it any longer? Has not blood enough been shed? My friends, if a child of yours were to fall into the fire, would you pull him out gradually? If he were to swallow a dose of laudanum sufficient to cause speedy death, and a stomach pump was at hand, would you draw the poison out by degrees? If your house were on fire, would you put it out piecemeal? And yet there are men who talk of gradual emancipation by force of ancient habit, and there are men in the Slave States who make of slavery a sort of idol which they are unwilling to part with; which, if it must be removed, they would prefer to see removed after a lapse of time and tender leave-takings.

"Slavery is a foul and monstrous idol, a Juggernaut under which thousands are crushed to death; it is a Moloch for whom the children of the land pass through fire. Must we consent that the number of the victims shall be diminished gradually? If there are a thousand victims this year, are you willing that nine hundred shall be sacrificed next year, and eight hundred the next, and so on until after the lapse of ten years it shall cease? No, my friends, let us hurl the grim image from its pedestal. Down with it to the ground. Dash it to fragments; trample it in the dust. Grind it to powder as the prophets of old commanded that the graven images of the Hebrew idolaters should be ground, and in that state scatter it to the four winds and strew it upon the waters, that no human hand shall ever again gather up the accursed atoms and mould them into an image to be worshiped again with human sacrifice."

When the war had terminated, it was the deliverance of the nation from all complicity with slavery that he regarded as its great and compensating result.

A few weeks after peace was reëstablished, his

feelings of patriotic pride and satisfaction over-
flowed in a letter of congratulation to Miss Sedgwick, in the course of which he said, "Never,
I think, was any great moral lesson so powerfully
inculcated by political history. What the critics
call poetic justice has been as perfectly accomplished as it could have been in any imaginary
series of events.

"When I think of this great conflict and its
great issues, my mind reverts to the grand imagery
of the Apocalypse — to the visions in which the
messengers of God came down to do his bidding
among the nations, to reap the earth, ripe for the
harvest, and gather the spoil of the vineyards;
to tread the winepress till it flows over far and
wide with blood; to pour out the phials of God's
judgments upon the earth and turn its rivers into
blood; and, finally, to bind the dragon and thrust
him down into the bottomless pit.

"Neither you nor I thought, until this war began, that slavery would disappear from our country until more than one generation had passed
away. Yet a greater than man has taken the work
in hand, and it is done in four years. It is a great
thing to have lived long enough to have seen this
mighty evil wrenched up from our soil by the roots
and thrown into the flames."

The war over, Bryant directed all his influence
and effort to the reparation of the graver financial
errors of the government, which the exigencies of
the preceding five years had, in the judgment of

patriots, palliated if not excused. He insisted upon the immediate repeal of the "legal tender act;" he exposed and denounced the schemes which were rife, especially in the Western and Southern States, for the increase of inconvertible currency, then popularly known as "soft money;" and he urged with unwonted vehemence the liberation of the industries and commerce of the country from the paralyzing burdens of what is euphuistically termed "a war tariff," and the accumulation in the treasury of wealth unnecessarily withdrawn from the channels of productive industry.

On the brief chart of Bryant's career which we are fashioning, it is only possible to set down the headlands of the route by which he journeyed. The topics we have enumerated constitute but a very inconsiderable portion of those which he had occasion to treat in the course of his long professional career, but they show the single-eyed, large-minded, and patriotic spirit with which he dealt with all public questions. It is doubtful if so wise, comprehensive, and edifying a system of political ethics as might be compiled from Mr. Bryant's editorial contributions to the "Evening Post" can be found elsewhere in the literature of our own or of any other country. I do not believe any man ever sat down to the discharge of a professional duty with a more resolute determination to exclude the influence of personal or selfish considerations. He repeatedly felt himself constrained to take the unpopular side on important public questions. His support

of General Jackson in his war against the United
States Bank aroused a feeling against his paper
among the merchants of New York, upon whom
its existence largely depended, which no one of
much less weight of personal character and authority could have surmounted. The attitude of his
journal upon the slavery question also stripped its
columns of most of its advertisements, and brought
it to the verge of bankruptcy.

During the riots of 1863, it enjoyed the distinction of being threatened by a reactionary mob, and
had not special measures of defense been season-
ably taken, it would doubtless have been sacked.[1]
His firmness, his fidelity to principle, his uncalcu-
lating devotion to the greatest good of the greatest
number, and the dignified and temperate way in
which he was accustomed to commend his views to
the public were not wasted, though at times they
seemed to contribute more to deplete than replen-
ish his exchequer. If many from that day turned

---

[1] The following note was sent in reply to one from his steward,
Mr. Cline, informing him that some one in the cars had been
overheard to say that " Bryant's house would have to blaze."

OFFICE OF THE EVENING POST.
NEW YORK, July 18, 1863.

DEAR SIR, — Mr. Henderson has just shown me your letter.
Four revolvers and ammunition will be sent down to you this evening. Mr. Godwin and Bryant (his grandson) know how they are
to be used, if you and others about you do not. You will, I
hope, be discreet in what you say, and though not believing too
much of what is reported, be ready for the worst. If John and
Jacob are willing to aid in the defense of the house, you may re-
munerate them. As to Thomas, I am sure I may depend on him
as one not easily frightened.

back from following him, there was probably no
man in the whole country who was personally more
respected. Even in Tammany Hall, where his
paper and political doctrines were publicly denounced, a quotation from his poems by its speakers would be received with rounds of applause.

During the earlier and less prosperous portions
of his editorial career, the poet and the journalist
wrestled with each other in the affections of Bryant
like Esau and Jacob in the womb of Rebecca.
There was probably no time during the first twenty
years of his connection with the "Evening Post"
that he would not gladly have abandoned all his
interests in the property for half of what he received from it later in a single year. This feeling
nearly mastered him during the bank war and the
monetary crisis which followed it. Writing to his
friend Dana in 1836, — he had already been seven
years on the "Post," — he says: —

"Plans for the future I have none at present,
except to work hard as I am now obliged to do; I
hope, however, the day will come when I may retire without danger of starving, and give myself
to occupations that I like better. But who is suffered to shape the course of his own life?"

In July following, he writes to his wife: —

" 'The Evening Post' was a sad, dull thing during the winter after Sedgwick [1] left it, and people

---

[1] During Mr. Bryant's absence the previous year in Europe,
his partner, Mr. Leggett, had been taken ill, and the columns of
the *Evening Post* were temporarily confided to Theodore Sedg-

were getting tired of it. I have raised it a good deal, so that it begins to be talked about and quoted. I must now apply myself to bringing it up to its old standard, after which I shall look for a purchaser. Dr. Anderson says he will find me one. I think from the attention he pays to politics, writing frequently, talking much, and coming to the office to read the papers we receive in exchange, that he may possibly become a purchaser himself."

How modest were his views of a retiring fortune in those days appears in a letter written to his brother John in September of the same year: —

"I think of making some disposition of my interest in the 'Evening Post,' and coming out to the Western country with a few thousand dollars to try my fortune. What do you think of such a plan? What could I do next summer or fall with a little capital of from three to five thousand dollars? Will you write me at large your views of the probability of my success, and of the particular modes of investment which would yield the largest profit? I am inclined to think that I might make money as fast as I can do it here, and with much less wear and tear of brains. Write me fully, but do not go too much into conjecture; speak only of what you know, or of what has actually happened. I have not been much pleased,

wick, Jr., a member of the New York bar and a nephew of Miss Sedgwick, the authoress. His discussion of public questions under the signature of "Veto" enjoyed quite a reputation in their day.

since my return, with New York. The entire
thoughts of the inhabitants seem to be given to
the acquisition of wealth; nothing else is talked
of. The city is dirtier and noisier, and more un-
comfortable, and dearer to live in than it ever was
before. I have had my fill of a town life, and begin to wish to pass a little time in the country. I
have been employed long enough with the management of a daily newspaper, and desire leisure for
literary occupations that I love better. It was not
my intention when I went to Europe to return to
the business of conducting a newspaper. If I were
to come out to Illinois next spring with the design
of passing the year there, what arrangements could
be made for my family? What sort of habitation
could I have, and what would it cost? I hardly
think I shall come to Illinois to live, but I can tell
better after I have tried it. You are so distant
from all the large towns, and the means of education are so difficult to come at, and there is so little
literary society, that I am afraid I might wish to
get back to the Atlantic coast. I should like, however, to try the experiment of a year at the West."

Again, in February of 1837, he reveals to his
friend Dana his yearnings for more leisure and less
care. "The gains you talk of I wish I could see.
The expenses of printing and conducting a daily
paper have vastly increased lately, and there is no
increase in the rate of advertisements, etc., to make
it up. I should be very glad of an opportunity to
attempt something in the way I like best, and am,

perhaps, fittest for; but here I am a draught-horse, harnessed to a daily drag. I have so much to do with my legs and hoofs, struggling and pulling and kicking, that, if there is anything of the Pegasus in me, I am too much exhausted to use my wings. I would withdraw from the occupation if I could do so and be certain of a moderate subsistence, for, with my habits and tastes, a very little would suffice. I am growing, I fear, more discontented and impatient than I ought to be at the lot which has fallen to me."

In the following year, 1837, he found himself obliged to give up any idea of selling or fleeing, for reasons assigned in the following letter to his brother John: —

"New York, *October 25th.*

"I am very much obliged to you for your kind offer, and if I were at liberty I should like nothing better than to pass a year in Illinois. But I am fastened here for the present. The 'Evening Post' cannot be disposed of in these times, and, on account of the difficulty of making collections, its income does not present an appearance which would enable me to sell it for its real value, even if I could find a purchaser. I am chained to the oar for another year, at least. The prospects of the journal are, however, improving, though I am personally no better for it at present. I am very much perplexed by the state of my pecuniary affairs. I have taken a house in town at as moderate a rent as I could find, and expect my family from the country in a very few days. I am obliged to practice the strictest frugality, but that I do not regard as an evil. The great difficulty lies in meeting the debts in which the purchase of the paper has involved me. When I went to Europe, the 'Evening Post' was producing a liberal income; Mr. Leggett, who conducted it, espoused very zealously the cause of the Abolitionists, and then was taken ill. The business of the establishment fell into the hands of a drunken and saucy clerk to manage, and the hard times came on. All these things had a bad effect on the profits of the paper, and when I returned they were reduced to little or nothing. In the mean time Mr. Leggett and myself had contracted a large debt for the purchase of the 'Evening Post.' He retired, and the whole was left on my shoulders. I have been laboring very diligently to restore the paper to a prosperous state, and begin to have hopes that I shall retrieve what was lost during my absence in Europe by careful attention to the business of the paper, properly so called. I cannot leave the establishment till I have put it in good order. Nobody will buy it of me. With so much to pay, and with a paper so little productive, I have been several times on the point of giving it up, and going out into the world worse than penniless. Nothing but a disposition to look at the hopeful side of things prevented me, and I now see reason to be glad that I persevered.

"I have no leisure for poetry. The labors in

which I am engaged would not, perhaps, be great
to many people, but they are as great as I can
endure with a proper regard to my health. I cannot pursue intellectual labor so long as many of
a more robust or less nervous temperament. My
constitution requires intervals of mental repose.
To keep myself in health I take long walks in the
country, for half a day, a day, or two days. I cannot well leave my business for a longer period, and
I accustom myself to the greatest simplicity of
diet, renouncing tea, coffee, animal food, etc. By
this means I enjoy a health scarcely ever interrupted, but when I am fagged I hearken to nature
and allow her to recruit. I find by experience
that this must be if I would not kill myself. What
you say of living happily on small means I agree
to with all my heart. My ideas of competence
have not enlarged a single dollar. Indeed, they
have rather been moderated and reduced by recent
events, and I would be willing to compound for
a less amount than I would have done three or
four years since. If I had the means of retiring, I would go into the country, where I could
adopt a simpler mode of living, and follow the
bent of my inclination in certain literary pursuits,
but I have a duty to perform to my creditors."

Among the unanswerable problems of history
which have exercised the ingenuity of speculative
minds, there are few, perhaps, of more interest to
Americans than those which would have been presented if some of the things that might have hap-

pened, and seemed likely to happen, had happened; if, for example, Columbus and his party had been lost on the voyage which resulted in the discovery of America, and if Milton, Cromwell, and the first Napoleon had executed the purpose, which each of them at one time seriously entertained, of seeking a refuge and a home on this side of the Atlantic. Of scarcely less interest would it be to his countrymen to be able to divine the consequences had Bryant's wish at this time to sell his paper and emigrate to the West been granted.

Bryant managed in a few years to retrieve the ground his journal had lost during his absence from the country, and from that time his paper, though once or twice threatened with disaster, always yielded him enough to give him peace of mind. Its revenues varied considerably at different periods, as its doctrines happened to be more or less in accord with those of the party upon which it was largely dependent, but it always proved a sure reliance for his needs, and occasionally for something more, though it never promised him affluence until he had reached a pretty advanced period of life. The average net earnings of his paper prior to 1849 was about $10,000 a year, of which his share was four tenths. Its net earnings for the year 1850 were a little less than $16,000; for the year 1860 it was over $70,000. From this time forth, I think it may be stated with confidence that Mr. Bryant experienced no privation which money could relieve. He not only was able to provide for all the personal needs of himself and family, but he had the chief if not the only privilege which makes wealth desirable, of ministering to the wants of others, and of extending substantial encouragement to those institutions of public beneficence which specially commended themselves to his taste and judgment.

We are all of us disposed at some stage, if not at every stage, of our lives to complain of the burdens we are required to carry, and of the difficulties with which we have to struggle like Milton's lion, "to get free our hinder parts." Few, however, are grateful, or at least as grateful as they should be, for the discipline and the training which they owe to these trials, and through which they acquire most of whatever capacities for usefulness and happiness they possess. Longfellow, during his professional life at Cambridge, was constantly groaning over the drudgery it imposed, and fancying that if he had nothing to do, he would do a great deal more. "Pardon me, oh ye souls," he wrote to one of his correspondents, "who, seeing education only from afar, speak of it in such glowing words. You see only the great pictures hanging in the light; not the grinding of the paint and the oil, nor the pulling of hair from the camel's back for the brushes."

Yet both of these gifted bards probably lived to realize that neither would have attained the rank they took, even as poets, not to say men, had their lives lacked their background of drudgery. A life of pleasure, "stretched upon the rack of a too easy chair," is of all lives the most miserable. There is no recreation where there is no work. The grinding of the paints may seem very hateful to the enthusiastic artist, who naturally fancies himself born for better things. But Longfellow, in this allusion to a sister art, seems to have overlooked the fact that the most renowned painters of the world not only ground their own paints, but prepared their own canvases, and even the walls which they decorated with their immortal frescoes.

Happily, Bryant was saved from the devices of his own heart and the *vita umbratilis* for which in his short-sightedness he yearned, and he lived to realize the wisdom so quaintly phrased by Quarles: —

> "Mechanic soul, thou must not only do
> With Martha, but with Mary ponder too,
> Happy the house where these two sisters vary,
> But most, when Martha's reconciled to Mary."

Among the rarest things to find in all literary history are men who have succeeded as well as Bryant in maintaining a conversancy with men and affairs without entirely losing their hold of the contemplative life.

Partly from sanitary considerations, but more to satisfy his craving for opportunities of indulging his love of nature, which amounted more nearly than anything else to a passion with him, he took advantage of the first surge of financial prosperity that overtook him to secure a country home. In

1843, he found on Long Island a place entirely to his taste. " It was near a little village afterward called Roslyn, overlooking an estuary of the Sound, — such a nook as a poet might well choose, both for its shady seclusion and its beautiful prospects; embowered in woods that covered a row of gentle hills, and catching glimpses of a vast expanse of water, enlivened in the distance by the sails of a metropolitan commerce. The estate was at first confined to a few acres only, on which he proposed erecting a house according to his taste, but he was soon enamored of a house already erected on it, and the next year made it his own. It was an old-fashioned mansion, built by a plain Quaker in 1787, containing many spacious rooms, surrounded by shrubberies and grand trees, and communicating by a shelving lawn with one of the prettiest of small fresh-water lakes." [1]

With this acquisition life bloomed with new charms for Bryant, and the toils of his profession were at last "sweetened to his taste." Nothing more was heard of selling the " Evening Post," nor of a new home in the wilderness. For the remainder of his life, from early spring until winter drove him to his city residence, he rarely spent less than two or three days of every week at his Roslyn home. Leaving his cares behind him in town, here he gave himself up " to keeping his friendships in repair," to nursing and developing all the vital energies and graces of his garden and farm;

[1] Godwin's *Life,* i. 408.

to cultivating a most intimate acquaintance with every tree and flower and fruit that they could be encouraged to produce, and in teaching them to become to his neighbors and friends the prolific instruments of a judicious and seasonable beneficence. Here it was his delight to receive his old friends, and to extend an unostentatious but welcome hospitality to distinguished strangers who were apt to think that "seeing the States" necessarily included a visit to Roslyn.

Partly to gratify a sentiment, but more in the hope of benefiting Mrs. Bryant's health, which already had become the subject of some solicitude, in 1865 Bryant became the proprietor of another country seat. Writing to an English correspondent, he says: "I have been passing a few weeks at a place to which I shall return in a day or two. I mean Cummington, my birthplace. Here I have repossessed myself of the old homestead and farm where my father and maternal grandfather lived, and have fitted it up and planted a screen of evergreens, from ten to twenty feet in height, back of it to protect it from the northwest winds, — though that is of little consequence in summer, — and here I pass several weeks in the warm season. The region is high, — nineteen hundred feet above the level of the sea; the summers are cool, the air Swisslike, and the healthiness of the country remarkable." . . .

His private letters from his country homes all breathe of the regenerating atmosphere in which they were penned. Those who only knew Bryant through the columns of his journal would hardly recognize his pen in the following letter to his venerable friend, and for some time pastor, the Rev. Dr. Dewey.

"NEW YORK, *April* 30, 1860.

" 'If we will have you, doctor? what words have passed thy lips unweighed?' If the earth will have the spring, — if the sunflower will have sunshine, — if the flock will have grass. You might as well put an 'if' between a hungry man and his dinner. You shall come to Roslyn, you and your Sultana, and shall be welcome, and treated *en rois*. If I were writing for the press I should not say '*en rois*,' for in public I hold it my duty to maintain on all occasions the supremacy and sufficiency of the English language; but I have said *en rois* because it came into my head. Come on and we will make the most of you both, and anybody else you choose to bring with you, — that our poor means allow. You shall not be walked out more than you absolutely choose, nor asked to look at anything. You shall have full leave to bury yourself in books, or write, or think, or smoke away your time, and I will make a provision of cigars for your idle hours, with the prudent toleration which the innocent have for the necessary vices of others. I have a coachman, and he shall take you about the country whenever you and Mrs. Dewey take a fancy for a ride. And having done this, I will neglect you, for I am afraid that is what you like, to your heart's content. And then if, — for I, too, must have my if, — if you will only stay over Sunday, you shall be asked to preach by our orthodox Presbyterian minister, who inquires when Dr. Dewey is expected, for he wants to ask him to preach. Come, then, prepared for a ten days' sojourn, with a stock of patience in your heart, and a sermon or two in your pocket, of your second or third quality, for we are quite plain people here, and anything very fine is wasted upon us.

" For any imperfections in my eulogy on Irving I beg you to consider the Historical Society as responsible ; they put it upon me without consulting me ; and at first I flatly refused, but I was afterward talked into consent. Besides the excuses of incapacity, unworthiness, and all that, I did not want the labor of writing the discourse. There has been no end of work with me the past winter. . . . Among other symptoms of age, I find a disposition growing up within me to regard the world as belonging to a new race of men, who have somehow or other got into it, and taken possession of it, and among whom I am a superfluity. What have I to do with their quarrels and controversies? I, who am already proposed as a member of the same club with Daniel Defoe and Sir Roger L'Estrange. Is it fitting that, just as I have taken my hat to go out and join the Ptolemies, I should be plucked by the elbow and asked to read a copy of silly verses, and say whether they are fit to be printed ? Besides, it seems to be agreed by everybody who is about my own age, or older, that the world is nowadays much wickeder than when they were young; and it is no more than it deserves to leave it to take care of itself as it can. But we will talk over these things when you come."

Again, three years later, he pleads for another visit from his reverend friend, written in a yet more frolicsome not to say rollicksome mood: —

" ROSLYN, *October* 5, 1863.

"Looking at your last a second time, it strikes me that you might, perhaps, expect that I should answer some part of it. Let me say, then, that we will give you a reasonable time to consider the question of coming to Roslyn, you and Mrs. Dewey, if you will only come at last, and before the days arrive described in the verses which you will find on the other leaf of this sheet. Mrs. Kirkland says she will come when you do.

" The season wears an aspect glum and glummer,
The icy north wind, an unwelcome comer,
Frighting from garden-walks each pretty hummer,
Whose murmuring music lulled the noons of summer,
Roars in the woods, with grummer voice and grummer,
And thunders in the forest like a drummer.
Dumb are the birds, — they could not well be dumber;
The winter-cold, life's pitiless benumber,
Bursts water-pipes, and makes us call the plumber.
Now, by the fireside, toils the patient thumber
Of ancient books, and no less patient summer
Of long accounts, while topers fill the rummer,
The maiden thinks what furs will best become her,
And on the stage-boards shouts the gibing mummer.
Shut in by storms, the dull piano-strummer
Murders old tunes. There's nothing wearisomer! "

It is true that for the first twenty years of his editorial career Bryant led a very laborious life, but it was not merely love of the quiet and leisure of an independent planter, nor aversion to the din and distraction of the city, that caused him to dream of exchanging his newspaper for a farm on the prairies. Hard work did not worry him; on the contrary, during all this period his health seemed constantly to improve, and the care which he took of it was so judicious that he was always in condition for literary work of any kind. He seemed to have no moods nor seasons when literary labor was to him more or less irksome than at other. His discontent with his position has been and will always be the common experience of all who attempt to impose upon their neighbors higher standards of duty than their neighbors are prepared to accept. Those paths always lead to Calvary and the Cross. Bryant's standards were very high. His editorial work was chiefly critical. To find fault with the conduct of large parties and of communities is never a gracious task, and is the less gracious the more it is deserved. Bryant was so constituted morally, that when he saw public abuses, especially in high places, he could not hold his peace. He felt like St. Paul that, did he keep silence, the very stones would cry out. He was not prone to calculate the consequences of publicly judging the rest of mankind by his own standards. He was once heard to quote in extenuation of his course the following majestic passage of Milton : —

" It is manifest with what small willingness I endure, to leave calm and pleasing solitariness, to embark upon a troublous sea of noises and harsh disputes; put from beholding the bright countenance of Truth in the quiet of delightful studies; but one of the meanest under service, if God by his secretary, conscience, enjoined it, it were sad for me if I should draw back."

The duty of the journalist to comment sometimes with severity upon the conduct of public men, and of men with whom he entertains or has entertained social relations, is one of the most unpleasant that his profession devolves upon him. It tends to drive him from public resorts and make him appear unsocial. It had these effects upon Bryant during the most active portion of his life as a journalist. He studied to so manage his critical function as to create the least possible friction, and was wont to cite to his editorial associates the example of Dr. Bartlett, the editor of a weekly paper in New York, especially addressed to English people, called " The Albion," who made it a rule " never to write anything of any one which would make it unpleasant to meet him the following day at dinner." Though Bryant thought well of this standard, it must be conceded that in the discharge of what he esteemed his duty as a journalist, he had somewhat reduced the number of people whom it would have been pleasant for him or them to meet at the same festive board. *Chacun a les défauts de ses vertus*, and Mr. Bryant was so constituted that no relations, social, political, or literary, could induce him to forget that in his editorial chair he was the trustee of the public, the sentinel of a sleeping army. As such he sometimes incurred the reproach of intolerance and uncharitableness, not from being too severe in his condemnation of wrong, but in his judgments of those to whom such wrongs were imputed, no one but the Master knowing the extenuating circumstances of every man's misconduct.

This loyalty to his profession disinclined him to partake of the hospitalities of those whose positions before the public were liable to bring them under his editorial guns. Hence his social relations through life were mostly with those who were contented with the honors and dignities which could be acquired and enjoyed in private stations.

Outside of the comparatively restricted number to whom his standards did not seem chimerical, he was by some regarded as a scold, by more as an impracticable guide. The editor of the "Herald" was in the habit of referring to him and his associates as "The Poets of the Post." Of course, by those who happened to be directly under the shadow of his frown, he was regarded as an enemy. He heard little from those who approved of and admired his work, while he was deafened with the clamor of those whose consciences were pricked, whose vanity was wounded, or whose schemes were thwarted by his denunciations. It seemed to him in those earlier stages of his journalistic experience that he was rowing against a strong current, without the hope of any assistance of wind or tide. Had he been willing simply to reflect the fads and fancies of the day, had he been able to permit his paper to drift with the tide, he might probably have found his employment lucrative, and himself a popular favorite.

Bryant's friend Dana had little faith in the efficacy of his methods of reforming and perfecting society, and was constantly urging him to stick to his poetry. He said to him, "Keep eye and heart upon poetry all that you can, amid bustle and anxiety. As to reforming the world, give all that up. It is not to be done in a day, nor, on your plan, through all time. Human nature is not fitted for such a social condition as your fancy is pleased with."

Dana was more nearly right than Bryant then supposed him to be, but far less nearly right than he supposed himself to be. Bryant, perhaps, exaggerated the importance of political organizations, criticism, and debate under republican institutions, overlooking the great and controlling fact that in a popular government the laws and their administration will always fairly express the average morality and intelligence of the community that makes them, and that the only way to secure higher standards of legislation and administration is to elevate the average of the morality and intelligence of the constituency. In saying, therefore, that the world was not to be reformed on Bryant's plan, Dana was perhaps the nearer right of the two; but the intimation of Dana that human nature is so constituted that the people are incapable of improving their government, and that they should be ruled by a hereditary or dynastic class, like convicts in a prison or a chain-gang, which was practically his view, was yet farther from the truth, as we think history is demonstrating. Paul fighting with the beasts at Ephesus, Dana must have deemed a mistake, a waste of energy, resurrection or no resurrection.

There is no doubt that in republics the government can only be improved substantially by raising the moral standard of the people. While not undervaluing nor neglecting ethical teaching, Mr. Bryant, in common with most men having to deal with public questions, expected more from political organizations and combinations than was to be realized from them, while later in life he became aware that governments like clocks would run down as they were wound up; that they are resultant forces, the directions of which are more or less affected by each individual member of the society for which it is constituted, and that the government which remains after we have done what we think best in our respective spheres is, on the whole, the government best suited for its constituency.

Though Bryant never consciously gave up to party what was meant for mankind, he was, nevertheless, in every proper sense of the word, a party man. While recognizing every man's primary responsibility to his own conscience, he did not pretend to think anybody wiser than everybody. In dealing, therefore, with all public questions he recognized fully the importance of combination. He as freely criticised the conduct of his own party as of any other, but he never broke with it unless and until it was convicted of subordinating the greater to the lesser interests of society. While its main tendencies were right, he submitted to its errors of detail. He broke with the Democratic party in 1848, refusing to support the candidature of General Cass for President; but not because of anything in the public life of General Cass which he did not admire, nor of much in the resolutions of the Convention which nominated him, which he frankly denounced, but because the Democratic party of the State in which he resided was not represented in the Convention by which Cass had been nominated. He insisted that the State of New York was entitled to a voice in the selection of a candidate for its support, and he was the less disposed to put up with her practical exclusion from the Convention because it was effected in the interests and at the behests of the partisans of slavery. With Cass's defeat he resumed his relations with his party, supporting all succeeding Democratic candidates until the nomination of Abraham Lincoln in 1860.[1]

[1] Writing to one of his brothers shortly after the nomination of Franklin Pierce to the Presidency by the Democratic party, and

The Democratic party at this election was divided by the slavery question, and presented two

John P. Hale by the Abolitionists, he vindicated his support of the former in the following terms: —

"The Free-Soil Party is now doing nothing. Its representatives in Congress have wasted their time till all chance of repealing or modifying the fugitive slave law is gone by, if there ever was any. They have left everything to be done by the journals. Now, at the end of the session, when it is too late for serious debate, Sumner gets up and wants to make a speech. They refuse to consider his resolution, as might have been expected. He might have stated the subject a score of times in the early part of the session. The whole conduct of the public men of the party has been much of a piece with this. What is the use of preserving a separate organization if such be its fruits? But, as I intimated, I see not the least chance of a repeal or change of the fugitive slave law. Its fate is to fall into disuse. All political organizations to procure its repeal are attempts at an impracticability. We must make it odious, and prevent it from being enforced. That the *Evening Post* can do, in a certain measure, just as effectively by supporting Pierce as Hale. Nay, it can do it far more effectually. A journal belonging to a large party has infinitely more influence than when it is the organ of a small conclave. In speaking against slavery, the *Evening Post* expresses the opinions of a large number of people; in exhorting them to vote for Mr. Hale it expresses the opinions of few. The Free-Soil members of Congress — Hale and Sumner, and many others — are not more than half right on various important questions. Freedom of trade is not by any means a firmly established policy in this country. I do not know where these men are on that question. They vote away the public money into the pockets of the Hunkers, — Collins, for example. The only certainty we have of safety in regard to these matters is in a Democratic administration.

"These are some of my reasons for supporting Pierce. I think the slavery question an important one, but I do not see what is to be done for the cause of freedom by declining to vote for the Democratic candidate.

"We of New York — the Democrats of the State, I mean —

candidates; neither, however, opposed to the extension of slavery into the free Territories, upon which point he was inexorable. The Republican party, which had been organized during the interval from the anti-slavery elements of both the old parties for the purpose mainly of resisting such extension, presented Abraham Lincoln as its candidate. As the triumph of either of the Democratic candidates would have practically resulted in disputing the right of the majority to rule, and in the subversion of the principles upon which our government was founded and upon which only it could hope to subsist, Mr. Bryant supported the Republican candidate.

These are, I believe, the only instances in his long career as a journalist in which he did not find it wise and expedient to put up with the evils of

will contend for the measures and principles we think right, let what will come of it. No man pledged against the prohibition of slavery in the Territories, or supposed to be hostile to it, will be able to get the vote of the State of New York. Any separate organization, however, would come to nothing. All parties formed for a single measure are necessarily short-lived, and are as much subject to the abuses and vices of party as any other — I have sometimes thought more so. I never mean to belong to any of them unless I see some very strong and compelling reason for it. The journalist who goes into one of these narrow associations gains by it no increase of independence in discussion, while he parts with the greater part of his influence. As to the influence of the administration, it is at this moment very insignificant in New York. It is strongest in the city, where the government patronage is greatest; but even here it is extremely feeble, and in the country it hardly exists. We are awaiting, as you see, what will grow out of the present state of things with no very sanguine hopes, and very indefinite notions of what the event will be."

the party in which he had enrolled himself, rather than fly to evils he knew not of in other organizations. Had he not ceased to take much interest in public affairs, and to participate in the active management of his paper, it is not unlikely that he would have broken with the Republican party during the later years of President Grant's administration, with which he was extremely dissatisfied. Though his paper rendered a perfunctory support to the Republican candidate of 1876, we feel authorized to affirm that he did not vote for him.

In dealing with facts, Mr. Bryant was not only conscientious, but cautious. In the whole of his long career he was rarely called upon to defend any statement of fact, or to qualify it. Though endowed by nature with a violent temper, he was singularly temperate in debate. He had a refined humor, and, when occasion required, was master of a scathing satire, but he was never tempted to indulge in either at the expense of his own dignity or that of the subject he might be treating. From his editorials it would not be difficult to extract some of the finest specimens of prose in our language, but unhappily they are so woven into the texture of events of transitory importance, and for the most part long since forgotten, that their fame, which in their day was not limited by the bounds of the country to which they were addressed, can hardly be expected to survive another generation.

The degree and kind of influence exerted by Mr. Bryant, or, indeed, by any other journalist upon human society, can only be properly appreciated by contemporary readers, for the reason that the work of the journalist never culminates in results which are traceable to their proper parentage. The soldier wins a battle, the lawyer wins his case, the statesman by his wisdom or his eloquence brings a nation to his feet, the philanthropist founds a durable public charity, the artist produces a masterpiece. In these results the toil and study of years are made intelligible and impressive. They not only address the imagination, but from what we see we are enabled to form a tolerably definite idea of the power required to achieve them. The work of a journalist offers no such appeal to the imagination. Like the sun upon the vegetation of our planet, the journalist leaves an impression upon the minds of many thousands every day, but, unlike the sun, these successive daily impressions do not culminate in a harvest. The world little recks their influence, dispensed like the familiar and unnoticed alternations of day and night, in shaping the thought and in building up the dignity, power, and resources of the nation.

Though, as has been already remarked, Bryant was not a man of moods and tenses, but owing to the regularity and simplicity of his life and his wise control of all his appetites was always in condition for any kind of intellectual exertion, he was not without some of the eccentricities of genius. He never liked to write for his journal except at his desk in his office. It cost him a special effort to do any work for the paper elsewhere, and it is hardly an exaggeration to say that he never wrote for the paper at his home. When the semi-centennial anniversary of the " Evening Post " was approaching, it was proposed to him to prepare for its columns a sketch of its career. He cheerfully accepted the task, and in order that he might be free from interruption he was advised to go down to his country-home at Roslyn and remain there until it was finished, and have such of the files of the paper as he might have occasion to consult sent to him there. He rejected the proposal as abruptly as if he had been asked to offer sacrifices to Apollo. He would allow no such work to follow him there. Not even the shadow of his business must fall upon the consecrated haunts of his muse. He rarely brought or sent anything from the country for the " Evening Post ; " but if he did, it was easy to detect in the character of the fish that they had been caught in strange waters. This separation of his professional from his poetical life must be taken into account in any effort to explain the uniform esteem in which he was always held as a poet by his country people, while occasionally one of the least popular of journalists.[1] Bryant's office desk was his newspaper Egeria. It was also a curiosity. Except for a space immediately in front of

[1] For a copy of this paper, which abounds in interesting memorials of one of the oldest journals in the country, see Appendix A.

him about two feet long and eighteen inches deep, his desk was usually covered to the depth of from twelve to twenty inches with opened letters, manuscript, pamphlets, and books, the accumulation of years. During his absence in Europe in 1859–60, his associate thought to do Bryant a good turn by getting rid of this rubbish and clearing his table so that he should have room for at least one of his elbows on the table. When he returned and saw what had been done, it was manifest from his expression — he said nothing — that what had been so kindly intended was regarded as anything but a kindness. He had also one habit in common with Pope,[1] of always writing his " copy " for the paper on the backs of these old letters and rejected MSS. One who was associated with him for many years in the management of the " Evening Post " affirms that he never knew Bryant to write an article for its columns on a fresh sheet of paper. He also used a quill pen, which he was in the habit of mending with a knife nearly as old as himself, and which might originally have cost him fifty cents. He has been heard to speak of this knife with affection, and to resent the suggestion that he should replace it with a better one. Every year had added a value to it which no new knife could possibly have in his eyes. The same attachment to old servants made him hold on to a blue cotton

---

[1] "Paper-sparing Pope" was an epithet bestowed by Swift upon the poet. A great part of his version of the Iliad was written upon the backs of letters.

umbrella which had very little to commend it either in fair weather or foul but its age. The ladies of his household at last, and when he was about setting out for Mexico, conspired against the umbrella, hid it away, and in its place packed a nice new silk one. He discovered the fraud that had been practiced upon him, turned his back upon the *parvenu*, and insisted upon the restoration of his old and injured friend to its accustomed post of honor by his side. To him age made everything sacred but abuses. He petted the old brutes of his barnyard and stables, and held to his old friends with hooks of steel, closing his eyes resolutely to everything about them which he could not admire. When his friends Verplanck and Tilden deprecated the nomination of Lincoln to the Presidency and opposed his election, preferring to leave the slavery problem to the sagacious ministrations of time, much as he regretted their course, and frankly as he denounced it, he never permitted it for one moment to disturb their friendly relations, or to interrupt their mutual confidences. He knew — no one better — that our affections are the growth of what in us is permanent, our opinions, of what is more or less changeable and transient.

History teaches nothing more persistently than the demoralizing influences which beset the possessors of extraordinary power, and she has preserved to us the names of very few who have been able to resist them. The enormous power wielded by the director of a free press who is in a position daily to address thousands, and perhaps hundreds of thousands, most of whom are but imperfectly qualified to test the value of his opinions, is very intoxicating. It is especially so to the junior members of the profession who have not previously been accustomed to any special deference for their utterances. The privilege of saying what one pleases, of whom one pleases, when and as often as one pleases; to discipline a president or a cabinet minister as if he were a school-boy or a culprit; to sneer at foreign sovereigns; to make or mar the fortunes of a new book or play; to "boom" or bankrupt a struggling corporation; to trifle with the character of eminent citizens, or with the peace of a social or domestic circle, is one which few can possess without abusing, nor without gradually getting to underestimate the rights and judgments of others, and to overestimate their own. Arrogance, conceit, rashness, and self-sufficiency are the infirmities to which the profession of journalism is most exposed, and which only the array of the higher qualities of human character can successfully resist.

It is no mean evidence of the solid foundations upon which Bryant's moral character was erected that he never betrayed under any temptations or provocations the intoxicating influence of newspaper despotism. No one could ever detect a purely personal end to serve, a personal grievance to avenge, a personal ambition or vanity to be gratified, in any line that he ever wrote for his journal.

If he had occasion to defend himself, his defense was sure to repose on public not on personal grounds. He regarded himself strictly as a trustee for the public, and bound to consecrate all the forces and influences of his paper to the public use. Hence, though an alert and aggressive combatant, and by his literary and moral eminence sure to give more or less of dignity and consequence to any assailant, it was not possible to engage him in a personal controversy, unless public considerations were involved, and then they were always placed in the front of the battle. In this respect, also, he was in his day an exceptional as well as a model journalist.

" In his intercourse with his colaborers and subordinates," wrote Mr. Godwin who was for many years his associate in the " Evening Post," " the impression produced by Mr. Bryant, after a certain reticence, which diffused an atmosphere of coldness about him, was broken through, was that of his extreme simplicity and sincerity of character. He was as transparent as the day, as guileless as a child, and as clear in his integrity as the crystal that has no flaw nor crack. His love of truth was so instinctive and controlling that he seldom indulged in an indirection of speech except in the indulgence of his wit, which often flashed like summer lightning through the dark clouds of debate. He used no polite terms merely because they were polite, a plain, uncompromising adherence to the letter of his phrase

seeming to him better than the most courtly affectation.
As he tried to see all things as they were in their real
relations to each other, so he tried to convey his percep-
tion and feeling of them to others as they were.   That
exquisite fidelity to nature which forms one of the
charms of his poetry pervaded his life and his utterances.
No amount of adulation or flattery — and these were
sometimes heaped upon him in unmeasured terms toward the latter part of his career — ever disturbed his
modest estimate of himself, or misled him into vanity or
presumption.   To those who stood near him there was
always something sublime in the severe yet single-
hearted and unassuming simplicity of his bearing.
Sensitive, as men of poetical temperament are apt to be,
his command of his irritabilities and passions was so
complete that he breathed an air perpetually serene and
bright." [1]

It is possible that his power as a journalist
might have been increased by a larger intercourse
with the world.   During the most active stages
of his professional career he saw comparatively
few people, save those who sought him at his
office, and these consisted largely, of course, of
those who had personal ends to serve by the visit.
This isolation made it so much easier for designing
men to disguise the antipathies, prejudices, and
selfishness which often prompted their suggestions.
A larger commerce with the world would have rec-
tified erroneous impressions sometimes left upon

[1] Letter addressed to the *Evening Post* from Carlsbad, Germany, June 15, 1878.

his mind by this class of parasites, who usually approached him on the moral side of his nature, because it was the most impressionable.

Though accustomed daily for more than half a century to discuss professionally the doings of our federal and state governments, he was never at Washington before the war, I believe, but once, except as a traveler passing through to some remoter point. He was once urged to visit the federal capital during an important crisis in our struggle for free labor and free speech. He declined, assigning as a reason that he had been there once, — I think it was during the administration of President Van Buren, — and found that he was more content with the judgment he formed in his office of the doings at the seat of government than with any he was able to form under the shadow of the Capitol. Once also during a critical period of the war he yielded reluctantly to the importunities of some friends, and went to Washington to urge a more vigorous prosecution of the war and the immediate emancipation of the slaves. He shrank too from the restraints which personal intercourse with the public servants imposed upon the freedom of his pen. According to his view, a journalist did less than his duty who did not strive at least to leave the world better than he found it; who did not wrestle with those social and political abuses which are amenable to public opinion. The reform of society, as he thought, like Mahomed's paradise, lies in the shadow of crossed swords. Controversy, therefore, always earnest and sometimes acrimonious with those whom he regarded as the Amorites, the Hivites, and the Perizzites of the land, was inevitable. With them he made no terms. He had no personal antagonisms, but he could not compromise or transact with those whom he regarded as the enemies of society.

CHAPTER VII.

THE POET.

As a poet, Bryant is to be judged by the quality rather than the quantity of his work. The sum of all his verse that he thought worth preserving did not exceed thirteen thousand lines. Of these, about one third were written before 1829. The double task of mastering his new profession and that of discharging its duties pretty effectually absorbed his time and thoughts for several of the succeeding years. He wrote but thirty lines in 1830, but sixty in 1831. In 1832, he wrote two hundred and twenty-two. It does not appear that he wrote any in 1833. In the ten years immediately succeeding 1829, he seems to have produced only eleven hundred and thirty-seven lines, or a trifle over one hundred lines a year. But though he produced comparatively little during this decade, he did not suffer the waters of "livid oblivion" to roll over him.

In 1831, he published a volume containing about eighty of his poems, in addition to those which had appeared in the pamphlet collection in 1821. He was induced to try the fortunes of this little volume by more impartial and less indulgent tests than those to which his verse had hitherto been subjected.

A friend had shown him a letter written by Washington Irving, from Madrid, in which occurred the following passage : —

"I have been charmed with what I have seen of the writing of Bryant and Halleck. Are you acquainted with them? I should like to know something about them personally; their view of thinking is quite above that of ordinary men and ordinary poets, and they are masters of the magic of poetic language."

Encouraged if not determined by these words of commendation from such a competent authority, Mr. Bryant sent a copy of his volume to Murray in London, and at the same time addressed the following note to Irving : —

"SIR, — I have put to press in this city a duodecimo volume of two hundred and forty pages, comprising all my poems which I thought worth printing, most of which have already appeared. Several of them I believe you have seen, and of some, if I am rightly informed, you have been pleased to express a favorable opinion. Before publishing the thing here, I have sent a copy of it to Murray, the London bookseller, by whom I am anxious that it should be published in England. I have taken the liberty, which I hope you will pardon a countryman of yours, who relies on the known kindness of your disposition to plead his excuse, of referring him to you. As it is not altogether impossible that the work might be republished in England, if I did not offer it myself, I could wish that it might be published by a respectable bookseller in a respectable manner.

"I have written to Mr. Verplanck desiring him to give me a letter to you on the subject, but as the packet which takes out my book will sail before I can receive an answer I have presumed so far on your goodness as to make the application myself. May I ask of you the favor to write to Mr. Murray on the subject as soon as you receive this? In my letter to him I have said nothing of the terms, which, of course, will depend upon circumstances which I may not know or of which I cannot judge. I should be glad to receive something for the work, but if he does not think it worth while to give anything, I had rather he should take it for nothing than that it should not be published by a respectable publisher.

"I must again beg you to excuse the freedom I have taken. I have no personal acquaintance in England whom I could ask to do what I have ventured to request of you; and I know of no person to whom I could prefer the request with greater certainty that it will be kindly entertained.

"I am, sir,

With sentiments of the highest respect,

Your obedient and humble servant,

WILLIAM CULLEN BRYANT.

"P. S. — I have taken the liberty to accompany this letter with a copy of the work."

Bryant received the following reply from Mr.

Irving, dated at Byron's former home, Newstead Abbey, January 26, 1832 : —

DEAR SIR, — I feel very much obliged to you for the volume you have had the kindness to send me, and am delighted to have in my possession a collection of your poems, which, separately, I have so highly admired. It will give me the greatest pleasure to be instrumental in bringing before the British public a volume so honorable to our national literature. When I return to London, which will be in the course of a few days, I will ascertain whether any arrangement can be effected by which some pecuniary advantage can be secured to you. On this head I am not very sanguine. The book trade is at present in a miserably depressed state in England, and the publishers have become shy and parsimonious. Besides, they will not be disposed to offer you anything for a work in print for which they cannot secure a copyright. I am sorry you sent the work to Murray, who has disappointed me grievously in respect to other American works intrusted to him ; and who has acted so unjustly in recent transactions with myself as to impede my own literary arrangements, and oblige me to look around for some other publisher. I shall, however, write to him about your work, and if he does not immediately undertake it, will look elsewhere for a favorable channel of publication.

Believe me, my dear sir,

With the highest consideration,

Very truly yours,

WASHINGTON IRVING.

Within a week from the date of this letter Mr. Irving received the following note from Murray : —

My dear Sir, — I received Mr. Bryant's poems yesterday, and I am very sorry to say it is quite out of Mr. Murray's power to do anything for him, or with them. I send the volume to you in compliance with your request.

> I am, dear sir,
> Yours very truly,
> J. Murray, Jr.

It seems to us now as if this reply or retort, whichever it was, might have been more courteous. How far its tenor was influenced by the quality of the poetry, how far by a national prejudice at that time more or less prevalent against anything American, and how far by the strained relations that chanced then to exist between the publisher and the sponsor of the poems, are questions which it is impossible and now, happily, unimportant to determine. As a publisher and man of business, Mr. Murray probably was not at fault in declining the poems. For a variety of reasons, none of which, I venture to think, go to their merits, Bryant's poetry has never touched a very sympathetic chord in England.[1]

Mr. Irving, however, was not discouraged by the repulse of Murray, and soon made arrangements with another house, and thus announced the success of his negotiations on the 6th of March : —

[1] A curious illustration of the lack of esteem for Bryant's poetry in England, and prevailing ignorance there of his life-work as a journalist, may be found in the recent edition of the *Encyclopedia Britannica*, which has found no place in its Walhalla for the name of William Cullen Bryant.

My dear Sir, — I send you a copy of the second edition of your work, published this day. You will perceive that I have taken the liberty of putting my name as editor, and of dedicating the work to Mr. Rogers. Something was necessary to call attention at this moment of literary languor and political excitement to a volume of poetry by an author almost unknown to the British public.

I have taken the further liberty of altering two or three words in the little poem of "Marion's Men," lest they might startle the pride of John Bull on your first introduction to him.

Mr. Andrews, the bookseller, has promised to divide with you any profits that may arise on the publication, and I have the fullest reliance on his good faith. The present moment, however, is far from promising to literary gains, and I should not be surprised if the returns were but trifling.

> Believe me, my dear Sir,
> Very respectfully and truly yours,
> WASHINGTON IRVING.

Wm. C. Bryant, Esqr.

Dana, who took more than a paternal pride in Bryant's poetry, choked a little over the dedication to Rogers. "I learn by to-day's paper," he wrote, "that the English edition of your poems has made its appearance with a dedication to Rogers by Irving. Samuel Rogers! never mind, dear sir, it will help to favor."

Rogers was not a great poet, but he was by no means an inferior critic, nor was there any poet in England in his time who did not value and desire his protection. He had the sagacity to discern, and the magnanimity to recognize everywhere and on all occasions, the merit of Bryant's poetry, and when Bryant called upon him later in London, he neglected no means of testifying his admiration and respect both for the poet and the man. It is interesting to those who knew Bryant's shyness and his undemonstrative ways with a new acquaintance to see how rapidly he entered into relations of affectionate intimacy with this venerable cynic, some evidences of which are disclosed in the following extract from an article which he allowed himself to write and print in the "Evening Post" on receiving the news of Rogers's death.

"The death of the poet Rogers," he said, "seems almost like the extinction of an institution. The world by his departure has one object the less of interest and reverence. The elegant hospitality which he dispensed for nearly three quarters of a century, and in which Americans had a large share, is brought to an end, and a vacuity is created which no Englishman can supply. Rogers loved to speak of his relations with Americans. 'Three American Presidents,' he used to say, ' have been entertained under my roof; '[1] and then he would enumerate, in his succinct way, the illustrious men, founders of our republic, or eminent in its later history, who had been his guests. He claimed an hereditary interest in our country. On the news of the battle of Lexington, his father put on mourning.

[1] Probably John Quincy Adams, Fillmore, and Van Buren.

'Have you lost a friend?' somebody asked him who saw this indication of sorrow. 'I have lost a great many,' was the answer; 'my friends in New England.'

"Rogers's breakfasts were the pleasantest social meetings that can be conceived of. There you met persons of every variety of intellectual and social distinction, eminent men and attractive women, wits, orators, dramatists, travelers, artists, persons remarkable for their powers of conversation, all of whom found themselves on the easiest terms with their venerable host, whose noon of life was reached in the last century. Even bores, in his society, which discouraged all tediousness, and in the respect which his presence inspired, seemed to lose their usual character, and to fall involuntarily into the lively and graceful flow of conversation of which he gave the example.

"The following little incident will show with how good a grace he could welcome a stranger to his hospitable dwelling. On one occasion he met an American for the first time [1] at a literary breakfast at the table of Mr. Everett, who, while abroad, was never wanting in obliging and friendly attentions to his countrymen. 'Where are you lodging?' he asked of the American. 'In St. James's Place,' was the answer. 'Come with me,' said Mr. Rogers, 'and I will show you the nearest way to St. James's Place.' He took his new acquaintance into that part of London which is sometimes called Bel-

[1] This was Mr. Bryant himself.

gravia, and pointed out to him the stately rows of spacious mansions lately erected to embellish the great capital of England; then passing through the Park of St. James, fresh in the beauty of early June, he arrived at the gate of a small garden. Taking a key from his pocket, he opened the gate, and, following a little walk among shrubbery and trees, on which innumerable sparrows were chirping, he entered a house by the back door, and introduced the American to his own home. After he had given him a little time to observe the objects of art which it contained, he dismissed him by the front door, which opened into St. James's Place. 'You see,' he said, 'that I have brought you by the nearest way to St. James's Place. Remember the house, and come to breakfast with me to-morrow morning.'

" The mention of sparrows in his garden reminds us of an anecdote of which they were the subject. 'I once used to feed sparrows,' said Mr. Rogers; 'but one day, when I was throwing them some crumbs for their breakfast, a gentleman said to me: "Do you see those birds on the tree yonder, how they keep aloof, and do not venture down, while those on the ground are feasting at their leisure? Those yonder are the females; these which you are feeding are the gentlemen sparrows; they keep their mates at a distance." Since that day I have fed sparrows no more.'

" Rogers began his poetical career early. One of his acquaintances was speaking of the little

well-known song of his, familiar to our grandmo-
thers : —

> "'Dear is my little native vale :
>   The ring-dove builds and warbles there;
> Close by my cot she tells her tale,
>   To every passing villager.
> The squirrel leaps from tree to tree,
> And shells his nuts at liberty.'

"'I wrote that song at sixteen years of age,'
said Mr. Rogers. Yet, though the production of
an immature age, it has all the better characteristics of his later poetry, and it shows how remarkably early they were acquired. In his ' Pleasures of
Memory,' very elaborately composed, he adopted
the carefully measured versification in fashion at
the time it appeared, with its unvaried periods,
its antithetic turns, and its voluntary renunciation
of the power of proportioning the expression to the
thought. In his ' Human Life,' a later and finer
poem, he shows that his taste had changed with
the taste of the age ; he broke loose from the old
fetters, indulging in a freer modulation of numbers, though not parting with any of their har-
mony and sweetness, and studying a more vigorous
and direct phraseology. ' Human Life ' is the best
of his longer poems, and that in which his genius
is seen to best advantage. It deals with life in its
gentler and less stormy moods, whether of pleasure
or of sadness, the sunshine and the shadows of
common life. The poem is of a kind by which a
large class of readers is interested, and contains
passages which once read are often recurred to,
and keep their place in the memory.

" The illustrated edition of his poems is the only work of the kind with which we are perfectly satisfied. To illustrate adequately by the pencil the writings of an eminent poet is one of the most difficult undertakings in the world. The fine taste of Rogers in the arts and his intimacy with the greatest artists of his country gave him a great advantage in this respect; and we have heard that the designs which embellish that edition of his works were selected from a much larger number made for that purpose.

" In approaching the close of a life so much prolonged beyond the usual lot of man, — a life the years of which circumscribed the activity of three generations, — he contemplated his departure with the utmost serenity. The state of man after death he called the great subject, and calmly awaited the moment when he should be admitted to contemplate its mysteries. ' I have found life in this world,' he used to say, ' a happy state ; the goodness of God has taken care that none of its functions, even the most inconsiderable, should be performed without sensible pleasure ; and I am confident that in the world to come the same care for my happiness will accompany me.'

" Mr. Rogers was of low stature, neither slightly nor sturdily proportioned; his face was rather full and broad than otherwise, and his complexion colorless. He always wore a frock-coat. ' I will not go to court,' he used to say, ' and for one reason among others, that I will not wear any other coat

than this.' 'The other day,' he once added, 'I
sent my clothes to the palace, and a man in them.'
The man whom he meant was Wordsworth, who
came to London as the guest of Rogers, in order
to attend court at the bidding of the Queen, and
to make his acknowledgments for the post of laureate, which had been bestowed on him. On that
occasion he wore the court suit of Mr. Rogers,
whose guest he was.

"In conversation, Mr. Rogers was one of the
most agreeable and interesting of men ; he was remarkable for a certain graceful laconism, a neatness and power of selection in telling a story or
expressing a thought, with its accessories, which
were the envy of the best talkers of his time. His
articulation was distinct, just deliberate enough to
be listened to with pleasure, and during the last
ten to twelve years of his life slightly — and but
very slightly — marked with the tremulousness of
old age.

"His ordinary manner was kind and paternal ;
he delighted to relate anecdotes illustrative of the
power of the affections, which he did with great
feeling. On occasion, however, he could say caus-
tic things ; and a few examples of this kind, which
were so epigrammatic as to be entertaining in their
repetition, have given rise to the mistake that they
were frequent in his conversation. His behavior
to the other sex was uncommonly engaging. He
was on friendly terms with his eminent literary
brethren, though they were enemies to each other ;

and, notwithstanding that his political opinions were those of the liberal school, his intimacies knew no party distinctions, and included men of the opposite sect."

The alterations in one of Bryant's poems which Irving had allowed himself to make before they were published had results which threatened for a time to prove most unfortunate. Mr. Leggett, who had just established the "Plaindealer," and who was justly incensed by a practice more or less prevalent among American publishers of mutilating foreign works which they were reprinting, by expunging passages likely to prove offensive to slaveowners, went quite out of his way to charge Irving with "literary pusillanimity" for changing in the "Song of Marion's Men" the line

"And the British foeman trembles"

into

"The foeman trembles in his camp."

This article naturally provoked Irving, who had recently returned from Madrid, and one of the results was a letter to the editor of the "Plaindealer," which I here give entire, as it is now to be found, I believe, only in the journals of that period, where it is no longer readily accessible.

To the Editor of the Plaindealer.

Sir, — Living at present in the country and out of the way of the current literature of the day, it was not until this morning that I saw your paper of the 14th of January, or knew anything of your animadversions on my conduct and character therein contained. Though

I have generally abstained from noticing any attack upon myself in the public papers, the present is one which I cannot suffer to pass in silence.

In the first place you have censured me strongly for having altered a paragraph in the London edition of Mr. Bryant's poems; and the remarks and comparisons in which you have indulged on the occasion would seem to imply that I have a literary hostility to Mr. Bryant and a disposition to detract from the measure of his well-merited reputation.

The relation in which you stand to that gentleman, as his particular friend and literary associate, gives these animadversions the greater weight, and calls for a real statement of the case.

When I was last in London (I think in 1832), I received a copy of the American edition of Mr. Bryant's poems from some friend (I now forget from whom), who expressed a wish that it might be republished in England. I had not at that time the pleasure of a personal acquaintance with Mr. Bryant, but I felt the same admiration for his poems that you have expressed, and was desirous that writings so honorable to American literature should be known to the British public, and take their merited rank in the literature of the language. I exerted myself, therefore, to get them republished by some London bookseller, but met with unexpected difficulties, poetry being declared quite unsalable since the death of Lord Byron. At length a bookseller was induced to undertake an edition by my engaging gratuitously to edit the work, and to write something that might call public attention to it. I accordingly prefixed to the volume a dedicatory letter addressed to Mr. Samuel Rogers, in which, while I expressed my own opinion of the poems, I took occasion to allude to the still more valuable approbation which I had heard expressed by that distinguished author, thus bringing the work before the British public with the high sanction of one of the most refined critics of the day. While the work was going through the press, an objection was started to the passage in the poem of " Marion's Men " —

> " And the British foeman trembles
> When Marion's name is heard."

It was considered as peculiarly calculated to shock the feelings of British readers on the most sensitive point, seeming to call in question the courage of the nation. It was urged that common decorum required the softening of such a passage in an edition exclusively intended for the British public; and I was asked what would be the feelings of American readers if such an imputation on the courage of their countrymen were inserted in a work presented for their approbation. These objections were urged in a spirit of friendship to Mr. Bryant, and with a view to his success, for it was suggested that this passage might be felt as a taunt of bravado, and might awaken a prejudice against the work before its merits could be appreciated.

I doubt whether these objections would have occurred to me had they not been thus set forth, but when thus urged I yielded to them, and softened the passage in question by omitting the adjective British, and substituting one of a more general signification. If this evinced " timidity of spirit," it was a timidity felt entirely on behalf of Mr. Bryant. I was not to be harmed by the insertion of the paragraph as it originally stood. I freely confess, however, that I have at all times almost as strong a repugnance to tell a painful or humiliating truth, unnecessarily, as I have to tell an untruth under any circumstances. To speak the truth on all occasions is the indispensable attribute of man ; to refrain from uttering disagreeable truths, unnecessarily, belongs, I think, to the character of a gentleman ; neither, sir, do I think it incompatible with fair dealing, however little it may square with your notions of plaindealing.

The foregoing statement will show how I stand with regard to Mr. Bryant. I trust his fame has suffered nothing by my republication of his works in London ; at any rate, he has expressed his thanks to me by letter, since my return to this country. I was therefore, I confess, but little prepared to receive a stab from his bosom friend.

Another part of your animadversions is of a much graver nature, for it implies a charge of hypocrisy and double dealing which I indignantly repel as incompatible with my nature. You intimate that "in publishing a book of my own, I prepare one preface for my countrymen full of *amor patriæ* and professions of home feeling, and another for the London market in which such professions are studiously omitted." Your inference is that these professions are hollow, and intended to gain favor with my countrymen, and that they are omitted in the London edition through fear of offending English readers. Were I indeed chargeable with such baseness, I should well merit the contempt you invoke upon my head. As I give you credit, sir, for probity, I was at a loss to think on what you could ground such an imputation, until it occurred to me that some circumstances attending the publication of my " Tour on the Prairies " might have given rise to a misconception in your mind.

It may seem strange to those intimately acquainted with my character that I should think it necessary to defend myself from a charge of duplicity, but as many of your readers may know me as little as you appear to do, I must again be excused in a detail of fact.

When my "Tour on the Prairies" was ready for the press, I sent a manuscript copy to England for publication, and at the same time put a copy in the press at New York. As this was my first appearance before the American public since my return, I was induced while the work was printing to modify the introduction so as to express my sense of the unexpected warmth with which I had been welcomed to my native place, and my general feelings on finding myself once more at home, and among my friends. These feelings, sir, were genuine, and were not expressed with half the warmth with which they were entertained. Circumstances alluded to in that introduction had made the reception I met with from my countrymen doubly dear and touching to me, and had filled my heart with affectionate gratitude for their unlooked-for kindness. In fact, misconstructions of my conduct and misconceptions of my character, somewhat similar to those I am at present endeavoring to rebut, had appeared in the public press, and as I erroneously supposed, had prejudiced the mind of my countrymen against me. The professions, therefore, to which you have alluded were uttered, not to obviate such prejudices, or to win my way to the good will of my countrymen, but to express my feelings after their good will had been unequivocally manifested. While I thought they doubted me, I remained silent; when I found they believed in me, I spoke. I have never been in the habit of beguiling them by fulsome professions of patriotism, those cheap passports to public favor; and I think I might for once have been indulged in briefly touching a chord, on which others have harped to so much advantage.

Now, sir, even granting I had " studiously omitted " all those professions in the introduction intended for the London market, instead of giving utterance to them after that article had been sent off, where, I would ask, would have been the impropriety of the act? What had the British public to do with those home greetings and those assurances of gratitude and affection which related exclusively to my countrymen, and grew out of my actual position with regard to them? There was nothing in them at which the British reader could possibly take offense; the omitting of them, therefore, could not have argued "timidity," but would have been merely a matter of good taste; for they would have been as much out of place repeated to English readers, as would have been my greetings and salutations to my family circle. if repeated out of the window for the benefit of the passers-by in the street.

I have no intention, sir, of imputing to you any malevolent feeling in the unlooked-for attack you have made upon me: I can see no motive you have for such hostility. I rather think you have acted from honest feelings, hastily excited by a misapprehension of facts; and that you have been a little too eager to give an instance of that "plaindealing" which you have recently adopted as your war-cry. Plaindealing, sir, is a great merit, when accompanied by magnanimity, and exercised with a just and generous spirit; but if pushed too far, and made the excuse for indulging every impulse of passion or prejudice, it may render a man, especially in your situation, a very offensive, if not a very mischievous member of the community. Such I sincerely hope and trust may not be your case; but this hint, given in a spirit of caution, not of accusation, may not be of disservice to you.

In the present instance I have only to ask that you will give this article an insertion in your paper, being intended not so much for yourself, as for those of your readers who may have been prejudiced against me by your animadversions. Your editorial position, of course, gives you an opportunity of commenting upon it according to the current of your feelings; and whatever may be your comments, it is not probable that they will draw any further reply from me. Recrimination is a miserable kind of redress in which I never indulge, and I have no relish for the warfare of the pen.

Very respectfully your obedient servant,
WASHINGTON IRVING.

In submitting this letter to his readers, Mr. Leggett, while modifying in no degree the opinion he had expressed of what he deemed the liberty Irving had taken with Bryant's verse, took pains to relieve Bryant from all responsibility for what he had written about it.

"It is proper," he began his comments, "that we should exonerate Mr. Bryant from any lot or part, directly or indirectly, in the remarks we made concerning what seemed to us (and we must be pardoned for saying what still seems to us) a piece of literary pusillanimity on the part of Mr. Irving. Whether our censure was called for or not, and whether well founded or not, we alone are responsible for having uttered it. Mr.

Bryant's first knowledge of the article, like Mr. Irving's, was derived from a perusal of the published 'Plaindealer,' placed in his hands in the regular course of distribution to subscribers. Nay, more, to disabuse not only Mr. Irving's mind, but the minds of those whom the phraseology of his communication in certain parts may mislead, candor requires us to state that, on various occasions, we have heard Mr. Bryant express the kindest sentiments towards Mr. Irving for the interest he took in the publication of a London edition of his poems, and for the complimentary terms in which he introduced them to the British public."

Not content with Leggett's declaration of his innocence of any responsibility for the strictures of the " Plaindealer," and a little moved by what seemed to him a slightly skeptical tone on this point in Irving's letter, Bryant sent to the " Plaindealer" the following : —

"TO THE EDITOR OF THE PLAINDEALER.

"SIR, — I read in your paper of the 28th of January a letter from Mr. Irving, partly in answer to a censure passed in a previous number upon an alteration made by him in the London edition of my poems. I was much surprised to find that he chose to consider me as in some degree answerable for your animadversions. Disliking as I do to speak of my private affairs in print, I was glad to see that you fully replied to his suspicions by declaring them utterly groundless. I find, however, that many of the friends of that distinguished author are still determined to make me, in some way or other, the instigator of an attack upon him, in return for the kindness he had shown in recommending my volume to the British public. I must, therefore, beg you to print this communication.

"Let me quote in the first place those passages in Mr. Irving's letter which have led me to ask of you this favor. Near the beginning he says, alluding to your animadversions and to me: —

"'The relation in which you stand to that gentleman as his particular friend and literary associate gives these animadversions the greater weight, and calls for a real statement of the case.'

"And again: —

"'The foregoing statement will show how I stand with regard to Mr. Bryant. I trust his fame has suffered nothing by my republication of his works in London; at any rate, he has expressed his thanks to me by letter since my return to this country. I was therefore, I confess, but little prepared to receive a stab from his bosom friend.'

"I cannot refrain from again expressing my surprise that with the proof of my real feelings in his hands, contained in the letter of which he speaks, Mr. Irving should have found it possible to connect me in any manner with the animadversions to which he alludes.

"I must, then, declare briefly that I highly appreciated the generosity of Mr. Irving in bringing my work before the British public with the great advantage of his commendation, and that although I should not have made the alteration in question,

I had no doubt that it was made with the kindest intentions, and never complained of it to anybody. If I had been disposed to complain of it privately, it would have been to himself; if publicly, it would have been under my own name; nor can I comprehend the disingenuous and pusillanimous malignity which would have led me to procure another to attack in public what I had not even ventured to blame in private.

"It is perhaps best that I should leave the matter here; merely remarking, in conclusion, that they who are acquainted with the literary as well as the political course of the ' Plaindealer '*know very well that its editor is not accustomed to shape his censures or his praises according to the opinions or the desires of others.

WILLIAM CULLEN BRYANT.

"NEW YORK, *February* 6, 1837."

The following rejoinder from Irving, which appeared in the "New York American," closed the discussion. Bryant has told us that his explanation "was graciously accepted, and in a brief note in the 'Plaindealer' Irving pronounced my acquittal." It is more difficult for us even now to acquit Mr. Leggett for his part in provoking this correspondence: —

To WILLIAM CULLEN BRYANT, ESQ.

SIR, — It was not until this moment that I saw your letter in the "Plaindealer" of Saturday last. I cannot express to you how much it has shocked and grieved me. Not having read any of the comments of the editor of the "Plaindealer" on the letter which I addressed to him, and being in the country, out of the way of hearing the comments of others, I was totally ignorant of the construction put upon the passages of that letter which you have cited. Whatever construction these passages may be susceptible of, I do assure you, sir, I never supposed, nor had the remotest intention to insinuate that you had the least participation in the attack recently made upon my character by the editor of the above mentioned paper, or that you entertained feelings which could in any degree be gratified by such an attack. Had I thought you chargeable with such hostility I should have made the charge directly and explicitly, and not by innuendo.

The little opportunity that I have had, sir, of judging of your private character, has only tended to confirm the opinion I had formed of you from your poetic writings, which breathe a spirit too pure, amiable, and elevated to permit me for a moment to think you capable of anything ungenerous or unjust.

As to the alteration of a word in the London edition of your poems, which others have sought to nurture into a root of bitterness between us, I have already stated my motives for it, and the embarrassment in which I was placed. I regret extremely that it should not have met with your approbation, and sincerely apologize to you for the liberty I was persuaded to take: a liberty, I freely acknowledge. the least excusable with writings like yours, in which it is difficult to alter a word without marring a beauty.

Believe me, sir, with perfect respect and esteem,

Very truly yours,   WASHINGTON IRVING.

THURSDAY MORNING, *February 16th.*

Of Bryant's rank and merits as a poet there is, and for some time to come is likely to be, a great diversity of opinion. A partial explanation of this may be found in the fact that the most enduring qualities of his verse are readily appreciated by only a comparatively restricted class even of those who read poetry. He was essentially an ethical poet. His inspiration was always from above. In the flower, in the stream, in the tempest, in the rainbow, in the snow, in everything about him, nature was always telling him something new of the goodness of God and framing excuses for the frail and the erring. His verses are the record of these lessons as far as he apprehended and could express them. The number who comprehend the full force of them at a single reading, however, is comparatively small. Every one of his verses will bear the supreme test of a work of literary art, which discloses a wider horizon and new merits at each successive perusal.

Bryant's whole life was a struggle, and a marvelously successful struggle, with the infirmities of the natural man. In his work, whether as journalist or poet, the moral elevation of himself and of his fellow - creatures was the warp of whatever theme might be the woof. But the ethical nature is always operating upon two parallel but quite separate lines. It is critical and denunciatory when dealing with error and wrong-doing; it is hopeful, joyous, and strengthening when it deals with the virtues and their triumphs. Bryant confined the exercise of the critical function of the moralist mainly to his newspaper; in his verse he sang the beauty and joys of holiness. As a journalist, he was prone to dwell upon wrongs to be repaired, upon evils to be reformed, upon public offenders to be punished. But when he donned his singing robes and retired from the clash and din of worldly strife, he went up into a mountain and sat, and angels ministered unto him; everything around him seemed eloquent of hope and cheer, of faith and love. The sight of the 'new moon' brings

> "Thoughts of all fair and youthful things—
>   The hopes of early years;
> And childhood's purity and grace,
> And joys that like a rainbow chase
>   The passing shower of tears.

> "The captive yields him to the dream
>   Of freedom, when that virgin beam
>   Comes out upon the air;
> And painfully the sick man tries
> To fix his dim and burning eyes
>   On the sweet promise there.

> "Most welcome to the lovers' sight
> Glitters that pure, emerging light;
>   For prattling poets say,
> That sweetest is the lovers' walk,
> And tenderest is their murmured talk,
>   Beneath its gentle ray.

> "And there do graver men behold
> A type of errors, loved of old,
>   Forsaken and forgiven;
> And thoughts and wishes not of earth

Just opening in their early birth,
    Like that new light in heaven."

The waning moon has its lesson also : —

"In thy decaying beam there lies
    Full many a grave on hill and plain
Of those who closed their dying eyes
    In grief that they had lived in vain.

"Another night and thou among
    The spheres of heaven shall cease to shine;
All rayless in the glittering throng
    Whose lustre late was quenched in thine.

"Yet soon a new and tender light
    From out thy darkened orb shall beam,
And broaden till it shines all night
    On glistening dew, and glimmering stream."

In the winds he finds a lesson which he com-
mends with exquisite grace to the impatient re-
formers of society.

"Yet oh, when that wronged Spirit of our race
    Shall break, as soon he must, his long-worn chains
And leap in freedom from his prison-place,
    Lord of his ancient hills and fruitful plains,
Let him not rise, like these mad winds of air,
To waste the loveliness that time could spare,
To fill the earth with woe, and blot her fair
    Unconscious breast with blood from human veins.

"But may he like the spring-time come abroad,
    Who crumbles winter's gyves with gentle might
When in the genial breeze, the breath of God,
    The unsealed springs come spouting up to light ;
Flowers start from their dark prisons at his feet,
The woods, long dumb, awake to hymnings sweet,
And morn and eve, whose glimmerings almost meet,
    Crowd back to narrow bounds the ancient night."

In the North Star he finds

> " A beauteous type of that unchanging good,
> That bright eternal beacon, by whose ray
> The voyager of time should shape his heedful way."

March, the most abused of all the months in the calendar, has a good word from Bryant.

> " The year's departing beauty hides,
>   Of wintry storms the sullen threat;
> But in thy sternest frown abides
>   A look of kindly promise yet.

> " Thou bring'st the hope of those calm skies,
>   And that soft time of sunny showers
> When the wide bloom on earth that lies,
>   Seems of a brighter world than ours."

In the beautiful boundless "firmament" he finds a charm

> " That earth, the proud green earth, has not,
> With all the forms, and hues, and airs,
>   That haunt her sweetest spot.
> We gaze upon thy calm pure sphere,
>   And read of Heaven's eternal year.

> " Oh, when amid the throng of men,
>   The heart grows sick of hollow mirth,
> How willingly we turn us then
>   Away from this cold earth,
> And look into thy azure breast,
> For seats of innocence and rest ! "

The " Fringed Gentian " preaches to him of Hope and Immortality.

> " Thou comest not when violets lean
> O'er wandering brooks and springs unseen,
> Or columbines, in purple dressed.
> Nod o'er the ground-bird's hidden nest.

"Thou waitest late and com'st alone,
    When woods are bare and birds are flown,
    And frosts and shortening days portend
    The aged year is near his end.

"Then doth thy sweet and quiet eye
    Look through its fringes to the sky,
    Blue — blue — as if that sky let fall
    A flower from its cerulean wall.

"I would that thus, when I shall see
    The hour of death draw near to me,
    Hope, blossoming within my heart,
    May look to heaven as I depart."

The river teaches him the processes of moral purification : —

"Oh, glide away from those abodes that bring
Pollution to thy channel and make foul
Thy once clear current ; summon thy quick waves
And dimpling eddies ; linger not, but haste,
With all thy waters, haste thee to the deep,
There to be tossed by shifting winds and rocked
By that mysterious force which lives within
The sea's immensity, and wields the weight
Of its abysses, swaying to and fro
The billowy mass, until the stain, at length,
Shall wholly pass away, and thou regain
The crystal brightness of thy mountain-spring."

To those who mourn the supposed degeneracy of their time he says : —

. . . "Despair not of their fate who rise
To dwell upon the earth when we withdraw.

·   ·   ·   ·   ·   ·   ·   ·   ·

"Oh no ! a thousand cheerful omens give
Hope of yet happier days whose dawn is nigh.
    He who has tamed the elements, shall not live
The slave of his own passions ; he whose eye

> Unwinds the eternal dances of the sky,
> And in the abyss of brightness dares to span
> The sun's broad circle, rising yet more high,
> In God's magnificent works his will shall scan
> And love and peace shall make their paradise with man."

Even natural death to him in his poetic mood had its sunny aspects. Instead of treating it as a penal institution only to be dreaded, the thoughts of which "come like a blight" over the spirit, —

> . . . " and sad images
> Of the stern agony, and shroud and pall,
> And breathless darkness and the narrow house,
> Make thee to shudder and grow sick at heart," —

he treats it as "a ministry of life," a change as natural, as inevitable, and as beneficent as the changes of the seasons, as the change from infancy to maturity, from hunger to satiety, from sleeping to waking, and from waking to sleeping; as no more the penalty of sin than it is the penalty of virtue; a change which the good are just as certain to experience as the wicked, the rich as the poor, the noble as the peasant. And therefore when the summons comes for us to take our

> " Chamber in the silent halls of death,"

we should obey it, not

> " Like the quarry slave at night
> Scourged to his dungeon, but sustained and soothed
> By an unfaltering trust, . . .
> Like one who wraps the drapery of his couch
> About him and lies down to pleasant dreams."

There are none who will gainsay any of the great truths which Nature was ever teaching this most faithful and devout of her disciples, but the

number of those who comprehend them is comparatively limited. " Every one that is of the truth
heareth his voice." But alas! how many of us are
still like Pilate, asking " What is truth?" To such
— and they unhappily constitute the great body
of what are commonly denominated " the reading
public " — the poetry of the passions and the appetites, the poetry which derives its inspiration
largely from our sensuous nature, from the lusts of
the flesh, the lusts of the eye, and the pride of
life, is the most attractive, and therefore most esteemed. But if, as Bryant taught and believed,
the world's moral standards are steadily rising,
and the supersensuous is gaining upon the sensuous life, or what Paul calls " the rudiments of the
world ; " if our affections are being gradually lifted
up from the verdure of the field which to-day is and
to-morrow is cast into the oven, to the hand that
clothes the field with this verdure, Bryant's poems
must grow in popular favor and take a rank in the
world's esteem which is reserved for no considerable proportion of English verse, justifying the
prediction of his friend Halleck : —

> " Spring's lovelier flowers for many a day
> Have blossomed on his wandering way ;
> Beings of beauty and decay
>   They slumber in their autumn tomb ;
> But those that graced his own Green River
>   And wreathed the lattice of his home,
>   Charmed by his song from mortal doom
> Bloom on and will bloom on forever." [1]

[1] It may interest the readers of these pages to be reminded of

What has been said will serve to explain the fact that Bryant was not the poet of " occasions."

what has been said of the rank and superior " staying power " of ethical poetry by an eminent poet whose genius gives great weight to his opinion, whatever may be thought of his example.

Byron, in the course of his once famous letter to the Rev. Mr. Bowles in defense of Pope, wrote:—

" In my mind the highest of all poetry is ethical poetry, as the highest of all earthly objects must be moral truth. Religion does not make a part of my subject; it is something beyond human powers, and has failed in all human hands except Milton's and Dante's, and even Dante's powers are involved in his delineation of human passions, though in supernatural circumstances. What made Socrates the greatest of men ? His moral truth —his ethics. What proved Jesus Christ the Son of God hardly less than his miracles ? His moral precepts. And if ethics have made a philosopher the first of men, and have not been disdained as an adjunct to his gospel by the Deity himself, are we to be told that ethical poetry, or didactic poetry, or by whatever name you term it whose object is to make men better and wiser, is not the very first order of poetry, and are we to be told this, too, by one of the priesthood ? It requires more mind, more wisdom, more power, than all the 'forests' that ever were 'walked' for their description and all the epics that ever were founded upon fields of battle. The Georgics are indisputably and, I believe, undisputedly even a finer poem than the Æneid. Virgil knew this. He did not order them to be burnt.

" The proper study of mankind is man. It is the fashion of the day to lay great stress upon what they call 'imagination' and 'invention,' the two commonest of qualities: an Irish peasant with a little whiskey in his head will imagine and invent more than would furnish forth a modern poem. If Lucretius had not been spoiled by the Epicurean system, we should have had a far superior poem to any now in existence. As mere poetry it is the first of Latin poems. What, then, had ruined it ? His ethics. Pope has not this defect. His moral is as pure as his poetry is glorious. . . . If any great natural or national convulsion could or should overwhelm your country in such sort as to sweep Great Britain from the kingdoms of the earth and leave only that, after

His muse was never prostituted to the service of his own or any public vanity or passion. When he put on his singing robes there was always something more or less pontifical in the rites that were to be celebrated. The spirit of poesy descended upon him only upon the Sabbaths of his soul. He seemed to lay aside for the time all worldly considerations, and to hold communion with the spirits of the just made perfect. If he took an occasion or a name for his theme, it must be one standing in universal and everlasting relations with humanity. He was, of course, constantly appealed to, to lend dignity to events of transient interest and local importance, and his ingenuity was constantly taxed to provide excuses for declining to become the poetical interpreter of fleeting popular emotions.

In a letter to Mr. Charles Sedgwick in 1865, he said : —

"It is not my intention to deliver a poem at Williams College, or anywhere else. I once delivered a Phi Beta Kappa poem at Cambridge, and that

all, the most living of human things, a dead language, to be studied and read and imitated by the wise of future and far generations, upon foreign shores ; if your literature should become the learning of mankind, divested of party cabals, temporary fashions, and national pride and prejudice, an Englishman anxious that the posterity should know that there had been such a thing as a British Epic and Tragedy, might wish for the preservation of Shakespeare and Milton; but the surviving world would snatch Pope from the wreck and let the rest sink with the people. He is the moral poet of all civilization ; and as such let us hope that he will one day be the national poet of mankind."

was forty-four years ago, but since that time I have uniformly declined all requests to do the like, and I get several every year. It is an undertaking for young men. If I could be put back to twenty-six years and my wife with me, I might do it again; youth is the season for such imprudence. I should never be able to satisfy myself in the composition of a poem on such an occasion; and then it should be an exceedingly clever thing, — not a work for the closet, though; and admirably read — read as you would read it, and as few can, not to bore the audience. You have observed that such poems, with few, very few exceptions, are unspeakably tiresome."

Writing to his brother John in 1874, he says: —

"The poem you speak of I suppose you hardly expected me to compose. Such things as occasional poems I have for many years left to younger men; besides which there is nothing more tiresome and flat than a poem read at a public celebration of any event; nothing more unintelligible, unless the poem be read with exceeding skill, and the better the poem is, the less, as a general rule, it is understood by a promiscuous assembly. The only use of verses on such occasions is when they take the shape of a short ode and are sung."

It was not, I think, merely a distaste, strong as it was, for this kind of work, but a well-grounded distrust of his ability to succeed in it, which in many if not most of these cases controlled his decision. It seems as though his muse could only breathe in the Empyrean. It would have stifled

in the mephitism of Grub Street. Anything that
localized or temporized his theme seemed to par-
alyze him. There were some circumstances in the
condition of the country in 1838, just after President Jackson's successful battle with nullification,
which persuaded him that he should accept an invitation from the New York Historical Society to
deliver a poem before that body on the occasion of
its fiftieth anniversary, when John Quincy Adams
was to deliver the oration. He wrote the poem in
four stanzas, to be sung by the choir, beginning

> " Great were the hearts, and strong the minds,
>   Of those who framed in high debate
> The immortal league of Love that binds
>   Our fair, broad empire, State with State."

It appeared to suit everybody but himself. It
was a temple that had not been built as he thought
the temples of the muses should always be built,
without the noise of hammer or of axe. He never
included it in any collection of his works.

He was requested to prepare an ode for the
opening ceremonies at the Universal Exhibition
of the Centennial year at Philadelphia. In his
reply to Mr. Hawley, the president of the commission, he said : —

"I am sensible of the compliment paid me in
requesting me to compose a poem for the Centennial Exhibition at Philadelphia. It will not be in
my power to comply with the request for several
reasons. One is old age, which is another form of
ill-health, and implies a decline of both the bodily

and mental faculties. Another is the difficulty of satisfying myself in writing verses for particular occasions, a circumstance which has of late caused me to decline all applications of this nature."

Set into an old Roman wall in an old town in the south of France may still be seen a memorial stone, on which are inscribed the words *Saltavit et placuit.* This is all the record we have of the life-work of a Roman slave who died at the age of fifteen. He was a popular favorite. He danced and he pleased. The same epitaph would answer for many popular poets. If Dryden had " debauched the stage," he said, " it was to please the prince ; " claiming in the words of the well-worn couplet that

"The Drama's laws, the Drama's patrons give,
And they who live to please must please to live."

Dr. Young also *saltavit et placuit.* He felt constrained to omit from the collection of what he termed his " Excusable Poems " many addressed to the people of the highest rank in England ; such as his " Epistle to Lord Lansdowne," his dedication of " The Last Day " to Queen Anne ; and of " The Force of Religion or Vanquished Love " to the Countess of Salisbury ; " The Poem on the Accession of George I.," and several others.

Bryant's muse begat no offspring which his descendants will ever blush to recognize.

It was Bryant's notion that the life should be a true poem of him who would himself be a true poet. Like Milton he drew the inspiration of his poems "neither from the heat of youth nor from the vapours of wine like that which flows at waste from the pen of some vulgar amourist or the trencher fury of some rhyming parasite," but from

> "Siloa's brook that flows
> Fast by the Oracle of God."

It is one of his great distinctions that he never wrote a line, either in verse or prose, that countenanced a degrading impulse, an unclean thought, a mischievous propensity, or an unmanly act; and this too in a period of our literature when for none of the poets most read could their most ardent admirers claim any one of these distinctions. Bacon pleaded the distinction between *vitia temporis* and *vitia hominis* in palliation of his official venality. Whatever force this distinction may have had in Bacon's case, it cannot be invoked to diminish in any degree the exceptional merit of Bryant's example. When he began to be known as a poet, the reign of baseness and brutality in literature which followed the restoration of the Stuarts in England, and "which," said Macaulay, "never could be recalled without a blush," had not come to an end. The most popular poets at the beginning of this century owed no inconsiderable share of their popularity to verses which would now scarcely receive hospitality from any respectable periodical. It is, we hope, with a pardonable pride that we allow ourselves to ob-

serve that the same exalted sense of the poet's
calling has characterized all the verse written in
the English tongue on this side of the Atlantic
that has enjoyed any considerable measure of popular favor. Following his own advice to the poet,
slightly paraphrased, —

> " He let no empty gust
>   Of passion find an utterance in *his* lay,
> A blast that whirls the dust
>   Along the crowded street and dies away ;
> But feelings of calm power and mighty sweep,
> Like currents journeying through the windless deep."

As water in crystallizing excludes all foreign in-
gredients, and out of acids, alkalies, and other solutions yields a crystal of perfect purity and sweetness, so his thoughts in passing into verse seemed
to separate themselves from everything that was
transient or vulgar. His poems have come to us
as completely freed from every trace of what is
of the earth earthy as if, like St. Luke's pictures,
they had received their finishing touch from the
angels.

Of poetic inspiration or the state of mind in
which poetry of a high order is produced, — that
exaltation of the faculties in which high thoughts
come into the mind and clothe themselves in apt
words, — Bryant's views serve to illustrate the
statement already made, that he was not a man of
moods and tenses, and that his seasons for productive labor did not alternate like the seasons of the
calendar year, or the ebb and flow of the tides.

" I cannot say," he wrote to a gentleman who had addressed him some inquiries upon the subject, " that in writing my poems I am directly conscious of the action of an outside intelligence, but I sometimes wonder whence the thoughts come, and they seem to me hardly my own. Sometimes in searching for the adequate expression, it seems suddenly darted into my mind like a ray of light into a dark room, and gives me a kind of surprise. I don't invoke the muse at all.

" It appears to me that inspiration has no more to do with one intellectual process than another, and that if there is such a thing it might be present as directly in the solutions of a problem of high mathematics as in a copy of verses."

Bryant seems never to have attempted to place his fame under the protection of a long poem. Of the one hundred and sixty poems which he left us, the average length is only seventy-five lines. He did not believe in long poems. It was a theory of his that short poems might perhaps be chained together with links of verse, so as to add some to their commercial but not to their poetical value; that a long poem was as impossible as a long ecstasy; that what is called a long poem, like " Paradise Lost " and the " Divine Comedy," is a mere succession of poems strung together upon a thread of verse; the thread of verse serving sometimes to popularize them by adapting them to a wider range of literary taste, or a more sluggish intellectual digestion. He was often urged by his friend

Dana, and indeed by most of his intimate friends, to undertake a long poem. In his younger days he seems to have dreamed of such a work, but early came to the conclusion that there was no such thing as a long poem, and if there was, that Apollo had not provided him with the sort of lyre to render it. Loyalty to his journal, too, may have had something to do with his never attempting it. Those who are most familiar with Bryant's poetry will now probably be agreed that the ethical, which in the language of a sister art is called the *motif*, of all his verse in which reflection ruled, subordinating if not excluding all the demonstrations of passion, would be fatal to the success of a long poem.

William Walsh, whom Dryden pronounced the best critic of his time in England, gave Pope a bit of advice which has become famous: "We had had great poets," he said, "but never one great poet that was correct," and he accordingly recommended Pope to make correctness his great aim.

Of the wisdom of this advice Bryant seems to have been more thoroughly penetrated than the poet to whom it was addressed. The correctness of his measure and the conscientious fidelity of his rhymes are apt to arrest the attention and compel the admiration of even the careless reader. No poet probably ever knew better than he the *technique* of the art of "building the lofty rhyme." Dana urged him to write a book on the laws of metre, of which at a very early age he had made himself

a master. And yet, though critics concur in pronouncing his verse unfailingly graceful and melodious, Mr. Bryant had no ear nor taste for music.
Whatever inconvenience or loss of enjoyment he
may have experienced from this insensibility, there
is no evidence that either his verse or prose suffered in consequence, while both, as asserted by an
accomplished English critic, "partook in an eminent degree of that curious and almost rarefied
refinement in which oddly enough American literature seems to surpass even the literature of the
Old World." [1]

[1] The French poet Malherbe exhibits another instance of a
poet who was a master of versification, though like Bryant destitute of the musical sense. D'Alembert says of him : —

"Malherbe, dont le vrai mérite est d'avoir mis le premier, dans
les vers français, de l'*harmonie* et de l'*élégance*, comme l'a dit lui-
même avec tant d'élégance et d'harmonie le législateur Des-
preaux.

"On prétend que ce même Malherbe, si sensible à l'harmonie
des vers, et qui en a été le créateur parmi nous, était absolument
démêlé d'oreille pour la musique. Plus d'un homme de lettres
célèbre a été dans ce cas, et même en a fait l'aveu. Juste Lipse
et Ménage étaient de ce nombre, sans parler de beaucoup d'autres. Le second de ces deux savans faisait pourtant des vers en
quatre langues, en latin, en grec, en italien *et même* en français.
Cette insensibilité musicale, même dans un poëte, est peut-être
moins surprenante qu'on ne pourrait le croire. La mélodie du
chant et celle des vers quoiquelles aient pour ainsi dire quelques
points d'attouchement communs sont trop séparées et trop diffé-
rents à d'autres égards, pour qu'une oreille vivement affectée de
l'une, soit necessairement entrainée et subjuguée par l'autre, sur-
tout si la melodie musicale est renforcée, pour ne pas dire trou-
blée par les effets bruyants de l'harmonie moderne: effets que
l'oreille delicate des anciens parait n'avoir pas sentis ou peut-
être qu'elle a reprouvés."

By some process as mysterious as the leafing of the forests or the swelling of the tides, Bryant managed to make himself familiar with most of the languages of the world that had a literature. Like Sir Henry Wotton, —

> " So many languages had he in store
> That only fame could speak of him in more."

Besides an acquaintance with the Greek and Latin tongues, which many who have made these studies a specialty might have envied, he had a critical knowledge of German, French, Spanish, Portuguese, Italian, and modern Greek, to which during his travels in the East he added more than a smattering of Arabic. When it is borne in mind that he acquired them all in the leisure economized from one of the most unrelenting professions, we can realize the amazing faculty, the high discipline and admirable husbandry of time and force, which enabled him like Ulysses " to do so many things so well." The French say, " Ce qui n'est pas clair n'est pas Français." Bryant thought that verses that were obscure were not poetry. His constitutional aversion to sham of all kinds no doubt had its share in begetting this aversion. He would as soon have invoked the aid of a brass band to secure an audience as to lend himself to any meretricious devices for extorting admiration. Such he regarded all surprising novelties of expression and all subtleties of thought which the common apprehension does not readily accept. He felt that no poem was fit to leave his hand if a word or a line in it betrayed affectation or required study to be understood.

His doctrine upon this subject is thus briefly set forth in his introduction to " A Library of Poetry and Song : " —

" To me it seems that one of the most important requisites for a great poet is a luminous style. The elements of poetry lie in natural objects, in the vicissitudes of human life, in the emotions of the human heart, and the relations of man to man. He who can present them in combinations and lights which at once affect the mind with a deep sense of their truth and beauty is the poet for his own age and the ages that succeed him. . . . The metaphysician, the subtle thinker, the dealer in abstruse speculations, whatever his skill in versification, misapplies it when he abandons the more convenient form of prose, and perplexes himself with the attempt to express his ideas in poetic numbers."

In a letter to the Century Club, on the occasion of Bryant's seventieth birthday, Edward Everett pays a special tribute to this quality of the poet's verse.

" I particularly enjoy Bryant's poetry because I can understand it. It is probably a sign that I am somewhat behind the age, that I have but little relish for elaborate obscurity in literature, of which you find it difficult to study out the meaning and are not sure you have hit upon it at last. This is too much the character of the modern English school. . . . Surprise, conceit, strange combinations of imagery and expression may be successfully managed, but it is merit of an inferior kind. The truly beautiful, pathetic, and sublime is always simple and natural and marked by a certain serene unconsciousness of effort. This is the character of Mr. Bryant's poetry."

He often amused himself with translating from foreign tongues the verses that particularly pleased him, and there were very few thus honored by his choice that were not to be congratulated upon the new garb in which he arrayed them. Later in life, and when invention became too fatiguing to be more than an occasional resource, he found in translation an agreeable employment. We find the first intimation of this in a note to Dana dated May, 1863.

"I have been looking over Cowper's translation of Homer lately, and comparing it with the original. It has astonished me that one who wrote such strong English in his original compositions should have put Homer, who wrote also with simplicity and spirit, into such phraseology as he has done. For example, when Ulysses in the fifth book of the Odyssey asks 'What will become of me.' Cowper makes him say : —

"'What destiny at last attends me?'

and so on. The greater part is in such stilted phrase, and all the freedom and fire of the old poet is lost."

Old age affected the quantity rather than the quality of Bryant's verse. We have lines written after he was eighty which will compare not unfavorably with anything he had written before. But his inspiration came at longer intervals, and for obvious reasons was less fervently invited. After seventy, when the grasshopper becomes a burden, he sought pleasant rather than exciting occupation for his mind, and this he found in transferring into English blank verse the works of the great master of Epic Poetry. "I find it a pastime," he wrote to his friend, Professor Alden. "At my time of life it is somewhat dangerous to tax the brain to any great extent. Whatever requires invention, whatever compels one to search both for new thoughts and adequate expressions wherewith to clothe them, makes a severe demand on the intellect and the nervous system, — at least I have found it so. In translating poetry, — at least in translating with such freedom as blank verse allows, — my only trouble is with the expression; the thoughts are already at hand."

It is with poets as with other men. When they are old they shall stretch forth their hands and another shall gird them. It was Bryant's choice not unnaturally when the time came for him to be girded to choose one of his own kind to gird him; to supply him with the invention and the thoughts for which he should only be required to supply the raiment.

In the fall of 1863, a translation of some passages from the fifth book of the Odyssey with which he had been amusing himself appeared in the " Atlantic Monthly," and at the close of 1863, he republished it in a collection of his more recent verses, which appeared under the somewhat depressing title of " Thirty Poems." The reception it met with from scholars as well as poets was so encouraging that he tried his hand with some passages of the Iliad. The death of Mrs. Bryant in the summer of 1866 increased his indisposition for severe work and his need for distracting employment. The translations from Homer answered this purpose so well that he finally resolved to translate the whole of the Iliad. He sailed on his sixth voyage to Europe in October of that year with a copy of Homer in his pocket, and a fixed purpose of rendering at least forty lines of the old Greek into English every day. He frequently exceeded this number, and as he became inured to the work, not unfrequently increased the number to seventy-five. This was his early morning work, and even after his return was never allowed to interfere with his customary professional avocations.

Writing to his brother John in February, 1869, he said : "I have just finished my translation of the twelfth book of Homer's Iliad. In regard to what you say about Homer I would observe that Pope's translation is more periphrastic than mine and will probably have several thousand more lines. I have yet somewhat more than seven thousand of the original to translate. Yesterday I translated sixty of the Greek, making some seventy or eighty in my shorter blank verse, but generally I cannot do so much, — sometimes not more than forty."

These first twelve books of his version of the Iliad were published by Fields, Osgood & Co., of Boston, in February, 1870, and the second volume, containing the remainder of the poem, in June of the same year.   In the preface he informs us that he began the work in 1865, but afterwards gave himself up to it the more willingly because it helped in some measure to divert his mind from a great domestic sorrow.   " I am not sure," he adds, " that, when it shall be concluded, it may not cost me some regret to part with so interesting a companion as the old Greek poet, with whose thoughts I have for four years past been occupied, though with interruptions, in the endeavor to transfer from his own grand musical Greek to our less sonorous but still manly and flexible tongue."

He tells us of his endeavor to be strictly faithful in his rendering, " to add nothing of his own, and to give the reader, so far as our language would allow, all that he found in the original."   He was at equal pains, he assures us, to preserve the simplicity of style of the old poet, " who wrote for the popular ear and according to the genius of his language.   I have chosen such English as offers no violence to the ordinary usages and structure of our own.   I have sought to attain what belongs to the original — affluent narrative style which shall carry the reader forward without the impediment of unexpected inversions and capricious phrases, and in which, if he find nothing to stop at and admire, there will at least be nothing to divert his attention from the story and the characters of the poem, from the events related and the objects described." He disagrees with Pope, who doubted whether a poem could be supported without rhyme in our language, unless stiffened with such strong words as would destroy the language itself. Bryant assigns as his reason for choosing blank verse for his Homer, that it enabled him to keep more closely to the original without any sacrifice either of ease or spirit. " The use of rhyme in a translation is a constant temptation to petty infidelities, and to the employment of expressions which have an air of constraint and do not the most adequately convey the thought." He did not adopt the ballad measure because the Homeric poems seemed to him beyond the popular ballads of any modern nation in reach of thought and in richness of phraseology. " If I had adopted that form of poetry," he says, " there would have been besides the disadvantage of rhyme, a temptation to make the version conform in style and spirit to the old ballads of our own literature in a degree which the original does not warrant, and which, as I think, would lead to some sacrifice of its dignity."

Bryant's reasons for preferring blank verse for this poem all have weight, and with a translator approaching his eightieth year they were conclusive. But no one can doubt that the position which Pope's version of Homer holds in our literature is very largely due to its measure and rhyme, nor that Bryant's translation would have been more widely popular, if less faithful, had it been tuned like Pope's to the popular ear. But to a person so conscientious about his rhymes, about the correctness of his verse and the fidelity of his translation, as Bryant, the use of rhyme implied an enormous increase of labor from which he shrank, and which would have deprived his task of what to him was its chief attraction, its recreatory character. Had he undertaken this task twenty or even ten years earlier, and given it the charm of rhyme, it would probably have soon extinguished forever all popular interest in every other translation in our language. Whether it would have stood as high in the estimation of scholars, whether the proportions of Homer to Bryant in it would have been the same as in this version, we have his own authority for doubting, but we should certainly have had a Homer which would have fascinated a larger number. Without rhyme, however, it was a great literary success. It was received with unqualified admiration by the highest poetical and scholarly authorities as well as by the press of his country.

"It is commended," he wrote to Dana, "in quarters where my original poems are, I suspect, not much thought of, and I sometimes fancy that possibly it is thought that I am more successful as a translator than in anything else, which you know is not the highest praise. I did not find the work of rendering Homer into blank verse very fatiguing, and perhaps it was the most suitable literary occupation for an old man like me, who feels the necessity of being busy about something and yet does not like hard work."

To his old pastor, Dr. Dewey, he wrote : —

" I can imagine that on laying down the volume you drew a long breath of relief — one of those grateful sighs significant alike of the trouble that has been taken and the satisfaction we feel that it is over. Do you remember Pope's line : —

" ' And Congreve loved and Swift endured my lays ' ?

It is not every poet that has a friend capable of enduring four hundred pages of his verse.

" I am really glad that you can speak so kindly of my translation. It is well received so far, and sells well, I 'm told, for so costly a publication. I am almost ashamed to see it got up in so expensive a manner. Democrat as I am, I would, if the matter had been left to my discretion, have published it in as cheap a form as is consistent with neatness and a good fair legible type. I like very well to see it in that large type, but I should have made it a book for persons of small means, that is to say if they chose to buy it."

Bryant realized, as he had apprehended he should, that the old Greek poet was too interesting a companion to part with without regret, and he determined, therefore, to postpone their parting as long as possible. Before the Iliad was through the press he had begun to translate the Odyssey.

Writing to his brother John on the 1st of July, 1870, he says : —

" I have begun the translation of the Odyssey, but I do not intend to hurry the task, nor even to translate with as much diligence as I translated the Iliad; so I may never finish it. But it will give me an occupation which will not be an irksome one, and will furnish me with a reason for declining other literary tasks and a hundred other engagements which I want some other excuse besides old age for declining."

The feeling that the number of working days in reserve for him at the most was very limited had its effect in securing for the Odyssey a precedence among his numerous engagements which had not been accorded to the Iliad, for by the close of April, 1871, the first volume of twelve books was in the printer's hands, and, before the year closed, the whole work was ready for the press. " There was no need," he wrote his publisher in April, " that you should exhort me to be diligent in putting the Odyssey into blank verse. I have been as industrious as was reasonable. I understand very well that at my time of life such enterprises are apt to be brought to a conclusion before they are finished. And I have therefore wrought harder upon my task than some of my friends thought was well for me. I have already sent forward the MSS. for the first volume. You may remember that I finished my translation of the Iliad within the time that I undertook, and this would have been done without any urging. In the case of the Odyssey, I have finished the first volume two months sooner than I promised. I do not think the Odyssey the better part of Homer except morally. The gods set a better example and take more care to see that wrong and injustice are discouraged among mankind. But there is not the same spirit and fire, nor the same vividness of description, and this the translator must feel as strongly as the reader. Let me correct what I have already said by adding that there is yet in the Odyssey one more advantage over the Iliad. It is better as a story. In the Iliad the plot is, to me, unsatisfactory, and there is, besides, a monotony of carnage — you get a surfeit of slaughter."

Again, on the 18th of June following, he writes to Dana : —

"I do not feel quite so easy in work as I did in translating the Iliad, for the thought that I am so old that I may be interrupted in my task before it is done rises in my mind now and then, and I work a little the more diligently for it, which perhaps is not so well."

Writing to his publishers in July, he betrayed the consciousness that he was getting nervous about finishing his work : —

"As I have finished another book of the Odyssey, I forward it to-day. But do not let your printers tread on my heels. It is disagreeable to be dunned for copy, and I cannot write as well when I have any vexation of that sort on my mind."

On the 7th of December, 1871, Bryant addressed the following brief note to his publishers: " I have sent you by mail the twenty-fourth and concluding book of my translation of Homer's Odyssey together with the table of contents for the second volume." It was in this unceremonious way he took leave of a task which had been his chief solace and recreation for six long years. Perhaps he dared not trust himself to say more of such a parting.

The reception of Bryant's Homer by his country people could not have been more cordial. Every one seemed proud of it. The conviction rapidly took possession of the scholarly public that the old Greek had never before been brought so near to readers of English, and that our literature had been permanently and substantially enriched. Neither of these convictions is likely to be shaken. No scholar has made the criticism of Bryant's Homer that Bentley made of Pope's.[1] Nor did any one ever claim to share with him the credit of any portion of his work.[2] While giving his readers the genuine spirit of Homer, Bryant has also

---

[1] "A pretty poem, Mr. Pope, but you must not call it Homer. "

[2] A large portion of the translation of the Odyssey appears now to have been done by a better scholar than Pope named Broome, and all the learning in the notes was gathered by him. Pope's reluctance to recognize the services of his collaborators provoked no end of lampoons, of which the following is one of the cleverest: —

> " By tricks sustained in poet-craft complete
> Retire triumphant to thy Twickenham seat.
> That seat the work of half-paid drudging Broome,
> And called by joking Tritons Homer's tomb."

given them one of the finest specimens of pure Saxon English in our literature. It will reward the curiosity of the philologist to note the large proportion of words of one syllable, the scarcity of words of three or more syllables, and the yet more conspicuous absence of words of Greek or Latin derivation.

The sale of the work was to Mr. Bryant at least one gratifying evidence of its merit. Up to May, 1888, 17,000 copies of the Iliad had been sold, yielding him in royalties $12,738. Of the Odyssey, 10,244 copies, yielding in royalties $4,713, making a total income from these translations up to the spring of 1888 of $17,451.

There is a moral for publishers and authors in the circumstance that while 3,283 copies of the more costly 8vo edition of the Iliad were selling, 5,449 copies of the 12mo edition in two volumes were disposed of. The royalties from the cheaper editions amounted to $4,713.60, while the royalties from the other edition amounted only to $811.80. This is exclusive of the copyright of $2,500, paid on the day of publication. Of the large paper copies of the Odyssey only 1,615 copies were sold to 7,229 of the cheaper editions, yielding royalties from the former of $321.05, and $2,392 from the latter.

In looking at the financial side of this publication one is irresistibly tempted to compare it with the only publication which invites such a comparison — the version of Homer made by Pope in the first quarter of the last century,[1] which Johnson called "the noblest version of poetry the world has ever seen," which the poet Gray said somewhat rashly no other translation would ever equal, and to which Gibbon ascribed "every merit but that of faithfulness to the original." Pope's Iliad was published in six volumes, for each of which Lintot, his publisher, was to pay £200, besides supplying Pope gratuitously with the copies for which he procured subscribers. The subscribers paid a guinea a volume, and as 575 subscribers took 654 copies, Pope received altogether £5,320 4s. By the Odyssey he seems to have made about £3,500 more, yielding a total profit of about £9,000. So that he could say with truth, "Thanks to Homer," he "could live and thrive, indebted to no prince or peer alive."

"No author," says Leslie Stephen,[2] "had ever made anything approaching the sum which Pope received, and very few authors, even in the present age of gold, would despise such payment."

The returns to Bryant from his Homer in about the same period of time after publication were but about $20,000 as against the returns to Pope of say $45,000, a little more than one third the latter sum. On the other hand, Pope's receipts were all realized mainly from the sale of only 654 copies or thereabouts. How many Lintot sold we do not know, but probably not more than as many more, or, at

[1] 1715–1726.
[2] *Alexander Pope*, in English Men of Letters, p. 62.

most, a thousand copies, which would make a total of 1,654 copies, while the sales of Bryant's version amounted to 17,000 copies, or more than ten times the number sold of Pope's version.

When it is considered that Bryant made no personal appeal to his friends and admirers, as Pope did, to buy his book; that he had no touter like Swift to bustle about in the ante-chambers of royalty, button-holing every considerable man he met, to say, *mutatis mutandis*, "the best poet in America has begun a translation into English verse, for which he must have them all subscribe, for the author shall not begin to print till I have a thousand guineas for him;" and that he never presented a copy of this or of any other publication of his with the view of securing a notice or review of it,[1] the success of his translation financially cannot be deemed to suffer by the comparison with its only rival.

It deserves to be noted here also that Pope, when he finished his Homer, was on the hither side of forty, and Bryant, when he finished his, was on the thither side of eighty.

---

[1] Not long after the publication of his *Thirty Poems*, Bryant wrote to Dana: —

"Acting on your suggestion, I have sent a copy of my *Thirty Poems* to President Hopkins, of Williams College, and have received from him a very kind note. In a letter to him accompanying the volume, I made you responsible for my sending it, for I never in my life sent a copy of my poems to anybody with the design to get a good word from them or to invite their notice of my writings in print."

Of the financial returns of his other poetical works we have no precise information, but it is quite safe to say that he realized many times as much from his Homer as from all the other verses he ever wrote. We have ample confirmation of this conclusion in two letters written, one in the earlier stage of his career, and the other near to its close.

Writing to Dana in April, 1832, and shortly after the publication of the volume of poems which Irving introduced to the British public, he said: —

"You ask about the sale of the book. Mr. Bliss tells me it is very good for poetry. I printed a thousand copies, and more than half are disposed of. As to the price, it may be rather high at $1.25, but I found that, with what I should give away and what the booksellers would take, little would be left for me if a rather high price was not put upon it. And so I told the publisher to fix it at a dollar and a quarter. If the whole impression sells it will bring me $300, perhaps a little more. I hope you do not think that too much. I have sent the volume out to England, and Washington Irving has had the kindness to undertake to introduce it to the English public. . . . As for the lucre of the thing on either side of the water, an experience of twenty-five years — for it is so long since I became an author — has convinced me that poetry is an unprofitable trade, and I am very glad that I have something more certain to depend upon for a living."

Later on in his experience he spoke of the poetical market with even less indulgence.

To Dana : —

" After all, poetic wares are not for the market of the present day. Poetry may get printed in the newspapers, but no man makes money by it for the simple reason that nobody cares a fig for it. The taste for it is something old-fashioned ; the march of the age is in another direction ; mankind are occupied with politics, railroads, and steamboats. Hundreds of persons will talk flippantly and volubly about poetry, and even write about it, who know no more of the matter, and have no more feeling of the matter, than the old stump I write this letter with."

The artistic taste of this country has so much improved in the last quarter of a century, that it would not be surprising if Bryant's original poems have yielded to his heirs already larger returns than they ever yielded their author.

Bryant, as we have seen, sprang into the world a poet full grown. His muse had no adolescence. As with Pindar, the bees swarmed in his mouth while yet a child. At eighteen he took his place as the first poet of the country, but not to realize the too common fate of such rare precocity and fall a prey to the envy of the gods, as Dryden puts it, who

" When their gifts too lavishly are placed
Soon they repent and will not make them last."

There is no evidence that Bryant's genius ever suffered from prematurity of development. He never wrote a poem from the day that " Thana-topsis " appeared until his death that was unworthy of his best, and the cadences yet linger in the air of those impressive lines with which in 1878 he commemorated the birthday of the hero of our Republic. Was there ever a more meritorious poem written by a youth of eighteen than " Thanatopsis " ? Was there ever a nobler and more Homeric thought more exquisitely set to verse than is developed in the three last of the following stanzas, written in his eighty-fourth year?

THE TWENTY-SECOND OF FEBRUARY.

Pale is the February sky,
And brief the mid-day's sunny hours;
The wind-swept forest seems to sigh
For the sweet time of leaves and flowers.

Yet has no month a prouder day,
Not even when the summer broods
O'er meadows in their fresh array,
Or autumn tints the glowing woods.

For this chill season now again
Brings, in its annual round, the morn
When, greatest of the sons of men,
Our glorious Washington was born.

Lo, where, beneath an icy shield,
Calmly the mighty Hudson flows!
By snow-clad fell and frozen field,
Broadening, the lordly river goes.

The wildest storm that sweeps through space,
And rends the oak with sudden force,

Can raise no ripple on his face,
Or slacken his majestic course.

Thus, 'mid the wreck of thrones, shall live
Unmarred, undimmed, our hero's fame,
And years succeeding years shall give
Increase of honors to his name.

CHAPTER VIII.

THE TOURIST.

BRYANT'S favorite and chief recreation was travel, partly because there is no escape from the importunate exactions of a daily journal but flight, partly because of the happy combination of rest and mental fertilization which travel affords. Few Americans have been as well equipped to enjoy travel as Bryant, and no one could enjoy it much more. His familiarity with the languages and literature of the countries he visited, his intelligent curiosity about everything which distinguished his own from other countries and peoples, and his love of nature that always grew by what it fed on, made him in the largest sense of the word a citizen of the world, a stranger nowhere, and welcome wherever a welcome was desirable. His first excursion that deserved to be dignified with the title of a journey was made in 1832 to visit his brothers, who upon the death of their father had with their mother sought a new home in the West, and had become the proprietors of a large landed estate in Illinois. He consumed two weeks in this journey, which is now made in about as many days. While crossing the prairies

between the Mississippi River and his brothers'
plantation, he encountered a company of Illinois
volunteers who were moving south to take a part in
what is commonly known as the "Black Hawk
War." They were led by a tall, awkward, un-
couth lad, whose appearance particularly attracted
Mr. Bryant's attention, and whose conversation delighted him by its breeziness and originality. He
learned many years afterwards, from one who had
belonged to the troop, that this captain of theirs
was named Abraham Lincoln.[1] Mr. Bryant little
dreamed as he scanned the ungainly stripling and
listened to his unweeded jokes that, some thirty
years later, it would become his duty to present
him to a New York audience and his privilege to
hear from these very lips "the decisive word of
the contest" which was to result in making this
captain of volunteers, for eight consecutive years,
President of the Republic; the central figure of
one of the most momentous wars that has ever yet
been waged among men, and the signer of the proclamation that delivered over six millions of people from slavery.

It was during this visit to his brothers that he
wrote of

> "The unshorn fields, boundless and beautiful
> For which the speech of England has no name,"

the closing lines of which, though found in every
"Reader" used in American schools, never stales,

[1] Godwin's *Life of Bryant*, i. 283.

and will always lend a classic interest to Bryant's first trip beyond the Alleghanies.

> "Still this great solitude is quick with life.
> Myriads of insects, gaudy as the flowers
> They flutter over, gentle quadrupeds,
> And birds, that scarce have learned the fear of man,
> Are here, and sliding reptiles of the ground,
> Startlingly beautiful. The graceful deer
> Bounds to the wood at my approach. The bee,
> A more adventurous colonist than man,
> With whom he came across the eastern deep,
> Fills the savannas with his murmurings,
> And hides his sweets, as in the golden age,
> Within the hollow oak. I listen long
> To his domestic hum, and think I hear
> The sound of that advancing multitude
> Which soon shall fill these deserts. From the ground
> Comes up the laugh of children, the soft voice
> Of maidens, and the sweet and solemn hymn
> Of Sabbath worshipers. The low of herds
> Blends with the rustling of the heavy grain
> Over the dark brown furrows. All at once
> A fresher wind sweeps by, and breaks my dream,
> And I am in the wilderness alone."

In June, 1834, Bryant took passage with his family in the sailing ship Poland for Havre, to receive his first impressions of the Old World. He spent a few weeks in Paris, a month in Rome, a month in Naples, two months in Florence, four months in Pisa, three months in Munich, and four months in Heidelberg. His studious sojourn at this renowned seat of learning was interrupted by intelligence of the dangerous illness of his editorial colleague, William Leggett, who became associated with him in the editorship of the " Evening Post "

very shortly after the death of Coleman.[1] Placing
his family in charge of friends, — not wishing to
expose them to the discomforts of a winter's voyage, — he sailed from Havre for New York in
February, 1836.

As we never have first impressions of anything
but once, it is interesting to note some of Bryant's
first impressions of France. On his journey from
Havre to Paris, he tells us in one of his letters to
the " Evening Post : " —

" We passed females riding on donkeys, the Old
Testament beast of burden, with panniers on each
side, as was the custom hundreds of years since.
We saw ancient dames sitting at their doors with
distaffs, twisting the thread by twirling the spindle
between the thumb and finger as they did in the
days of Homer. A flock of sheep was grazing on
the side of a hill; they were attended by a shep-
herd and a brace of prick-eared dogs, which kept
them from straying, as was done thousands of
years ago. Speckled birds were hopping by the
sides of the road ; it was the magpie, the bird of
ancient fable. Flocks of what I at first took for
the crow of our country were stalking in the fields,
or sailing in the air over the old elms ; it was the
rook, the bird made as classical by Addison as his
cousin the raven by the Latin poets. . . .

[1] Leggett was a native of New York, had been a midshipman
in the navy, and had written some tales and verses which attracted Mr. Bryant's attention. The wags of the opposition
called them " The Chaunting Cherubs."

"As we drew nearer to Paris we saw the plant which Noah first committed to the earth after the deluge — you know what that was, I hope — trained on low stakes, and growing thickly and luxuriantly on the slopes by the side of the highway. Here, too, was the tree which was the subject of the first Christian miracle, the fig, its branches heavy with the bursting fruit just beginning to ripen for the market."

He was in raptures with the Italian atmosphere, which surpassed his expectations, but in other respects he was disappointed with Italian scenery : —

"The forms of the mountains are wonderfully picturesque, and their effect is heightened by the rich atmosphere through which they are seen, and by the buildings, imposing from their architecture, or venerable from time, which crown the eminences. But if the hand of man has done something to embellish this region, it has done more to deform it. Not a tree is suffered to retain its natural shape, not a brook to flow in its natural channel. An exterminating war is carried on against the natural herbage of the soil. The country is without woods and green fields; and to him who views the vale of the Arno 'from the top of Fiesole,' or any of the neighboring heights, grand as he will allow the circle of the mountains to be and magnificent the edifices with which the region is adorned, it appears, at any time after midsummer, a huge valley of dust, planted with low rows of the pallid and thin-leaved olive, or the more dwarfish maple on which the vines are trained. The simplicity of nature, so far as can be done, is destroyed; there is no fine sweep of forest, no broad expanse of meadow, or pasture ground, no ancient and towering trees clustered about the villas, no rows of natural shrubbery following the course of the brooks and rivers. The streams, which are often but the beds of torrents dry during the summer, are confined in straight channels by stone walls and embankments; the slopes are broken up and disfigured by terraces; and the trees are kept down by constant pruning and lopping, until half way up the sides of the Apennines, where the limit of cultivation is reached, and thence to the summit, is a barren steep of rock, without herbage or soil."

Venice, he found, as many others have done, "the most pleasing of the Italian cities."

At a post house in the Tyrol where he stopped on a Saturday his refection was limited to soup maigre and fish, "the post-master telling us that the priest had positively forbidden meat to be given to travelers. Think of that! — that we who had eaten wild boar and pheasants at Rome under the very nostrils of the Pope himself and his whole conclave of cardinals, should be refused a morsel of flesh on an ordinary Saturday at a tavern on a lonely mountain in the Tyrol by the orders of a parish priest."

In September, 1845, he found an opportunity of returning to Europe. After spending about two months in England, he devoted the succeeding three months to the principal places of interest in France, Belgium, Holland, Germany, Switzerland, and Italy, returning to his country and work in November.

In England, Bryant felt the reflex influence of his fame as a poet more distinctly than he had felt it ten years before on his visit to the Continent. This was due in part to the publication in the interval of the collection of his poems which appeared in London under the editorial auspices of Mr. Irving. Mr. Everett, then our Minister at the English Court, called upon him promptly, and invited him to meet some of the prominent literary men at breakfast. Samuel Rogers, Monckton Milnes (the late Lord Houghton), and Tom Moore were of the number. How Rogers drove him home to his lodgings, gave him a general invitation to his breakfasts, and how they contracted before they separated a warm personal regard for each other, which only increased with their years, has been already told. From Bryant's diary it appears that Rogers's house was always open to him as a favored guest. Presented to London society under such auspices, it is needless to say that before he left England he was brought into relations with most of the literary celebrities of London. He attended Parliament several times, went to a Corn Law meeting, at which addresses were made by Cobden, Fox, and Bright, where he heard some lines cited from his "Hymn to the

City," which, say the reports of the day, were received with such prolonged applause that he was obliged to acknowledge the compliment by rising and bowing to the audience.[1] Upon the invitation of one of the managers of the British Association he went to Cambridge to attend one of its meetings. He here became acquainted with Dr. Lyell, Dr. Buckland, Sir John Herschel, Hallam the historian; breakfasted and lunched with Dr. Whewell, had his health proposed at a dinner at which Professor Sedgwick presided, and at Sheffield was taken to see the venerable James Montgomery, "a light made man, in a huge black silk cravat that filled his neck beyond the chin, rather

[1] In his address at the dinner given him by the Free Trade League of New York in 1868, Bryant gives the following reminiscence of this meeting: —

"Mr. President: we must follow up with vigor the advantage we have gained, and when the people speak. Congress must and shall give way. I remember that, when in the time of the famous Corn-Law agitation in England, an agitation for cheap bread, — and our agitation is for cheap iron, cheap fuel, and cheap clothing, — I heard Cobden, Bright, and Fox discuss the question of free trade in corn before an immense assemblage crowded into Drury Lane Theatre. Fox insisted that the only method to move the British Ministry with Peel at its head was to move the people. He quoted the old rhyme —

> "When the wind blows then the mill goes;
> When the wind drops then the mill stops,"

and he parodied it thus: —

> "When the League blows then the Peel goes,
> When the League stops then the Peel drops."

"The league followed his advice and blew vigorously, and Peel brought in a bill to repeal the restrictions on the trade in breadstuffs, and England had cheap bread."

thin faced, with a thin, long nose; his conversation agreeable but not striking." At the urgent solicitation of Crabb Robinson he drove over to call upon Wordsworth, whom he found "in his garden in a white broad-brimmed, low-crowned hat." The guests walked with him over his grounds, took tea at six, and left at ten in the evening.[1]

He thought Edinburgh "the finest city he ever saw," and Glasgow not without claim to the epithet "beautiful." What seems to have impressed him most in the latter was "the good sense of the people in erecting the statues which adorn their public squares only to men who have some just claim to distinction. Here are no statues, for example, of the profligate Charles II., or the worthless Duke of York, or the silly Duke of Cambridge, as you will see in other cities; but here the marble effigy of Walter Scott looks from a lofty column in the principal square, and not far from it is that of the inventor Watt; while the statues erected to military men are to those who, like Wellington, have acquired a just renown in arms."

[1] "Mr. Bryant often recurred in conversation to his pleasant visit to Wordsworth, but one always suspected that, much as he reverenced the poet, he was not very strongly impressed by the man. Wordsworth had a way of talking of himself and his poetry which must have seemed strange if not ludicrous to one so habitually reticent in the same respects as our traveler. . . . After his return, Mr. Bryant sometimes amused his more intimate friends with imitations of Wordsworth's reverent manner of repeating his own verses — not, however, in a way that lessened respect for the venerable bard." — Godwin's *Life*, ii. 9.

He listened on the Sabbath to a sermon from "a comfortable-looking professor in some new theological school. It was quite commonplace, though not so long as the Scotch ministers are in the habit of giving. . . . At the close of the exercises he announced that a third service would be held in the evening. 'The subject,' he continued, 'will be "The Thoughts and Exercises of Jonah in the Whale's Belly." ' "

At Ayr, he wondered that, "born as Burns was in the neighborhood of the sea, which is often swelled into prodigious waves by the strong west winds that beat on this coast, he should yet have taken little, if any, of his poetic imagery from the ocean, either in its wilder or its gentler moods. But his occupations were among the fields, and his thoughts were of those who dwelt among them, and his imagination never wandered where his feelings went not." He visited the monument to Burns erected near the bridge, which he found "an ostentatious thing, with a gilt tripod on its summit. . . . The wild rose and the woodbine were in full bloom in the hedges, and these to me were a better memorial of Burns than anything which the chisel could furnish."

In March, 1849, and immediately after the memorable schism in the Democratic party which resulted in the nomination of Van Buren for President by the Free Soil party, the consequent defeat of Cass, and the election of Taylor to the Presidency, Mr. Bryant visited Cuba by way of the Carolinas and Florida. He spent a week on a cotton plantation in South Carolina, another week in Florida; was received by the Governor-General at Havana, passed several days on a coffee estate at Matanzas, went by rail to San Antonio in a car built at Newark, drawn by an engine made in New York, and worked by an American engineer; breakfasted at the inn of La Punta on rice and fresh eggs and a dish of meat so highly flavored with garlic that it was impossible to distinguish the species of animal it belonged to. He visited a cock-pit in which a man "with a gray beard, a grave aspect, and a solemn gait was training a game-cock in the virtue of perseverance;" witnessed a cock-fight, a masked ball, a murderer garroted, and slavery in some of its most inhuman phases. He was absent on this excursion about two months.

In June, and only a few weeks after his return from Cuba, he sailed again on his third trip to Europe. After a few days in London he visited the Orkney and Shetland Islands, Iona and Staffa. In August, he passed over to the Continent, spent a few days in Paris, and then proceeded to Switzerland and Bavaria, returning to the United States in December. During his brief stay in London he was again warmly received by Rogers, to whom he was specially indebted for an introduction to, and a good deal of attention from, the most eminent artists of that day in England. At their first meeting on this visit Rogers, then over eighty, said to him, "You look hearty and cheerful, but our poets all seem to be losing their minds. Campbell's son is in a madhouse, and if his father had been put there during the later years of his life it would have been the proper place for him. Bowles became weak-minded ; and as for Southey, you know what happened to him. Moore was here the other day, and I asked him how long he had been in town. 'Three or four days,' he said. 'What, three or four days, and not let me know it!' 'I beg pardon,' said he, putting his hand to his forehead, 'I believe I came to town this morning.' As to Wordsworth, a gentleman who saw him lately said to me, 'You will not find Wordsworth much changed, he still *talks* rationally.' "

On returning from the Shetland Islands, which he left reluctantly, he called upon Lord Jeffrey, "who," he wrote in his diary, "talked eloquently of Puseyism, which he said was a fashion, — an affectation having no root in any great principle of human nature; appealing neither to mysticism nor rationalism, the two great parties of the religious world — and which could only be temporary." Bryant's impressions of Abbotsford were unsatisfactory. "The fellow at the gate was tipsy and crusty, and the woman at the house flushed and peremptory, not allowing the inside to be seen, because the house was shut up."

Bryant found the Continent bristling with bayonets, and having all the air of conquered provinces; nearly every city worth visiting was "in a state of siege." Soldiers filled the streets and all the public squares of Paris. "Those," he wrote, "who maintain that France is not fit for liberty need not afflict themselves with the idea that there is at present more liberty in France than her people know how to enjoy."

He found the cities along the Rhine also crowded with soldiers, Heidelberg full of Prussian troops, and every other man he met in the streets a soldier; he entered Stuttgart "with a little army." From Geiselingen to Ulm, on the Danube, "the road was fairly lined with soldiers walking or resting by the wayside, or closely packed in the peasants' wagons." At Munich, he hoped for better things, but in vain. "They were everywhere placed in sight as if to keep the people in awe." So weary had he become of the perpetual sight of the military uniform and other symbols of repression and oppression that when he reached Switzerland, where no *gens d'armes* challenged his movements, where no one asked for his passport, nor for the keys to his baggage, he "could almost have kneeled and kissed the shores of the hospitable republic." He returned to his country and duties in December.

In November, 1852, Bryant sailed again into the East, Egypt and Syria being his objective points. On his way through London he passed an evening at the house of Mr. Chapman, the publisher, where, it appears by his diary, he met "a blue-stocking lady, who writes for the 'Westminster Review,' named Evans." A few days later, he learned that this blue-stocking was Miss Marian Evans, since celebrated as " George Eliot." He met there also Herbert Spencer, Louis Blanc, and Pierre Leroux. He arrived in Paris the evening before the proclamation of the Empire; saw the new emperor escorted to the palace of the Tuileries, and was impressed " by the utter absence not only of enthusiasm, but even of the least affectation of enthusiasm," in the crowd which surrounded him. From Paris he proceeded through Lyons, Marseilles, and Nîmes to Genoa, whence he sailed to Naples. After a flying visit to Pompeii, Amalfi, Pæstum, Nocera, and Malta, he embarked for Alexandria, whence without delay he proceeded to Cairo, where he spent a week, and thence up the Nile as far as the first cataract, in which sixteen days were consumed. From Cairo he set out across the desert for Jerusalem, where, after fifteen days' camel-riding, he arrived on the 13th of February. After bathing in the Jordan and the Dead Sea, visiting Nazareth, the Lake of Tiberias, Mount Carmel, Acre, Tyre, Sidon, Beyrout, Damascus, and Baalbec, he sailed to Constantinople; thence went to Smyrna, Athens, Corfu, Trieste, Venice, Florence, Rome, Cività Vecchia, and Marseilles. After spending ten or twelve days in Paris, and a day or two in London, he returned to New York in May, 1853.

In May, 1857, Mr. Bryant crossed the Atlantic for the fifth time, not on this occasion for his own pleasure, but for Mrs. Bryant's health, which for two or three years had given him more or less solicitude. They landed in Havre on the first of June. After a short stay in Paris, they traveled through Belgium and Holland to Heidelberg, thence through Switzerland, where they did not tarry, and France to Bagnères de Luchon. By November, they were at Madrid, and in January, 1858, at Naples. On this journey Mrs. Bryant was attacked with a catarrhal fever, which assumed so grave a character at Naples as to detain them there about four months instead of the one month which they had reserved for that city. They left in May for Rome, where they passed about a fortnight. They returned through Venice in July to Paris, where they tarried a couple of weeks, and then left for England, returning to the United States in August, but unhappily without accomplishing the primary purpose of their expedition. "I brought back Mrs. Bryant," he wrote to Dr. Dewey, "nearly as well as she was when I carried her off to Europe, and gaining strength so steadily that I have great hopes of soon seeing her even better than she was there."

It was in the spring of this year, as already stated, that Bryant purchased the Bryant homestead at Cummington, mainly to test the effects of the Berkshire air upon her still languishing health. He built a new house to insure the greater advantage to her from the atmospheric accessories, and when it was finished in the spring of 1866 invited all his relations from Illinois to join him there in "hanging the pot." The pleasure and benefits for which he had so considerately planned were not to be realized. Mrs. Bryant's health that summer declined so rapidly that early in July he was compelled to notify his brothers and their families, already assembled at Cummington, that his wife was too ill to meet them there. She survived but a few weeks, and on the 27th she was where — to use Bryant's own words : —

> "He who went before thee to prepare
> For his meek followers, shall assign thy place."

In reply to a letter of condolence from his friend Dana, he wrote : —

"I know, my dear friend, that she is happier where she is now than even her generous sympathies made her here, yet when I think of the suffering which attended her illness of eleven weeks, of the patience with which she compelled herself to endure it, and of her strong desire to do God's will, I cannot help feeling a sharp pang at the heart, notwithstanding that I am able to think of her as now beyond the reach of death, pain, and decay, with the Divine person whose example of love and beneficence she sought to copy with the humblest estimate of her success. In this point of view my grief may be without cause, but there is yet another way to look at it. I lived with my wife forty-five years, and now that great blessing of my life is withdrawn, and I am like one cast out of Paradise and wandering in a strange world. I hope yet to see all this in the light of which you speak — the light in which 'death duplicates those who are taken from us.' Meantime, I perceive this: that the example set me by her whom I have lost — of absolute sincerity, of active benevolence, and of instant and resolute condemnation of whatever is unrighteous and inhuman — is more thought of and cherished by me than during her lifetime, and seems invested with a new sacredness."

Among the papers found upon Bryant's table when he left for Mexico was the following sketch of an uncompleted poem which can scarcely be fully appreciated by any who have not experienced a similar bereavement, but which no one can read without being moved by its pathetic tenderness. Mr. Bryant had then been a widower seven years.

> " The morn hath not the glory that it wore,
>   Nor doth the day so beautifully die,
> Since I can call thee to my side no more,
>   To gaze upon the sky.
>
> " For thy dear hand, with each return of Spring,
>   I sought in sunny nooks the flowers she gave ;
> I seek them still, and sorrowfully bring
>   The choicest to thy grave.
>
> " Here where I sit alone is sometimes heard,
>   From the great world, a whisper of my name,
> Joined, haply, to some kind, commending word,
>   By those whose praise is fame.
>
> " And then, as if I thought thou still wert nigh,
>   I turn me, half forgetting thou art dead,
> To read the gentle gladness in thine eye,
>   That once I might have read.

" I turn, but see thee not; before my eyes
    The image of a hillside mound appears,
Where all of thee that passed not to the skies
    Was laid with bitter tears.

" And I, whose thoughts go back to happier days,
    That fled with thee, would gladly now resign
All that the world can give of fame and praise,
    For one sweet look of thine.

" Thus, ever, when I read of generous deeds,
    Such words as thou didst once delight to hear,
My heart is wrung with anguish as it bleeds
    To think thou art not near.

" And now that I can talk no more with thee
    Of ancient friends and days too fair to last,
A bitterness blends with the memory
    Of all that happy past.

" Oh, when I —
" ROSLYN, 1873."

In a brief memoir written immediately after her
death for the eyes of his daughters alone, Mr.
Bryant said : —

" I never wrote a poem that I did not repeat to
her and take her judgment upon it. I found its
success with the public precisely in proportion to
the impression it made upon her. She loved my
verses and judged them kindly, but did not like
them all equally well." [1]

The health of his younger daughter, worn by
watching and anxiety, now required his special attention, and under the impression that change of

[1] Godwin's *Life of Bryant*, ii. 246.

scene and climate might be advantageous to both,
they sailed again in a French steamer for Havre,
in October, 1866.   After a fortnight in Paris they
went to Amélie-les-Bains, in the eastern Pyrenees.
In January, they left for the south of Spain, and
in February, they were in Florence.   Here Bryant
was invited by Garibaldi to accompany him ·to
Venice, whither he was going to celebrate the
withdrawal of the Austrians from Italy.   No one
who knew Bryant would need be told that he preferred to adhere to his original purpose of taking
his daughter to Rome, where he arrived in March.
They were soon driven thence by the heat, and
were at Dresden in April, having visited on their
way Ancona, Trieste, Vienna, Salzburg, Munich,
and Nuremberg.   They were again in Paris early
in May, 1867, in England in July, where they remained until the 24th of August, passing much of
their time in Wales, and returned to New York
again in September.   This was the sixth and last
of Mr. Bryant's trips beyond the Atlantic.   While
in Rome and later in Florence on this trip, he met
Hawthorne more or less familiarly.   In his "French
and Italian Note-Books," Hawthorne has given a
striking sketch of Bryant and the impression the
poet left upon him.

" May 22.   Yesterday, while we were at dinner, Mr.
Bryant called.   I never saw him but once before, and
that was at the door of our little red cottage in Lenox,
he sitting in a wagon with one or two of the Sedgwicks,
merely exchanging a greeting with me from under the

brim of his straw hat, and driving on. He presented himself now with a long white beard, such as a palmer might have worn as the growth of his long pilgrimages; a brow almost entirely bald and what hair he has quite hoary; a forehead impending, yet not massive; dark, bushy eyebrows and keen eyes, without much softness in them; a dark and sallow complexion; a slender figure, bent a little with age, but at once alert and infirm. It surprised me to see him so venerable; for, as poets are Apollo's kinsmen, we are inclined to attribute to them his enviable quality of never growing old. There was a weary look in his face, as if he were tired of seeing things and doing things, though with certainly enough still to see and do, if need were. My family gathered about him, and he conversed with great readiness and simplicity about his travels, and whatever other subject came up, telling us that he had been abroad five times, and was now getting a little homesick, and had no more eagerness for sights. . . .

"His manners and whole aspect are very particularly plain, though not affectedly so; but it seems as if in the decline of life, and the security of his position, he had put off whatever artificial polish he may have heretofore had, and resumed the simple habits and deportment of his early New England breeding. Not but what you discover, nevertheless, that he is a man of refinement, who has seen the world, and is well aware of his own place in it. He spoke with great pleasure of his recent visit to Spain. I introduced the subject of Kansas, and methought his face forthwith assumed something of the bitter keenness of the editor of a political newspaper while speaking of the triumph of the administration over the Free Soil opposition. I inquired whether he had seen S——,[1] and he gave a very sad account of him as he appeared at their last meeting, which was in Paris. S——, he thought, had suffered terribly, and would never again be the man he was; he was getting fat; he talked continually of himself, and of trifles concerning himself, and seemed to have no interest for other matters; and Mr. Bryant feared that the shock upon his nerves had extended to his intellect, and was irremediable. He said that S—— ought to retire from public life, but had no friend true enough to tell him so. This is about as sad as anything can be. I hate to have S—— undergo the fate of a martyr, because he was not naturally of the stuff that martyrs are made of, and it is altogether by mistake that he has thrust himself into the position of one. He was merely, though with excellent abilities, one of the best of fellows, and ought to have lived and died in good fellowship with all the world.

"Bryant was not in the least degree excited about this or any other subject. He uttered neither passion nor poetry, but excellent good sense, and accurate information, on whatever subject transpired; a very pleasant man to associate with, but rather cold, I should imagine, if one should seek to touch his heart with one's own. He shook hands kindly all round, but not with any warmth of gripe, although the ease of his deportment had put us all on sociable terms with him."

Upon the completion of his translation of the Homeric poems, Bryant felt the need of such relaxation and diversion as he could not secure at

[1] Charles Sumner, then in Paris under treatment for the bruises he had received in the senate chamber from a member of Congress named Brooks, of South Carolina.

home, and decided to seek them in a trip to Mexico. Accompanied by his brother John, his younger daughter, a niece, and his friend John Durand, he sailed on the 25th of January, 1872, for Nassau, where he stopped two weeks, thence to Havana, where he spent a week, thence to Vera Cruz, where he arrived on the 27th of February, thence by rail and stage to the City of Mexico. He remained in the capital about a fortnight, and then returned leisurely to the coast, visiting Puebla and Orizaba on the way. They returned by way of Havana, and reached home again before the end of April. During his stay in Mexico he was received with very conspicuous attention. No foreigner, it was said, had ever been received in Mexico with more. Not only President Juarez and his cabinet, but the literary and scientific notabilities of the country vied with each other in heaping honors upon him.

"To no extrinsic influences," said a Mexican print of the day, "can be attributed the honors and hospitality so lavishly conferred upon him. They were the spontaneous outpourings of a grateful people, who never forget an act of kindness and justice, and who had not forgotten that when Mexico was friendless, Mr. Bryant became her friend. They were the responsive echoes of the gifted and talented of the land, who appreciated his lofty genius; they were the tokens of the admiration of high talents and noble aspirations entertained by our society."

Upon his return from his trip to Europe in 1850, Bryant was persuaded to collect into a volume

and publish the letters he had sent to his journal from time to time during his several excursions
into foreign lands and in the remoter parts of his
own country. He called them " Letters of a Traveler." In the winter of 1869, he published a sup-
plementary volume containing the letters written
subsequently to the first publication. To these he
gave the title of " Letters from the East." Had
he written freely of what he saw and heard, these
letters would have been of rare interest and value,
for wherever he traveled he saw, if not all, very
many of the most interesting people. But his notions of the sanctity of private hospitality were so
strict that it is scarcely an exaggeration to say that
in all his published letters cannot be found the
name of a single person from whom he received
hospitality or whose acquaintance he made in any
private circle. In his preface to " Letters of a
Traveler," he says, " The author might have made
these letters more interesting to readers in general,
if he had spoken of distinguished men to whose
society he was admitted ; but the limits within
which this may be done with propriety and without
offense are so narrow and so easily overstepped
that he has preferred to abstain altogether from
that class of topics."

It is needless to say that the epistolary echoes
of a tourist, from which all notice of the people he
meets are rigorously excluded, could hardly possess
a very lively interest, whoever might be the writer ;
and Bryant put a just estimate upon his letters

when he said that "the highest merit such a work
can claim, if ever so well executed, is but slight."
They have a certain value, however, which time
will add to, more than it will subtract from. They
are written in faultless English and faultless taste ;
they show what, in the lands he visited, specially
attracted his attention ; and they paint many pictures and disclose many social and political conditions which, in progress of time, would hardly be
credited upon less unimpeachable authority. His
letters from the East are by far the most interesting, for there he encountered none of the restrictions which impoverished his letters from Europe.
He was at liberty to speak freely of everything he
saw and of everything he felt among the Mussul-
men, and he made of it an exceedingly entertaining
book. It possesses a consecutiveness of narrative,
too, which is wanting in the previous collection,
and was written after he had become more familiar
with the world and with the manners of many
men, and when his judgment was fully ripe. But
all of them have delighted his many personal
friends and admirers, in deference to whose wishes
rather than to his own judgment he put them into
volumes. It is very possible that they will add
little, if anything, to his fame as a man of letters,
but it is certain that they lend proportion and
dignity to his character as a member of human
society.

CHAPTER IX.

THE ORATOR.

An English critic, writing of Bryant a few weeks after his death, said, " He was so accomplished, so graceful, so impressive a speaker, that he only just failed to be an orator." This is not a criticism to quarrel with, but it is a judgment to be accepted with conditions. It can hardly be said that any of his discourses which have survived him were eloquent in the common acceptation of that word, for they lacked the fire and enthusiasm which we expect from a speaker inspired by an audience; but had he been accustomed to earn his bread by his tongue instead of his pen, had he occupied a seat in our halls of legislation, or remained at the bar, or in a position where the attention of large audiences was to be held, it would be difficult to name any faculty of heart or mind that was lacking to have won for him the reputation of an orator, had he courted such a reputation. He had an acute sensibility for the choicest forms and highest powers of expression; he had a marvelous memory, and was singularly alive to every sentiment that appealed to our higher nature and most refined sympathies. His aversion to every form of disingenuousness, too, was so uncompromising, and his judgments were so considerate and free from the delusions of partisanship, that he was always sure of a sympathetic and confiding audience. What he might have achieved as an orator is now largely a matter of conjecture. He left the bar before his talents as a public speaker had been tested; he never took a seat in any deliberative body; and the occasions upon which he appeared before the public were usually of a more or less academic character, where one would have hardly looked for the higher flights of eloquence from even the most accomplished orator. In any judgment of Bryant, the fact must never be lost sight of that it was his first and chief ambition from childhood to be a poet; to the Spirit of Poesy he was always so loyal that he would not allow himself to flirt, even, with any other kind of fame. He seemed to take no pride in being one of the best prose writers of his day, nor of being one of the most successful public speakers. It is easy to see by what he did, both as a journalist and platform speaker, that he might have excelled himself in both characters if he had desired to. But he preferred that posterity should know him as a poet, and was content that all his other work should be just good enough not to impair his poetical repute.[1]

---

[1] "I honor Mr. Bryant," says a distinguished contemporary poet, "for his laborious life, and admire him for the determination which kept him a poet through it all. The child was father to the man, and the man never forgot the child's birthright of song,

About twenty of Bryant's discourses have been preserved. Most of them were delivered after his position at the head of American literature was secure, and upon occasions when no other person could have filled his place.

His first effort of an oratorical nature in New York was at a meeting of the National Academy of Design, held in commemoration of Thomas Cole, the artist, in the spring of 1848. It is no disparagement of this performance to say that it would be the least missed perhaps of any of his elaborate discourses. He had been very intimate with Cole,

— the divine birthright which revealed him to himself, which brightened his brooding youth, sustained him through his struggling manhood, and consecrated him in his old age. The chambers of his mind were crowded with guests whom he would not have chosen if he had been free to choose, but there was one chamber into which they never penetrated, — into which nothing common ever penetrated, in that it was the innermost sanctuary of his soul. The poems that he wrote in New York and elsewhere were of the same general character as those that he wrote at Cummington, the only difference between them being that the later ones are riper and more mature than the earlier ones, larger in intention and scope, of broader and higher significance, more thoughtful and meditative, more serious and dignified, more purely poetical and imaginative, — in a single word, of greater distinction. What separates them from all other American poems is imagination, which was the supreme quality of his genius, and which, while it is nowhere absent from his verse, is omnipresent in his blank verse, which is the best that has been written by any modern poet whatever, — the most sustained, the most impressive, the most unforgettable. No one can read 'Thanatopsis,' 'The Prairies,' 'The Antiquity of Freedom,' and 'The Flood of Years' without feeling that Mr. Bryant was a great poet." — Richard H. Stoddard, in *Lippincott's Magazine*, November, 1889.

was fond of him, and he held in great respect the kind of cleverness which, till then, he had not seen much of in any one but Cole. It was, however, so manifestly inspired by feelings of personal regard as to lack something of the judicial impartiality which gives so much dignity to his later discourses.

The death of James Fenimore Cooper furnished the next, I might say the first, occasion for his appearance as the official interpreter of a national emotion. His discourse on this occasion and his address on the death of Irving are models of commemorative oratory. With a grateful appreciation of everything in the life and work of both that entitled them to the gratitude and admiration of posterity, there is not a lineament exaggerated nor a merit overlooked or overstated, while the criticism is so discriminating and amiable that the most loyal friend of either could find nothing in them to which they could take exception. Upon the deaths of Halleck in 1868 and of Verplanck in 1870, it was to Bryant that every eye turned as the fittest person to say the last word at their tombs.

The charms of these four discourses entitle them to a permanent place in our literature, and it is safe to say that no judgment that may hereafter be passed upon either of these eminent writers, not conforming substantially with that pronounced in these discourses, is likely to endure.

During the later years of his life there was no one whose presence was more sought for on public occasions in New York than Mr. Bryant, and he rarely refused these applications unless he could offer a satisfactory excuse, though he never encouraged them, and sometimes lost patience at the frequency and pertinacity with which they were pressed upon him.

All his discourses are conspicuous by a "virginal modesty," and the absence of all apparent effort to withdraw the interest of his audience from the occasion to himself. He never seemed to ask or expect fame from his speeches, and yet he never made a speech, however unpreparedly, that did not by its elevation of thought, or its scholarly allusions, or its cheerful humor, or its graces of form, or some or all these qualities combined, betray what Confucius was wont to call "the superior man," nor one which does not possess some charm sure to beguile the attention of the most indifferent reader.

At the dinner given to the late Professor Morse in 1868, he made a brief address in which there were passages that would add a leaf to the chaplet of any orator, ancient or modern. Speaking of Morse's great invention he said : —

"There is one view of this great invention which impresses me with awe. Beside me at this board, along with the illustrious man whom we are met to honor, and whose name will go down to the latest generations of civilized man, sits the gentleman to whose clear-sighted perseverance, and to whose energy, — an energy which knew no discourage-

ment, no weariness, no pause, — we owe it that the
telegraph has been laid which connects the Old
World with the New through the Atlantic Ocean.
My imagination goes down to the chambers of the
middle sea, to those vast depths where repose the
mystic wire on beds of coral, among forests of
tangle, or on the bottom of the dim blue gulfs,
strewn with the bones of whales and sharks, skele-
tons of drowned men, and ribs and masts of foun-
dered barks, laden with wedges of gold never to be
coined, and pipes of the choicest vintages of earth
never to be tasted. Through these watery soli-
tudes, among the fountains of the great deep, the
abode of perpetual silence, never visited by living
human presence and beyond the sight of human
eye, there are gliding to and fro, by night and by
day, in light and in darkness, in calm and in tempest, currents of human thought borne by the elec-
tric pulse which obeys the bidding of man. That
slender wire thrills with the hopes and fears of
nations ; it vibrates to every emotion that can be
awakened by any event affecting the welfare of the
human race. A volume of contemporary history
passes every hour of the day from one continent to
the other. An operator on the Continent of Europe gently touches the keys of an instrument in
his quiet room, a message is shot with the swiftness
of light through the abysses of the sea, and before
his hand is lifted from the machine the story of re-
volts and revolutions, of monarchs dethroned and
new dynasties set up in their place, of battles and

conquests and treaties of peace, of great statesmen fallen in death, lights of the world gone out and new luminaries glimmering on the horizon, is written down in another quiet room on the other side of the globe.

"Mr. President, I see in the circumstances which I have enumerated a new proof of the superiority of mind to matter, of the independent existence of that part of our nature which we call the spirit, when it can thus subdue, enslave, and educate the subtilest, the most active, and in certain of its manifestations the most intractable and terrible, of the elements, making it in our hands the vehicle of thought, and compelling it to speak every language of the civilized world. I infer the capacity of the spirit for a separate state of being, its indestructible essence and its noble destiny, and I thank the great discoverer whom we have assembled to honor for this confirmation of my faith."

Darwin's theory of the consanguinity of man and the lower animals was rarely if ever, in so few words, put more effectively on the defensive than in Bryant's brief address at a Williams College Alumni dinner in 1871. "Admitting," he says, "that we are of the same flesh and blood as the baboon and the rat, where does he find his proof that we are improving instead of degenerating? He claims that man is an improved monkey; how does he know that the monkey is not a degenerate man, a decayed branch of the human family, fallen away from the high rank he once held, and haunted

by a dim sentiment of his lost dignity, as we may
infer from his melancholy aspect? Improvement,
Mr. President and gentlemen, implies effort: it is
up-hill work; degeneracy is easy: it asks only
neglect, indolence, inaction. How often do the
descendants of illustrious men become the most
stupid of the human race! How many are there,
each of whom we may call

        " ' The tenth transmitter of a foolish face ' !

— a line of Savage, the best he ever wrote, worth
all his other verses put together — 'The tenth
transmitter of a foolish face' — and that face
growing more and more foolish from generation to
generation. I might instance the Bourbon family,
lately reigning in Spain and Naples. I might instance the royal family of Austria. There is a
whole nation, millions upon millions, — our Chinese
neighbors, — of whom the better opinion is that
they have been going backward in civilization from
century to century. Perhaps they wear the pig-
tail as an emblem of what they are all coming to
some thousands of years hence. How, then, can
Mr. Darwin insist that if we admit the near kindred of man to the inferior animals we must believe that our progress has been upward, and that
the nobler animals are the progeny of the inferior?
Is not the contrary the more probable? Is it not
more likely that the more easy downward road has
been taken, that the lower animals are derived
from some degenerate branch of the human race,

and that, if we do not labor to keep the rank we hold, our race may be frittered away into the meaner tribes of animals, and finally into animalculæ? Then may our Tweeds become the progenitors of those skulking thieves of the Western wilds, the prairie-wolves, or swim stagnant pools in the shape of horse-leeches; or astute lawyers may be represented by foxes, our great architects by colonies of beavers, our poets by clouds of mosquitoes famished and musical; our doctors of divinity — I say it with all respect for the cloth — by swarms of the mantis, or praying insect, always in the attitude of devotion. If we hold to Darwin's theory, — as I do not, — how are we to know that the vast multitudes of men and women on the earth are not the ruins, so to speak, of some nobler species, with more elevated and perfect faculties, mental, physical, and moral, but now extinct?

"Let me say, then, to those who believe in the relationship of the animal tribes, that it behooves them to avoid the danger which I have pointed out by giving a generous support to those institutions of wholesome learning, like Williams College, designed to hold us back from the threatened degeneracy of which there are fearful portents abroad — portents of moral degeneracy, at least. Let them move before we begin to squeak like bats or gibber like apes; before that mark of the brute, the tail, has sprouted, or, at least, while it is in the tender germ, the mere bud, giving but a faint and indistinct promise of what it may become when the owner shall coil its extremity around the horizontal branch of a tree and swing himself by it from one trunk of the forest to another. If any one here be conscious of but a friendly leaning to the monkey theory, let him contribute liberally to the fund for putting up a building where the students of Williams College can be cheaply boarded; if the taint have struck deeper, let him found a scholarship; if he have fully embraced the theory, let him, at any sacrifice, found a professorship, and then, although his theory may be wrong, his practice in this instance will be worthy of universal commendation."[1]

It is not difficult to imagine the effect of the following passage in a speech delivered at a mass meeting held in 1874 to denounce the issue of more irredeemable paper: —

"Will you hear an anecdote illustrative of this topic? It was some forty years ago that a tall, thin gentleman, in a long great-coat and a cap, stalked into the Mechanics' Bank in this city. He leisurely took from his pocket-book a five-dollar note of the bank, and laying it before the teller, requested its payment. The teller said, 'We do not pay our notes.' The tall, thin man — who it appeared was John Randolph — put on his spectacles and read the note in a high-keyed voice. '"The president and directors of the Mechanics' Bank promise to pay the bearer five dollars, value

[1] Whether as a specimen of his logic or his humor, is not this worthy of Dr. Franklin at his best?

received." There, I want the five dollars which you promise to pay.' 'But we do not pay,' rejoined the teller; the banks have suspended payment.' 'Oh, stopped payment! Then let me tell you what to do. Take the sledge-hammer out of the hand that hangs over your door, and in its place put a razor.' My friends, if Congress should be moved by this clamor to disgrace the country by issuing more notes, the condition of whose existence is to be dishonored, may we not take a hint from this anecdote? What business will the king of birds — the eagle, whose flight is above that of all other fowls of the air — have on an escutcheon which this policy will disgrace in the eyes of the world? Let his image then be blotted out; obliterate also the stars of heaven; efface the stripes of morning light which should be the promise of a day of glory and honor, and, instead of those emblems, let the limner draw on the broad sheet the image of a razor huge enough to be wielded by the Giant Despair, — a gentleman with whom, if this demand for more paper-money be granted, we are destined to scrape a closer acquaintance than we have enjoyed yet, — and on the enormous blade let the words be inscribed, in staring letters, ' Warranted to shave.' "

I ask indulgence for one more specimen of Bryant's oratory, taken from a speech made at a dinner given him by the Free Trade League in New York in 1868.

" Yet there is a certain plausibility in what the

protectionists say when they talk of home industry, and a home market, — a plausibility which misleads many worthy and otherwise sensible people, — sensible in all other respects, and whom as men I admire and honor. There are clever men among them who bring to their side of the question a great array of facts, many of which, however, have no real bearing upon its solution. There is a plausibility, too, in the idea that the sun makes a daily circuit around the earth, and if there were any private interests to be promoted in maintaining it, we should have thousands believing that the earth stands while the sun travels round it. 'See for yourself,' they would say. 'Will you not believe the evidence of your own senses? The sun comes up in the east every day before your eyes, stands over your head at noon, and goes down in the afternoon in the west. Why, you admit the fact when you say, "the sun rises," "the sun sets," "the sun is up," "the sun is down." What a fool was Galileo, what nonsense is the system of Copernicus, what trash was written by Sir Isaac Newton!'

"I remember a case in point, an anecdote I once heard in Scotland. A writer to the signet, that is to say an attorney named Moll, who knew very little except what related to the drawing up of law papers, once heard a lecture on Astronomy in which some illustrations were given of the daily revolution of the earth on its axis. The attorney was perplexed and bewildered by this philosophy

which was so new to him, and one day, his
thoughts frequently recurring to the subject, he
looked up from his law-papers and said: 'The
young mon says the warld turns roond. It's vera
extraordinar'. I've lived in this place sax and
thretty years and that grass-plot preserves the same
relative poseetion to the house that it had sax and
thretty years sin', and yet the young mon says the
warld turns roond. It's vera extraordinar'.' Here
was a man who was not to be taken in by this nonsense about the earth revolving on its axis, and if
there were any real or imaginary pecuniary advantage to be gained by denying it, Mr. Moll would
have a whole army of his way of thinking, many of
them far wiser and better informed in other respects than he."

Bryant was accustomed to think over and mem-
orize and not infrequently write out what he wished
to say, when he had sufficient notice of what was
expected of him,[1] though his most unpremeditated

---

[1] His memory once, and for the first time, served him a scurvy
trick, which depressed him very much. A friend of his who witnessed it has made the following account of the scene: "It was
at a public dinner, I think, and during the last decade of his life,
that he was called upon and expected to speak. He had not proceeded far in his discourse when he stopped, obviously having lost
its thread. He stood a few seconds in silence and then sat down.
Before another speaker had been called upon, however, he rose
again and resumed his speech, but alas! only for a sentence or
two. He lost the thread again, sat down, and made no farther
effort to resume. On leaving the hall I joined him, and we
walked together to his house. As soon as we were alone in the
street, he said in a tone which showed plainly how much the utterance cost him, 'I see I must attempt no more public speeches;

speeches had merits all their own. I do not recall
a single one which did not contain something that
was worthy of preservation. It cannot be said that
his elocution added much to the effectiveness of his
discourse. His voice was not rounded and full nor
very flexible, and therefore lent but little force or
light and shade to his discourse; nor did he ever
wholly overcome a certain monotony of manner
which made the hearer of the poem read before
the Phi Beta Kappa Society at Cambridge in
1821[1] exclaim, "If Everett had read this poem,
what a sensation it would have produced!" His
modesty and utter self-effacement always more
than made up with his audience for any lack of
elocutionary skill. I cannot better conclude what
I have to say of Bryant as a platform speaker than
with the following extract from some comments

my memory never served me such a trick before in all my life.'
I comforted him as well as I could by saying that he had been
too fatigued by the labors of the day, and that I had no doubt
after suitable rest he would find his memory just as faithful a
servant and friend as ever. The fact that his memory could tire,
and like himself was growing old, not merely in years, was a
revelation to him. Painful as is the spectacle always of a speaker
betrayed before an audience by his memory, there was one most
gratifying incident in the case I have described. No power of
eloquence from Mr. Bryant's lips could have drawn from that
audience the manifestations of sympathy for him which followed
the suspension of his speech, and which said as plainly as if uttered in words, 'No matter about the speech; nothing you have
said, nothing you could have said, nothing you have left unsaid,
could make us love and respect you more or less than we do
now.' "

[1] *The Ages.*

upon his "Discourses" from the pen of the late George Ripley, one of the most learned and judicious literary critics of his time.

"He was always the honored guest of the evening, and the moment in which he was to be called upon to speak was awaited with eager expectation that never ended in disappointment. He was singularly happy in seizing the tone of the company, no matter what were the circumstances or the occasion; his remarks were not only pertinent, but eminently felicitous; with no pretensions to artificial eloquence, he was always impressive, often pathetic, and sometimes quietly humorous, with a zest and pungency that touched the feelings of the audience to the quick.

"On more important public occasions, when the principal speech of the day was assigned to him, he discharged the trust with a tranquil dignity of manner, a serene self-possession, and an amplitude of knowledge and illustration that invariably won the admiration of the spectators. His last address of this kind, delivered on the day of his fatal attack, at the unveiling of the bust of Mazzini in Central Park, was a masterpiece of descriptive oratory, unsurpassed by any of his previous efforts for a similar purpose. Never was there a more just or feeling tribute to the Italian patriot. Seldom has been presented a more discriminating analysis of a great political career, or a finer portraiture of the admirable qualities of a noble and heroic personage."

CHAPTER X.

PUBLIC HONORS.

THOUGH occupied most of his life in shaping the opinions of his country people upon questions of public policy, Bryant never held any political office or dignity.[1] Under a popular government, the representative man is usually as near to the average of the popular intelligence and morality as the machinery provided for ascertaining public opinion permits. Our government's trusts are therefore rarely confided, or its honors bestowed, upon the comparatively restricted class of "superior men," and for the very sufficient reason that this class would not fairly represent the wishes of the great majority, which it is the proper function of popular governments to consult. There are none, probably, who would hesitate to admit that Bryant's standards, morally and intellectually, were too far above the average of his countrymen to make him in any political sense a representative man. Niagara is not a representative waterfall.

[1] His brief discharge of the duties of Tithing-man, Town Clerk, and Justice of the Peace during the moulting season of his career as a lawyer at Great Barrington hardly suffices to qualify this statement.

It is not easy to conceive of any important public
station in which Bryant would have proved acceptable to so large a number as many of his contemporaries, in both those respects his inferiors, would
have proved, or of any public office which would
not have gained from him more dignity and consideration than it could confer.

Republics in our day and " with all the modern
improvements " have in this respect no particular
advantage over any of their predecessors.   The
stream of popular favor never rises higher than
its fountain, and public honors, like kissing, go as
much by favor now as when Cæsar's barber was
made a senator, and honored with a gorgeous monument for his noisy hostility to Pompey.[1]

Though Bryant never received, nor if offered
would probably have accepted, any of those honors
and distinctions which are commonly regarded as
the only satisfactory reward of the successful poli-

[1] Some Roman wag proposed the following epitaph for the
tomb of this barber, whose name was Licinus : —

"Marmoreo Licinus tumulo jacet, at Cato parvo,
    Pompeius nullo ; "

which may be thus Englished : –

"For Licinus we built a tomb of marble, oh how tall!
    For Cato but a little one, for great Pompey none at all."

This epitaph recalls the fact that the commissioners of the New
York Central Park, in order to prevent the erection of a monu-
mental statue within its precincts to the notorious Tweed, made
a rule that no monument should be placed in the Park in honor of
any one who had not been dead five years, which rule for that
period, at least, excluded a bust of Bryant which was offered to
the commissioners, and before that time expired Tweed was in
the Tombs.

tician, he had no lack of public distinction and popular consideration, such, too, as governments have not to give.

Upon his return in 1836 from his first trip to Europe, he was invited to accept a public dinner by the most eminent literary men in the country, Irving, Halleck, Verplanck, and Paulding heading the list, that "they might express their high sense of his literary merits and estimable character," and congratulate him upon his safe return.

Out of the excess of his modesty Bryant declined this honor. "I cannot but feel," he said in his reply, "that although it might be worthily conferred upon one whose literary labors had contributed to raise the reputation of his country,[1] I who have passed the period of my absence only in observation and study have done nothing to merit such a distinction."

While absent in Europe in 1858, he was elected a Regent of the University of the State of New York. The mail following that which bore to him the intelligence brought me the following letter: —

"My dear Sir, — I learn, through the newspapers, that I have been elected by the New York Legislature a Regent of the University. I will not affect to undervalue the favorable opinion of so respectable a public body, manifested in so spontaneous a manner, without the least solicita-

[1] Obviously alluding to what Irving had done during his absence in Europe, and who did accept a dinner upon his return.

tion on the part of my friends, and I beg that this letter may be used as an expression of my best thanks.

"There are, however, many motives which make it necessary for me to decline the appointment, and among these are my absence from the country, the inconvenience of combining the duties of the place with the pursuits in which I am engaged when at home, and my aversion to any form of public life now, by my long habit made, I fear, invincible. I therefore desire by this letter to return the appointment to the kind hands which have sought to confer it upon me, confident that some worthier person will easily be found, who will bring the necessary alacrity to the performance of its duties.

"I am, dear sir, very truly yours,

W. C. BRYANT."

To JOHN BIGELOW.

It was no mean compliment to Bryant's eminence of character that when Abraham Lincoln came to deliver a lecture in New York immediately after his famous canvass for the senatorship with Senator Douglas in Illinois, that the politicians stood aside and Bryant was invited to preside. "It was worth the journey to the East," said Mr. Lincoln, "to see such a man."

It has rarely fallen to the lot of any man of letters to receive during his lifetime a more grateful tribute of affection and respect than was bestowed upon Bryant on his seventieth birthday, November

3, 1864. The Century Club, of which he had been one of the founders, resolved to make it the occasion of a festival in his honor. All the prominent men of letters and artists of the country participated. Bancroft, then president of the Century, greeted Bryant on his arrival with a brief address. "Our tribute to you," he said, " is to the poet, but we should not have paid it had we not revered you as a man. Your blameless life is a continuous record of patriotism and integrity; and passing untouched through the fiery conflicts that grow out of the ambition of others, you have, as all agree, preserved a perfect consistency with yourself, and an unswerving unselfish fidelity to your convictions."

Bryant's reply was singularly happy and becoming, the more so as there was nothing more difficult for him than to talk about himself.

"I thank you, Mr. President," he said, "for the kind words you have uttered, and I thank this good-natured company for having listened to them with so many tokens of assent and approbation. I must suppose, however, that most of this approbation was bestowed upon the orator rather than upon his subject. He who has brought to the writing of our national history a genius equal to the vastness of the subject has, of course, more than talent enough for humbler tasks. I wonder not, therefore, that he should be applauded this evening for the skill he has shown in embellishing a barren topic.

" I am congratulated on having completed my seventieth year. Is there nothing ambiguous, Mr. President, in such a compliment? To be congratulated on one's senility! To be congratulated on having reached that stage of life when the bodily and mental powers pass into decline and decay! Lear is made by Shakespeare to say,

" ' Age is unnecessary ; '

and a later poet, Dr. Johnson, has expressed the same idea in one of his sonorous lines : —

" ' Superfluous lags the veteran on the stage.'

You have not forgotten, Mr. President, the old Greek saying, —

" ' Whom the gods love die young,' —

nor the passage in Wordsworth : —

. . . " ' Oh, sir, the good die first,
And they whose hearts are dry as summer dust,
Burn to the socket.'

" Much has been said of the wisdom of Old Age. Old Age is wise, I grant, for itself, but not wise for the community. It is wise in declining new enterprises, for it has not the power nor the time to execute them; wise in shrinking from difficulty, for it has not the strength to overcome it; wise in avoiding danger, for it lacks the faculty of ready and swift action, by which dangers are parried and converted into advantages. But this is not wisdom for mankind at large, by whom new enterprises must be undertaken, dangers met, and difficulties surmounted. What a world would this be if it were made up of old men! — generation succeeding generation of hoary ancients who had but a dozen years or perhaps half that time to live! What new work of good would be attempted? What existing abuse or evil corrected? What strange subjects would such a world afford for the pencils of our artists — groups of superannuated gray-beards basking in the sun through the long days of spring, or huddling like sheep in warm corners in the winter time; houses with the timbers dropping apart; cities in ruins; roads unwrought and impassable; weedy gardens and fields with the surface feebly scratched to put in a scanty harvest; decrepit old men clambering into crazy wagons, perhaps to be run away with, or mounting horses, if they mounted them at all, in terror of being hurled from their backs like a stone from a sling. Well it is that in this world of ours the old men are but a very small minority.

"Ah, Mr. President, if we could but stop this rushing tide of time that bears us so swiftly onward, and make it flow towards its source; if we could cause the shadow to turn back on the dial-plate! I see before me many excellent friends of mine, worthy to live a thousand years, on whose countenances years have set their seal, marking them with the lines of thought and care, and causing their temples to glisten with the frosts of life's autumn. If to any one of them could be restored his glorious prime, his golden youth, with its hyacinthine locks, its smooth, unwrinkled brow, its fresh and rounded cheek, its pearly and perfect teeth, its lustrous eyes, its light and bounding step, its frame full of energy, its exulting spirits, its high hopes, its generous impulses, and, added to all these, the experience and fixed principles of mature age, I am sure, Mr. President, that I should start at once to my feet, and propose that in commemoration of such a marvel, and by way of congratulating our friend who was its subject, we should hold such a festivity as the Century has never seen nor will ever see again. Eloquence should bring its highest tribute, and Art its fairest decorations to grace the festival; the most skillful musicians should be here with all manner of instruments of music, ancient and modern; we would have sackbut, and trumpet, and shawm, and damsels with dulcimers, and a modern band three times as large as the one that now plays on that balcony. But why dwell on such a vain dream, since it is only by passing through the darkness that overhangs the Valley of the Shadow of Death that man can reach his second youth?

"I have read, in descriptions of the Old World, of the families of princes and barons coming out of their castles to be present at some rustic festivity, such as a wedding of one of their peasantry. I am reminded of this custom by the presence of many literary persons of eminence in these rooms, and I thank them for this act of benevolence. Yet I miss among them several whom I had wished rather than ventured to hope that I should meet on this

occasion. I miss my old friend Dana, who gave so
grandly the story of the Buccaneer in his solemn
verses. I miss Pierpoint, venerable in years, yet
vigorous in mind and body, and with an undimmed
fancy; and him whose pages are wet with the tears
of maidens who read the story of Evangeline; and
the author of 'Fanny and the Croakers,' no less
renowned for the fiery spirit which animated his
'Marco Bozzaris;' and him to whose wit we owe the
'Biglow Papers,' who has made a lowly flower of
the wayside as classical as the rose of Anacreon;
and the Quaker poet, whose verses, Quaker as he
is, stir the blood like the voice of a trumpet calling
to battle; and the poetess of Hartford, whose
beautiful lyrics are in a million hands, and others,
whose names, were they to occur to me here as in
my study, I might accompany with the mention of
some characteristic merit. But here is he whose
aerial verse has raised the little insect of our fields
making his murmuring journey from flower to
flower, the humble-bee, to a dignity equal to that of
Pindar's eagle; here is the Autocrat of the Breakfast Table — author of that most spirited of naval
lyrics, beginning with the line : —

"'Ay, tear her tattered ensign down;'

here, too, is the poet who told in pathetic verse the
story of Jephtha's daughter; and here are others,
worthy compeers of those I have mentioned, yet
greatly my juniors, in the brightness of whose rising
fame I am like one who has carried a lantern in

the night, and who perceives that its beams are no longer visible in the glory which the morning pours around him.

"To them and to all the members of the Century, allow me, Mr. President, to offer the wish that they may live longer than I have done, in health of body and mind, and in the same contentment and serenity of spirit which has fallen to my lot. I must not overlook the ladies who have deigned to honor these rooms with their presence. If I knew where, amid, myrtle bowers and flowers that never wither, gushed from the ground the Fountain of Perpetual Youth so long vainly sought by the first Spanish adventurers on the North American continent, I would offer to the lips of every one of them a beaker of its fresh and sparkling waters, and bid them drink unfading bloom. But since that is not to be, I will wish what, perhaps, is as well, and what some would think better, that the same kindness of heart which has prompted them to come hither to-night may lend a beauty to every action of their future lives. And to the Century itself, — the dear old Century, — to whose members I owe both the honors and the embarrassments of this occasion, — to that association, fortunate in having possessed two such presidents as the distinguished historian who now occupies the chair and the eminent and accomplished scholar and admirable writer who preceded him, I offer the wish that it may endure, not only for the term of years signified by its name, — not for one century only, but for ten centuries, — so that hereafter, perhaps, its members may discuss the question whether its name should not be changed to that of the Club of a Thousand Years, and that these may be centuries of peace and prosperity, from which its members may look back to this period of bloody strife, as to a frightful dream soon chased away by the beams of a glorious morning."

But the tributes from others, present or absent, were naturally the more significant features of the occasion. Poems were read by Dr. Holmes, Bayard Taylor, Boker, Stoddard, T. Buchanan Read, Julia Ward Howe. Other poems were read from Whittier, Lowell, H. T. Tuckerman, Dr. Allen, Rev. H. N. Powers, and several others who were unavoidably absent. Letters of congratulation were also read from the Danas, Everett, Longfellow, Pierpont, Verplanck, Halleck, Sprague, Charles T. Brooks, Miss Sedgwick, Goldwin Smith, Dr. Walker, Bishop Coxe, and others with whose names the public is less familiar.

Of Dr. Holmes's verses, which were illuminated by the earnestness with which they were pronounced, the following were in his happiest vein :

. . . .

"How can we praise the verse whose music flows
　　With solemn cadence and majestic close,
　　Pure as the dew that filters through the rose ?

"How shall we thank him that in evil days
　　He faltered never, — nor for blame nor praise,
　　Nor hire, nor party, shamed his earlier lays?

"But as his boyhood was of manliest hue,
    So to his youth, his manly years were true,
    All dyed in royal purple through and through!

· · · · · · · · ·

"Marbles forget their message to mankind:
    In his own verse the poet still we find,
    In his own page his memory lives enshrined,

"As in their amber sweets the smothered bees,
    As the fair cedar, fallen before the breeze,
    Lies self-embalmed amidst the mouldering trees."

· · · · · · · · ·

Emerson's speech concluded as follows. "Before I sit down, let me apply to him a verse addressed by Thomas Moore to the poet Crabbe, and Moore has written few better: —

"'True bard, and simple as the race
        Of heaven-born poets always are,
    When stooping from their starry place
        They're children near but gods afar.'"

Of the following lines from a poem of the Rev. H. N. Powers, all who are familiar with Bryant's poetry will recognize the peculiar felicity.

"Earth's face is dearer for thy gaze,
        The fields that thou hast traveled o'er
    Are fuller blossomed, and the ways
        Of toil more pleasant than before.

"The April pastures breathe more sweet,
        The brooks in deeper musings glide,
    Old woodlands grander hymns repeat,
        And holier seems the Autumn-tide.

"The crystal founts and summer rains
        Are haunted now with pictured grace,
    The winds have learned more tender strains
        And greet us with more kind embrace.

" More meekly pleads each flowret's eye,
　　On gentler errands comes the snow,
And birds write on the evening sky
　　More gracious lessons as they go.

" The clouds, the stars, the sea, the grave,
　　Wide prairie wastes and crowded marts,
All that is fair, and good, and brave,
　　In peaceful homes and gen'rous hearts,

" Through thee their wondrous meanings tell :
　　And as men go to work and pray
Feeling thy song's persuasive spell
　　Love's face seems closer o'er their way."

The Rev. John Pierpont, who was prevented by age and infirmities from coming to the festival, sent a letter, from which the following is an extract : —

"At first I said within my heart I'll go —
But second thoughts forbade me to engage,
At such a time, in such a pilgrimage,
My health infirm, and my age
— (For more than half my eightieth year is spent) —
Admonish me to stay at home content,
And worship, like the Sabian, from afar,
Kissing my hand towards our brightest star."

Lowell, detained at home by a serious domestic affliction, sent some verses — of which it was the least of their merits that they paid the tribute of a discriminating homage to a senior brother of Parnassus — entitled " On Board the Seventy-Six."

" Our ship lay tumbling in an angry sea,
Her rudder gone, her main-mast o'er the side ;
Her scuppers from the waves' clutch staggering free,
Trailed threads of priceless crimson through the tide ;
Sails, shrouds, and spars with hostile cannon torn,
We lay awaiting morn.

"Awaiting morn, such morn as mocks despair;
And she that bore the promise of the world
Within her sides, now hopeless, helmless, bare,
At random o'er the wildering waters hurled,
The wreck of battle drifting slow a-lee,
Not sullener than we.

"But one there was, the Singer of our crew,
Upon whose head Age waved his peaceful sign,
But whose red heart's-blood no surrender knew;
And couchant under brows of massive line,
The eyes, like guns beneath a parapet,
Watched, charged with lightnings yet.

"The voices of the hills did his obey;
The torrents flashed and tumbled in his song;
He brought our native fields from far away,
Or set us mid the innumerable throng
Of dateless woods, or where we heard the calm
Old homesteads' evening psalm.

"But now he sang of faith to things unseen,
Of freedom's birthright given to us in trust,
And words of doughty cheer he spoke between,
That made all earthly fortune seem as dust,
Matched with that duty, old as time and new,
Of being brave and true.

"We, listening, learned what makes the might of words, —
Manhood to back them, constant as a star;
His voice rammed home our cannon, edged our swords,
And sent our boarders shouting; shroud and spar
Heard him and stiffened; the sails heard and wooed
The winds with loftier mood.

"In our dark hour he manned our guns again;
Remanned ourselves from his own manhood's store;
Pride, honor, country, throbbed through all his strain;
And shall we praise? God's praise was his before;
And on our futile laurels he looks down,
Himself our bravest crown."

N. P. Willis, in his letter accepting the invitation of the Century Club, said of Bryant: —

"His present eminence among all parties, as the unquestioned first poet of the country, has been gained by him in connection with a career which has its daily trials and temptations, — a career which no one but an experienced editor of a newspaper would be likely fully to appreciate. Let me call the attention of the brother poets who are to celebrate his birthday to the undimmed lustre of the laurels worn so long. . . . For him to have thus set himself the task, and come from it as does Bryant, — the acknowledged most independently reliable editor, as well as the most irreproachable first poet, is an example not given us by the ancients."

Stoddard's admirable lines were read by Bayard Taylor. The spirit of them may be gathered from the first seven stanzas.

"VATES PATRIÆ."

November 3, 1794 — November 3, 1864.

There came a woman in the night,
  When winds were whist, and moonlight smiled,
Where, in his mother's arms who slept,
  There lay a new-born child.

She gazed at him with loving looks,
  And while her hand upon his head
She laid, in blessing and in power,
  In slow, deep words she said:

"This child is mine. Of all my sons
  Are none like what the lad shall be, —
Though these are wise, and those are strong,
  And all are dear to me.

" Beyond their arts of peace and war
    The gift that unto him belongs, —
To see my face, to read my thoughts,
    To learn my silent songs.

" The elder sisters of my race
    Shall taunt no more that I am dumb;
Hereafter I shall sing through him,
    In ages yet to come ! "

She stooped and kissed his baby mouth,
    Whence came a breath of melody,
As from the closed leaves of a rose
    The murmur of a bee !

Thus did she consecrate the child,
    His more than mother from that hour,
Albeit at first he knew her not,
    Nor guessed his sleeping power.

. . . .

Edward Everett wrote a cordial letter, the more cordial from the fact that upon questions of public policy growing out of the slavery controversy Mr. Bryant and he had not been in sympathy. Among other things, he said: " The taste, the culture, and the patriotism of the country are, on this occasion, in full sympathy alike with those who weave and with him who wears the laurel wreath. Happy the community that has the discernment to appreciate its gifted sons, — happy the poet, the artist, the scholar, who is permitted to enjoy, in this way, a foretaste of posthumous commemoration and fame ! "

Boker read some fervent verses, which closed with the following lines : —

"I have not a prayer
That would not clamber up the heavenly air,
To kneel before the splendor of the Throne,
If thus another blessing could be sown
In the fair garden of your blooming days,
Already fragrant with a nation's praise,
Bright with the wreaths the total world hath given
And warm with love that's sanctified by Heaven."

To crown the notable features of this memorable ovation, the most esteemed artists of the country, among them Durand, Huntington, Kensett, Eastman Johnson, Church, Gifford, Gray, Colman, Lafarge, Leutze, Hennessey, J. G. Brown, Bierstadt, McEntee, and Hicks, united in presenting Bryant with a portfolio of pictures from their respective easels. The presentation was made through Huntington, the president of the Academy of Design, in reply to whose brief discourse Mr. Bryant, among other things, said : —

" I shall prize this gift, therefore, not only as a memorial of the genius of our artists, but also as a token of the good will of a class of men for whom I cherish a particular regard and esteem."

It is worthy of being noted here that there was no journal of importance in the land that did not make the seventieth anniversary of Bryant's birth the theme of respectful and more or less eulogistic and discriminating comment.

In the winter of 1867, Bryant retired from the presidency of the American Free Trade League, a position which he had held from its origin. In recognition of the services he had rendered to the cause, not merely as an officer of the League, but more especially through the columns of his journal, his associates tendered him a public dinner on the 30th of January, 1868. All the most prominent free-traders of the country were present, or represented there in some form, to testify their appreciation of the work he had done for the emancipation of the industry and commerce of the nation. Bryant's address on the occasion, of which we have already cited a specimen, [1] was altogether admirable.

In the spring of 1874, Bryant was elected an honorary member of the Russian Academy of St. Petersburg, where most of his poems had already become known through a translation made by Professor Katejeneff, himself a member of the Academy.

On reaching his eightieth birthday, there was a spontaneous impulse all over the country to celebrate it. It was finally determined to present him with an address, to be followed, as soon as it could be prepared, by a vase commemorative of his literary career. The address, which Mr. Godwin tells us was signed by thousands of names, was presented to him at his house in Sixteenth Street by Jonathan Sturges, one of the most estimable and esteemed citizens of New York. [2] In presenting it, he said : —

---

[1] See p. 210.

[2] Mr. Sturges's useful career was terminated by death the following week.

" We have come, dear Mr. Bryant, to congratulate you upon reaching the ripe age of eighty years in such vigor of health and intellect; to thank you for all the good work that you have done for your country and for mankind; and to give you our best wishes for your happiness. For more than sixty years you have been an author, and from your first publication to your last you have given to us and our children the best thought and sentiment in the purest language of the English-speaking race. For more than fifty years you have been a journalist, and advocated the duties as well as the rights of men, with all the genuine freedom, without any of the license, of our age, in an editorial wisdom that has been a blessing to our daughters as well as our sons. You have been a good citizen and true patriot, ready to bear your testimony to the worth of your great literary contemporaries, and steadfast from first to last in your loyalty to the liberty and order of the nation. You have stood up manfully for the justice and humanity that are the hope of mankind and the commandment of God. We thank you for ourselves, for our children, for our country, and for our race, and we commend you to the providence and grace of Him who has always been with you, and who will be with you to the end. We present to you this address of congratulation, with signatures from all parts of the country, and with the proposal of a work of commemorative art that shall be sculptured with ideas and images from your poems, and be full of the grateful remembrances and affections of the friends who love you as a friend, and the nation that honors you as the patriarch of our literature."

Mr. Bryant's reply, brief as it was, was very impressive. After fitly returning thanks for the kind words of the address, he said : —

" I have lived long, as it may seem to most people, however short the term appears to me when I look back upon it. In that period have occurred various most important changes, both political and social, and on the whole I am rejoiced to say that they have, as I think, improved the condition of mankind. The people of civilized countries have become more enlightened, and enjoy a greater degree of freedom. They have become especially more humane and sympathetic, more disposed to alleviate each other's sufferings. This is the age of charity. In our day, charity has taken forms unknown to former ages, and occupied itself with the cure of evils which former generations neglected.

" I remember the time when Bonaparte filled the post of First Consul in the French Republic, for I began early to read the newspapers. I saw how that republic grew into an empire; how that empire enlarged itself by successive conquests on all sides, and how the mighty mass, collapsing by its own weight, fell into fragments. I have seen from that time to this, change after change take place, and the result of them all, as it seems to me, is that the liberties and rights of the humbler classes have been more and more regarded, both in framing and executing the laws. For the greater part of my own eighty years it seemed to me, and I think it seemed to all, that the extinction of slavery was an event to be accomplished by a remote posterity. But all this time its end was approaching, and suddenly it sank into a bloody grave. The union of the Italian principalities under one head, and the breaking up of that anomaly in politics, the possession of political power by a priesthood, seemed, during the greater part of the fourscore years of which I have spoken, an event belonging to a distant and uncertain future, yet was it drawing near by steps not apparent to the common eyes, and it came in our own day. The people of Italy willed it, and the people were obeyed.

" There is yet a time which good men earnestly hope and pray for, — the day when the population of the civilized world shall prepare for a universal peace by disbanding the enormous armies which they keep in camps and garrisons, and sending their soldiery back to the fields and workshops, from which, if the people were wise, their sovereigns never should have withdrawn them. Let us hope that this will be one of the next great changes.

" Gentlemen, again I thank you for your kindness. I have little to be proud of, but when I look round upon those whom this occasion has brought together, I confess that I am proud of my friends."

The vase was presented in the following June. In reply to addresses from Dr. Osgood and from Mr. Whitehouse, the artist, Bryant managed with singular grace and felicity as usual to keep his modesty in the foreground without the least appearance of trying to make a virtue of it. After thanking everybody entitled to thanks, and commending everything entitled to commendation, he said : —

"And now a word concerning the superb vase which is before me, the work of artists who are the worthy successors of Benvenuto Cellini, and eminent in their department. It has been greatly admired by those who have seen it. I remember to have read, I think some half century ago, a definition of the term genius, —making it to consist in the faculty of accomplishing great results by small means, — the power, in short, which an individual has of overcoming difficulties by a forecast and vigor not possessed by others, converting obstacles into instruments of success. This vase I may call a product of genius both in the design and the execution, for who would suppose that any skill of the artist could connect with such a subject as he had before him images so happily conceived, so full of expression, and so well combining expression with grace ? My friends, we authors cultivate a short-lived reputation ; one generation of us pushes another from the stage. The very language in which we write becomes a jargon, and we cease to be read ; but a work like this is always beautiful, always admired. Age has no power over its charm. Hereafter some one may say, ' This beautiful vase was made in honor of a certain American poet, whose name it bears, but whose writings are forgotten. It is remarkable that so much pains should have been taken to illustrate the life and writings of one whose works are so completely unknown at the present day.' Thus, gentlemen artists, I shall be indebted to you for causing the memory of my name to outlast that of my writings."

This anniversary was celebrated in Chicago the same evening by the Chicago Literary Club. This occasion derived a special interest from the presence of the poet's brothers, Arthur and John C. Bryant. The Rev. Dr. Robert Collyer presided; an admirable address was pronounced by the Rev. Horatio N. Powers, and the Bryant brothers entertained the company with many reminiscences of the youth of their illustrious brother, from whom an amusing letter was also read. After thanking the club for the honor they were doing him, " to which," he said, " on looking back upon my past life, I feel that I have no claim, and am therefore the more indebted to their generosity," he continued: " I cannot be present, but my good wishes will be with the members. I hope that they will find the banquet as pleasant, the conversation as entertaining, the speeches, if any, as eloquent, and the viands as well flavored, as if the members had met to celebrate the birthday of some better man. Now I think of it, there must have been born on the 3d of November a great many excellent persons, of both sexes, to whose virtuous lives the world is under great obligations. Will not my friends of the Literary Club pass to the credit of these persons such share of the honors of their festival as I am not worthy of, and thus square the account?"

In the winter of 1874–75, Bryant was invited with his family by Governor Tilden to visit him at the Executive Mansion in Albany. Their acquaintance had commenced when Tilden, a lad in roundabouts, was brought by his father to the office of the "Evening Post," in the "heated term" of the United States Bank controversy. Young Tilden soon after came to live in New York, where the acquaintance ripened rapidly into a friendship which never terminated. In the later years of his life, Bryant often spoke of the impressions left upon him by this precocious stripling, whose considerate manner and conversation made him appear but for his size and dress rather the eldest of the party. Bryant learned to attach such value to his judgment that he rarely took any important step, whether in private or professional matters, without counseling with him.

While a guest of the governor, both branches of the legislature tendered Bryant a public reception, a compliment which had never before been paid in this country to a man of letters. Lieutenant-Governor Dorsheimer, the president of the Senate, in presenting him to that body said: —

"I need not recall to you the career of your guest. Every American knows the incidents of that long and honorable life. Still less need I impress upon you the merits of his writings. You remember the glowing words with which in his youth he taught the love of nature and the Christian's faith. You have all seen him seated among the lengthening shadows of evening, and heard him repeat in English as pure as the English of Addison and Goldsmith Homer's undying song.

"I know that I utter your heartfelt wishes when I express the hope that the blessings which have been so abundantly given to him may be continued, and that his life may still be spared to the country whose institutions he has defended, whose liberties he has widened, and whose glories he has increased."

In acknowledging the courtesy of the Senate, of which its president had been the interpreter, Bryant said : —

"You will pardon me if, on rising to say a few words in acknowledgment of the honor conferred upon me, I find myself somewhat embarrassed on account of the novelty of the occasion. There is a little story, a story some two thousand years old, recorded originally in Greek, I believe, — for the Greeks had their jest-books as well as the English, — in which it is related that a man lost his little child and made a funeral. A considerable concourse came together of his friends and acquaintances, and as he appeared before them he made an apology for the smallness of the infant corpse. [Laughter.] I find myself in a similar condition. I see before me the representatives of the different parts of our great, powerful, and populous State. I see men who come from our rich and beautiful valleys, from the grand and picturesque mountain regions of the north of the State, from the banks of our glorious rivers, from the borders of our immense lakes, from populous towns and pleasant villages ; towns that are the seats of trade and industry, cities noisy with the bustle of business and commerce, or resounding with the clash of looms, or the blows of the ponderous hammers in our manufacturing establishments.

" You come, gentlemen, as representatives of the arts, of the wealth and industry of this great State. On my part I have nothing to offset against this great array, except what you see before you, and that is an object certainly disproportionately small compared with this imposing ceremony.

" I have nothing to say, therefore, except to return my thanks for the great honor you have done me, and to add my wishes for your future career. My wish is that this session may prove honorable to yourselves and useful to the community ; that it may be closed with credit, and that it may be long remembered for the service it has done and the benefit it has conferred on the State to which you belong."

Bryant was then presented to the assembly by the Speaker, Mr. McGuire, as one who, " as poet, journalist, sage, statesman, and man, had written his name in ineffaceable letters on the annals of his country and in the hearts of his countrymen."

To this, Bryant replied : —

"Gentlemen of the Assembly: I cannot take to myself the flattering words which have been uttered by the presiding officer of this Assembly. It would be the utmost stretch of self-admiration to do so. You will allow me, therefore, gentlemen, to put a great deal of what has been said so well, or a great deal of the honor of the reception, to the credit of old age. Old men, my friends, are rarities, and rarity, you know, is often an element of value. Things that are not useful are sometimes rated at a high value on account of the circumstance that they are rarely to be met with. If pebbles were scarce they would not be picked up and thrown at dogs, but would be sought after and collected by mineralogists, and deposited in cabinets to be gazed at with admiration.

"I therefore find it proper, and no other than proper, that I should divide a part of this honor — the greater part of this honor — with those of my colleagues who are remnants of a generation passed away and overlooked in the flood of waters in which we must sink and be submerged. I can therefore only return my sincere thanks for the honor, both in their names and in my own, and to add my best wishes that the deliberations of this Assembly may ever be conclusions just and honest; that no desire for self-aggrandizement or for pecuniary profit may ever taint its reputation; and that the labors performed in this session may be hereafter recorded as an honor to you, and to the credit of the State which you represent."

At the conclusion of his remarks, which were received with a curious enthusiasm, the Assembly adjourned for half an hour, to give the members of both houses an opportunity of being personally presented to their guest.

In the following year, Tilden was nominated by the Democratic party for the Presidency. It may not be inappropriate here to state that when the propriety of nominating Mr. Tilden for governor was under discussion in 1874, Bryant said to me that he hoped Tilden would accept the nomination if offered, and if he did, that he should vote for him. It was noticeable through the canvass which followed that, though the "Evening Post" supported the Republican ticket, not a line appeared in its columns calculated to depreciate Tilden in the estimation of its readers. Whether Bryant voted for Tilden or not I never heard, but I presume he did, for he with many others of his party were opposed to the election of President Grant for a third term, and a vote for General Dix, who was the Republican candidate for governor, was generally regarded as equivalent to an approval of the reëlection of Grant.[1]

[1] The judgment which Bryant formed of Grant, a judgment which history is likely to accept, was thus briefly stated in a letter to the Rev. Dr. H. N. Powers, dated July 15, 1877 : —

"I am glad to hear anything good of General Grant, and thank you for the anecdote of him given in your letter. His administration was, in modern phraseology, ' a failure.' I am willing to give him credit for any instance of good sense in perceiving his mistakes and frankness in acknowledging them, like that related in your letter. I was bitterly disappointed in General Grant, yet

I may also mention here that while Mr. Bryant was a guest of Governor Tilden at Albany, they were both present at a large dinner party given to the governor on his birthday. Mr. Bryant proposed Tilden's health, adding that as he had made so good a governor, the public probably would not be displeased if his present position were to prove a stepping-stone to one more elevated.

By the light of these facts and the great personal esteem which I knew Bryant entertained for the governor, I felt encouraged to address him the following letter: —

ALBANY, *August* 27, 1876.

MY DEAR MR. BRYANT, — It has been one of my dreams for several months that your name should head the Tilden Electoral Ticket this fall for the Presidency. It has not been practicable for me to see you since the St. Louis Convention, and I am now obliged to ask the governor's secretary, Mr. Newell, to do me the favor to convey to you the expression of my sincere hope that if named as an elector you will not decline.

You need not be told how gratifying such a nomination would be to Governor Tilden, nor need I recapitulate to you the many obvious reasons why you should

I see no reason to doubt his honesty. He had in the beginning of his administration, I think, some notions of what he ought to do, but they were not very clear, and the people he had about him, and who were not chosen as his associate, with the sagacity which I expected, contrived to confuse them still farther, and at last he gave us an administration with all the faults of the worst which had preceded it. But his part in the history of his country is at an end, and I suppose that the merits of his military career will be hereafter more looked at than the errors of his political administration."

desire to oblige his friends, a large proportion of whom are your pupils, with the use of your name.

The course of the "Evening Post," of course, somewhat disappoints me and others who like me embarked in this effort at administrative reform for no mere personal ends. To all such it would be an unspeakable satisfaction to know that you would not decline to charge yourself with the duty of taking their vote to Washington and depositing it for the candidates who in their judgment represent the best hope of the country.

Let me pray that if the convention which is to meet on Wednesday next should desire, you will not pain your friends by refusing them and your country this service.

I remain as ever, my dear Mr. Bryant,

Very sincerely yours,　　JOHN BIGELOW.

To this appeal I received the following disappointing though not altogether unexpected reply :

"CUMMINGTON, MASS., *August* 28, 1878.

"MY DEAR MR. BIGELOW, — Your letter of yesterday which has just been put into my hands was an utter surprise to me. There are many reasons why I must decline allowing my name to be placed on the Tilden Electoral Ticket, some of which you will, I think, understand without my referring to them. Others relate to the character and composition of the two political parties in the field, and to the letters of acceptance written by the two candidates for the Presidency. Such as they are, they constrain me with a force which I cannot resist to decline acting on the suggestions made in your letter. It gives me great pain to refuse anything to the friends of a man whom I esteem and honor as

I do Mr. Tilden, whom I know to be so highly accomplished for the most eminent political stations, whose opinions of the proper province and objects of legislation and government have been formed in the same school as my own, and who, so far as he is not obstructed by the party to which he belongs, will, I am sure, act not only with ability and integrity, but with wisdom, in any post to which the voice of his countrymen may call him.

"I am, dear sir,

Faithfully yours,

W. C. BRYANT."

HON. JOHN BIGELOW.

Though I was satisfied in my own mind that Bryant regarded Tilden as in every respect much the fitter of the two candidates for the Presidency, I did not underestimate the difficulties which he would encounter in publicly associating himself with the fortunes of a candidate which the journal he was supposed to, but in fact did not then, control[1] would be doing its utmost to defeat. When I wrote to him, I was not aware that a few days before the receipt of my letter the following correspondence had passed between him and a Republican friend, which must have made it practically impossible for him to entertain my proposal, even though, but for such correspondence, he might have been not indisposed to embrace it.

[1] The *Evening Post* had, a few years before, been converted into a stock company, of which Bryant owned only half, but not a majority, of the shares.

NEW YORK, *August 23, 1876.*

MY DEAR MR. BRYANT, — I notice by the press that you still linger at Cummington, where I hope that you are enjoying the nature you so well depict, and take all the comfort you so well deserve. In a casual conversation with Mr. Henderson [1] a few days since, I mentioned the impression that prevailed that he was now the editor in fact, as his son-in-law, Sperry, was managing editor of the "Post." He said that nothing could be more incorrect, that Mr. Bryant was the responsible editor, and inspired as he controlled the political course. I suppose this impression, which prevails to a considerable extent, arises from the fact of Mr. Henderson's supposed controlling influence in the stock of the "Post," as well as your known friendship for Governor Tilden, for whose election both Mr. Godwin and Bigelow are lending their influence. I do not know that you care about all this, but there are a good many intelligent and independent voters who depend somewhat on the coming of the "Post" to lead them to act wisely at the coming election, but they want to know if Mr. Bryant and the "Post" are still as of yore one and the same. Mr. Henderson knows of my writing you this letter, saying you would confirm what he said to me, which I have quoted to you.

Faithfully yours,   J. C. DERBY.

"CUMMINGTON, MASS., *August 28, 1876.*

"To J. C. DERBY, ESQ.

"DEAR SIR, — I do not wonder that many thoughtful persons are undecided as to which

---

[1] Isaac Henderson, a stockholder and the business manager of the *Evening Post.*

candidate they shall support in the coming election of President. Both parties aim at the same ends. Which has the best candidate or which party can be most depended upon to adopt and enforce the necessary measures are the questions which people are asking. If you look only to the candidate, Mr. Tilden is the best, the most of a statesman, the soundest and most enlarged in opinion, and, I think, of the firmest character. If you look at the parties by which the candidates are brought forward, the Republican party is the most to be relied on — although both parties, judged by the proceedings of their representatives in Congress, are greatly degenerate, and whichever of them obtain the ascendancy, those who look for a complete radical, thorough reform will be disappointed. Some changes will doubtless be made for the better, but those who expect all abuses in the administration of the government to be done away will find their mistake. As to the hard money question, it seems to me that it is safest with the Republicans. The Democratic party of the West is deeply infected with the inflation heresy. It is now smothered temporarily, but as soon as the election is over it will break out again with violence. The Republican party is most free from its influence. As to the civil service reform, which both parties profess to desire, Mr. Tilden has not pledged himself to abstain from the vicious practice of turning out indiscriminately all whom he shall find in office in case he is elected.

He only promises to look carefully into their characters and qualifications. I infer that all whom he finds in office must go out. Who will answer for him that all whom he appoints will be worthy of their places? Thousands and tens of thousands will flock to Washington for these places, all of them good ' Democrats,' and it will be absolutely astonishing if a large number of those who are appointed do not turn out to be rogues. Hayes, who only promises to send adrift the unworthy, will have an easier task, and leisure to exercise a just discrimination. As to the revenue laws, which are without doubt one cause of the hard times, neither Mr. Tilden nor Mr. Hayes has spoken of any reform to be made. Perhaps the chance of an enlightened revision of these laws is best in case the Democrats obtain the ascendancy, but how slight the prospect of such a revision is I leave to be inferred from the late proceedings of the Democratic House of Representatives. You see, therefore, that when we come to compare the prospect of reform under one of the two parties with that under the other, a man who is slow in forming conclusions might be forgiven for hesitating. Yet the greater number of those dissatisfied Republicans who came to the Fifth Avenue Conference, including most of the wisest heads among them, have acquiesced in the nomination of Hayes. The Cincinnati Convention did not give them all they wanted, but came so near to it that they thought it the wisest course to be content, and not to separate from the party with which they had hitherto acted. I thought the same thing in regard to the 'Evening Post,' namely, that it would not be well to detach itself from the party which had carried the country through the civil war until it was forced to do so by the signs of a hopeless degeneracy. There may have been some things in the 'Evening Post' which I have not agreed with altogether, being at so great a distance from it that I could not be expected to influence it in everything, but, in the main, it has treated Mr. Tilden with marked respect.

Yours truly, W. C. BRYANT."

A friend of Tilden's to whom the last letter was shown called Bryant's attention to the fact that the most conspicuous, and the only conspicuous, case of civil service reform which had been witnessed in the whole country up to that time had occurred under Tilden's administration, and right under his eyes at Albany; that his Secretary of State had selected as Superintendent of the Census a Republican,[1] upon the advice of the Hon. Francis A. Walker, Superintendent of the Federal Censuses of 1870 and 1880, also a Republican; that all his clerks, at one time over eighty in number, were selected by a competitive examination in which this Republican superintendent was the sole arbiter, and that three fourths at least of all the clerks consisted of Republicans.

[1] The late C. W. Seaton, who was afterwards associated with Francis A. Walker in digesting the census of 1880, and subsequently succeeded him as superintendent.

It was subsequent to, and doubtless in consequence of, this information that Bryant supplemented his first letter to Derby with the following : —

"Cummington, Mass., *September* 4, 1876.

"Dear Mr. Derby, — I did not write my previous letter for publication, and beg that you will not let the press get hold of it. I have a fear that I may have done injustice to Mr. Tilden in regard to the reformation of the civil service. If so, his letter of acceptance was the cause. I looked it over for some condemnation of the bad practice, so long followed, of turning out of office all the men of the beaten party after an election. I found no such condemnation, and inferred that he meant to leave himself at liberty to follow the practice. I have since learned that he had in many instances appointed men of the Republican party to office in his gift, solely on account of their competency and character. This was nobly done, but he will have great difficulty in resisting the pressure which will be brought to bear upon him, in order to force him to make a clean sweep of the public offices and fill them with men of his own party. I am willing, however, to take this as a proof of Mr. Tilden's present disposition, and hope that it will not be overcome by the force which will assuredly be brought against it.

Yours very truly,   W. C. Bryant."

Mr. Godwin tells us " Mr. Bryant voted at the election in November, but how he voted no one was ever able to learn. Members of each of the leading parties claimed his name, but when himself questioned on the subject, he smiled, and said that the ballot was a secret institution."

Mr. Godwin is correct in stating that Bryant voted at the election in November, but not quite correct in implying that he voted for either Presidential candidate. He did not vote the Electoral ticket at all. If I had not this assurance upon perfectly competent authority, I think it could be fairly inferred from the situation. Had Bryant voted for Hayes, the candidate of his party, there would have been no occasion to make a mystery of it. Neither would he ever have been guilty of anything so much like duplicity as to vote secretly for Tilden, while before the world in his paper he was understood to be recommending Hayes to the support of his readers. Had he voted for Tilden, the readers of the " Evening Post," at least, were certain to be the first to be taken into his confidence. He preferred Tilden to Hayes as a President, but the Republican to the Democratic as a party.

Only a few days after the election, he wrote to a lady in Scotland : —

" This is Evacuation Day, the day when in the Revolutionary War we saw the last of the red-coated soldiery. But we celebrate it no longer; we have other things to think of now ; we have chosen a President, and are trying to find out who it is. We shall be gainers at any rate. Let who will be awarded the Presidency, his administration is sure

to be better than the present one. I have never
before felt so little interest in a contest for the
Presidency. Both parties profess to have the same
ends in view; both have put up able and well-in-
tentioned men for candidates. Tilden is the abler
and the more thoroughly a statesman, and I think
the more persistent of the two in any course he has
marked out for himself; but his party has suffered
in character by the late rebellion, which forced
many of the best people to join the Republican
party."

In November, 1877, the Goethe Club gave Bryant
a reception, at which the Rev. W. R. Alger delivered an elaborate address. On closing, he said: —

" And now, Mr. Bryant, we thank you for consenting
to allow us this pleasant opportunity for greeting and
meeting you, and expressing something of our feeling
towards you. May the guardian fellowship of God sur-
round you and crown you with every gracious gift until
the end."

The length of the addresses which were made at
and about him were a little embarrassing to Mr.
Bryant, who was made by the force of circumstances an assenting party to a sort of conspiracy
to praise him; but he disengaged his responsibility and modesty together by some felicitous banter
about old age, behind which he was fond of taking refuge, and which proved in the later years of
his life an inexhaustible fountain of amusement

as well as of excuses. After thanking Mr. Alger
and Dr. Ruppaner, the president of the Club, for
the compliments they had paid him, but which he
insisted that he could not accept as his due, he
went on : —

"You will therefore allow me to ascribe the
kindness which has been shown me this evening to
a cause which you will admit to be sufficiently obvious, namely, to the long life which I have led,
— the late old age which I have reached, — an existence prolonged considerably beyond the common
lot. One who has passed rather inoffensively beyond the milestones which mark the stages of life
up to fourscore is looked upon by the rest of mankind with a certain compassionate feeling. He
cannot do much more mischief, they naturally and
justly think, and therefore may safely be praised.
His further stay upon the earth is necessarily short,
and it is therefore a charitable thing to make that
short stay pleasant. Beside, he has become, by reason of his very few coevals, a sort of curiosity, — a
rare instance, — and rarity often gives value and
price to things which are in themselves intrinsically
worthless.

"Let me pursue this thought a little further.
There have been various attempts to give a concise
definition of the term 'man,' founded on some peculiarity which distinguishes the human race from
all other animals, our fellow-inhabitants, of this
planet. Some have defined man as a talking animal,
notwithstanding the instance of the parrot, a bird

which sometimes talks as well as certain members
of Congress; some as a laughing animal, although
there is a laughing hyena; and some as a cooking
animal, the only animal that roasts chestnuts,
overlooking the ancient tradition of the monkey
who used the paws of the cat to draw the nuts from
the fire. I will venture to give another definition,
to which, I think, no objection can well be made.
I would define man as the animal that delights in
antiquities. No other creature gathers up the relics of past years and deposits them in museums
and guards them with care and points them out to
the wonder of others. It is only man who digs
among the ruins of cities destroyed long ago, in
order to unearth the domestic implements and personal adornments of the human race when it was
yet in its infancy, as Schliemann and others are
doing, thinking themselves fortunate in proportion
to the rudeness and clumsiness, in other words the
antiquity, of these objects. If we were to hear of
monkeys turning up the earth among old tombs in
search of the earrings and necklaces of those who
lived in the time of the Trojan war, we should be
struck with amazement, and word would at once be
sent to Darwin by his disciples that here was a
new proof of the doctrine of evolution.

"But older than Priam and Agamemnon are the
remains of the lake dwellers of a distant period of
the world's history, when men lived in habitations
built on floats over the water, and used only implements of stone, the use of metals not being yet

discovered. Stone axes and stone spear-heads have been fished up from the mud of these waters, the tokens of a time when warriors hammered each other to death with rude weapons of flint and granite. These have been diligently collected and daintily handled and laid up in cabinets of curiosities, and gazed at and wondered at and made the subject of books and elaborate treatises, and lighter magazine articles. All their value consists in the many years which have elapsed since they were shaped by the workmen of a rude and simple age.

" Offer one of these stone axes to a woodman to be used in his vocation, and he would reject it with scorn. He might by great efforts bruise down a tree with it, but he could not be said to cut it down. Offer it to a butcher that he may use it in felling an ox, and he would laugh at the clumsy implement, and demand an axe of metal. Rejected as it would be for lack of utility in ministering to our necessities or our comforts, it is yet made much of; it is written about and talked about, and men see in it a whole chapter of the history of mankind.

" I have thus shown how natural it is that those who are left to grow very old become by that circumstance alone the objects of kind attention. For such testimonials of this kindness as I have received this evening I return, along with my acknowledgments, my good wishes also. May you all who hear me yet become antiquities, not after the fashion of the stone axes which I have described, but after the manner of the pole star, which, century after century, has guided by its useful light the navigator on the sea and the wanderer on the land. May you become antiquities like the venerable mountains, which attract the clouds and gather the rains into springs and rivulets, and send them down to give life and refreshment to the fields below. May you become antiquities like the blessed and ancient sun, which ripens the harvests of the earth for successive generations of mankind, and at the end of every day leaves in the western sky a glorious memory of his genial brightness."

It is hardly necessary to say that this address was followed with great applause, the greater for the skill with which Bryant saved his personal dignity without the slightest sacrifice of his imperturbable good nature.

It is not only on these exceptional occasions to which we have referred that the evidences of respect, admiration, and reverence for Bryant as a poet, as a journalist, and as a man are to be sought; they welled up more or less profusely from every fountain of public opinion throughout the country. He was an honorary member of pretty much every Historical, Philosophical, Antiquarian, and Statistical society; of every Academy of Artists and Men of Letters, and of every college society in the United States of sufficient consideration to feel at liberty to proffer the compliment.

The homage that is paid to a public man who has offices and honors to bestow, whose smile confers credit and influence, and whose frown may threaten disaster, is always more or less tainted with the suspicion that it is to the functionary and not to the man it is paid. So the homage that is paid to the dead is often much more liberal than to the living, from the fact that the object of it is no longer in any one's way, and praising him interferes with no one's advancement, and affords an eligible opportunity of earning a reputation for magnanimity at a trifling cost.

When it is considered that Bryant never held any public office, that he never controlled any patronage, that he was not accustomed to borrow from occasions any factitious influence, it must, I think, be conceded that the respect and reverence with which he inspired his countrymen, and the homage which they so freely and abundantly accorded to him during his lifetime, are among the things in their history which do them infinite honor, and which testify most faithfully to their correct appreciation of what is good and great in human character.

CHAPTER XI.

PERSONAL AND DOMESTIC HABITS.

ONE of Milton's contemporaries tells us " that the poet's vein never happily flowed but from the autumnal equinox to the vernal; and that whatever he attempted at other times was never to his satisfaction, though he courted his fancy never so much."

What is here said of Milton might be said in a way, with more or less propriety, of most eminent writers, but not of Bryant. As has been already observed in these pages, he was not a man of moods and tenses. He never seemed one day less ready than another for any kind of intellectual exertion. Till years began to tell upon his nervous energy, which was not until very late in life, he seemed always ready to do his best of any kind of work. This is so rare a quality that it can only be explained by the pains he took for the conservation of his health and the religious control which he maintained over all his appetites. Like St. Paul, he treated his body as God's temple, and, to an almost inconceivable extent, resisted every inclination tending to unfit it for its holy office. He was born with a very delicate constitution. One who was a student in Dr. Bryant's office tells us, —

"The poet was puny and very delicate, and of a painfully delicate nervous temperament. There seemed little promise that he would survive the casualties of early childhood. In after years, when he had become famous, those who had been medical students with his father when he was struggling for existence with the odds very much against him delighted to tell of the cold baths they were ordered to give the infant poet in a spring near the house early mornings of the summer months, continuing the treatment, in spite of the outcries and protestations of their patient, so late into the autumn as sometimes to break the ice that skimmed the surface." [1]

Shortly after he settled as a lawyer at Great Barrington, he represented himself to a correspondent as "wasted to a shadow by a complaint of the lungs." This weakness of the chest, to which both his father and sister had succumbed, led him soon after his arrival in New York to discontinue the use of tea, coffee, spices, and all stimulating condiments; to eat sparingly of meat, and to take a great deal of bodily exercise.

It is easy to persuade ourselves that he was largely indebted for his ability to contend successfully with morbid hereditary tendencies, and for his extraordinary vigor and longevity, to the attention he was thus compelled to give to the care of his health in early life. It is an extraordinary fact

[1] Dawes's Centennial Address at Cummington, June 26, 1879.

that, starting life with such a limited capital of health, he lived to be an octogenarian without ever having been confined to his bed from illness, except his last, within the recollection of any of his offspring, and with all his bodily senses in apparently unimpaired perfection. He never used spectacles, and his hearing to the last seemed perfect.

Bryant has happily left us a brief account of his sanitary discipline in a letter to an acquaintance who had asked of him the secret of his uninterrupted health. If the value of his example as set forth in this letter to Joseph H. Richards, Esq., could be properly impressed upon the youth of our country, it would probably prevent far more disease than all the medical schools of the land will ever supply the skill to cure.

"New York, *March 30th.*

. . . "I rise early, at this time of the year about half past five; in summer, half an hour or even an hour earlier. Immediately, with very little encumbrance of clothing, I begin a series of exercises, for the most part designed to expand the chest, and at the same time call into action all the muscles and articulations of the body. These are performed with dumb - bells, — the very lightest, covered with flannel, — with a pole, a horizontal bar, and a light chair swung round my head. After a full hour, and sometimes more, passed in this manner, I bathe from head to foot. When at my place in the country, I sometimes shorten my exercises in the chamber, and, going out, occupy myself in some work which requires brisk motion. After my bath, if breakfast be not ready, I sit down to my studies till I am called. My breakfast is a simple one — hominy and milk, or, in place of hominy, brown bread, or oatmeal, or wheaten grits, and, in the season, baked sweet apples. Buckwheat cakes I do not decline, nor any other article of vegetable food, but animal food I never take at breakfast. Tea and coffee I never touch at any time; sometimes I take a cup of chocolate, which has no narcotic effect, and agrees with me very well. At breakfast I often take fruit, either in its natural state or freshly stewed.

"After breakfast I occupy myself for a while with my studies; and when in town, I walk down to the office of the 'Evening Post,' nearly three miles distant, and after about three hours return, always walking, whatever be the weather or the state of the streets. In the country I am engaged in my literary tasks till a feeling of weariness drives me out into the open air, and I go upon my farm or into the garden and prune the fruit trees, or perform some other work about them which they need, and then go back to my books. I do not often drive out, preferring to walk. In the country I dine early, and it is only at that meal that I take either meat or fish, and of these but a moderate quantity, making my dinner mostly of vegetables. At the meal which is called tea I take only a little bread and butter with fruit, if it be on the table. In town, where I dine later, I make but two meals a day. Fruit makes a considerable part of my diet, and I eat it at almost any hour of the day without inconvenience. My drink is water, yet I sometimes, though rarely, take a glass of wine. I am a natural temperance man, finding myself rather confused than exhilarated by wine. I never meddle with tobacco, except to quarrel with its use.

"That I may rise early I, of course, go to bed early: in town as early as ten; in the country somewhat earlier. For many years I have avoided in the evening every kind of literary occupation which tasks the faculties, such as composition, even to the writing of letters, for the reason that it excites the nervous system and prevents sound sleep. My brother told me not long since that he had seen in a Chicago newspaper, and several other Western journals, a paragraph in which it was said that I am in the habit of taking quinine as a stimulant, that I have depended on the excitement it produces in writing my verses, and that in consequence of using it in that way I have become as deaf as a post. As to my deafness, you know that to be false; and the rest of the story is equally so. I abominate drugs and narcotics, and have always carefully avoided anything which spurs nature to exertions which it would not otherwise make. Even with my food I do not take the usual condiments, such as pepper and the like."

To the habits of life outlined in this letter, Bryant faithfully adhered to the end of his days.

Not many weeks before his death, and when recovering from a slight indisposition which he had been describing to me (he was then approaching his eighty-fourth year), I said, " I presume you have reduced your allowance of morning gymnastics." "Not the width of your thumb nail," was his prompt reply. " What," said I, " do you manage still 'to put in' your hour and a half every morning?" "Yes," he replied, " and sometimes more; frequently more." This I have always regarded as a signal triumph of character. As the glaciers testify to the incalculable power of the sun which piles them up on the peaks of the loftiest mountains, so this resolute and conscientious prosecution of a toil which directly furthered no personal or worldly end, which added nothing of value to his stock of knowledge, which gratified neither his own nor any other person's vanity or ambition, which deprived him of no trifling proportion of the best working hours of his day, testified with unimpeachable authority to the heroic moral forces of which his will, his tastes, his ambition, were always the patient and faithful servants.

Soon after his settlement in New York, his attention was directed to the Hahnemannian theory of medical science, which had just been introduced into the United States by Dr. Hans B. Gram, and which he finally accepted as the system of cure having most pretensions to a scientific character. When later a society of homœopathic physicians was organized, he was elected its first president. In a letter written to his old friend, the Rev. Dr. Dewey, in January, 1842, he recapitulates the subjects then occupying most of public attention, and among them he enumerates homœopathy, which he says "is carrying all before it. Conversions are making every day. Within a twelvemonth the number of persons who employ homœopathic physicians has doubled. A homœopathic society has been established, and I have delivered an inaugural lecture before it, — a defense of the system which I am to repeat next week. The heathen rage terribly, but their rage availeth nothing." Bryant's faith in this system of medication grew with his years; and he became quite expert in its application to the ordinary ailments of his family and dependents. His lecture did much to commend homœopathy to the public confidence, though his extraordinary vigor of body and mind was more convincing to most persons than anything he could write or preach.

It is a curious coincidence that his death was the result not of disease but of a fall, and that the only alarm he ever experienced about his health, after he embraced homœopathy, was also in consequence of a fall. As he was going to his office one morning, — he was then in his eightieth year, — he slipped on the street and fell. To this accident he makes the following playful allusion in a letter to Miss C. Gibson, one of his very few regular correspondents : —

"I am sorry to hear that your health does not improve as a consequence of your rambles and sojourns on the continent. Will it never be so ordered that health, like some diseases, will become contagious? What a blessing it would be for some of us if a good constitution were catching, like the small-pox! if freedom from pain, and gayety of spirits, and the due and harmonious action of all our physical organs, could be given off from one to another, by a kind of infection! But, if that were the case, the bad as well as the good would have the advantage of it, and derive from it strength for their guilty purposes, so that, on the whole, the present arrangement need not be disturbed. . . . My own health, concerning which you expressed so kind a concern, is very good again. Only my lame shoulder reminds me now and then, and not very importunately by neuralgic twinges and shootings of pain, of the unlucky bruise which it had from my fall on Broadway. It always seems to me that there is a kind of disgrace in falling to the ground. Drunken people fall. As I got up, I thought to myself, 'Nobody, at least, is here who knows me.' At that very moment a gentleman, whom I did not know, asked: 'Are you hurt, Mr. Bryant?' 'Of course not,' I answered, and I marched off down town as if I had just come from my door."

During his visit to Europe in 1857, he left his place in charge of Mr. George B. Cline, the teacher of the public school in Roslyn, whose personal merits and professional accomplishments had won his respect and confidence. Not long after his return, his worldly affairs now warranting the expense, he engaged Mr. Cline to give him his whole time, and to discharge all the duties commonly confided to the steward of an English estate. He was eminently fortunate in this arrangement, which relieved him from all involuntary care of his country properties, while insuring a skillful as well as faithful execution of his wishes in their management. In whatever quarter of the world he might be, Bryant never seemed to lose sight of his landed properties, nor to become indifferent to the details of their management, of which a voluminous correspondence with Mr. Cline still bears testimony.

From Heidelberg, in 1857, he writes : —

"There is scarcely anything you could tell me about Cedarmere [the name of his place at Roslyn] that I should not be glad to know. When a time arrives in which there is less to do than usual, I should like to have the alders cut away about the pond, particularly on the east side where they are beginning to form thickets. In cold weather, also, when the thing is practicable, I should like to have some loads of sand brought from Mott's bank — it being understood that he is to be paid for it — and the swampy hollow under the Jargonelle pear-tree south of the garden filled up with it."

From Paris, he writes : —

"In regard to the trees on the hill and those near the boat-house which did not put forth leaves this spring, I should be glad if you could ascertain by any marks upon them to what varieties of fruit they belonged, that you could replace them. If they were pears, the best way would be to plant others in their place this fall as soon as the leaves begin to drop. If they were cherry or plum trees, the best time, according to my experience, is to plant them early in the spring, and to mulch the ground about their roots, that they may not suffer by the hot dry weather of the ensuing summer. . . . In addition to what I have already said concerning the things I wish to have done on the farm, I have at present only to say that I should like a small crop of wheat put in this fall, that I may have something to eat when I return."

From Madrid, he writes : —

"I should like the business of the farm to be so planned that there would be some leisure left for certain jobs, such as keeping the fences in neat repair, ditching, draining a little, patching up a thousand things that always want looking to, and working in the garden. . . . For the next year, beginning with April, I wish you to make such arrangements in regard to the workmen employed on the place as you may think most judicious, and in regard to the cows kept on it, to do just as you would if the farm belonged to you."

From Cadiz, he writes : —

"I wish you to write Mr. Dawes [who super-

vised the place at Cummington] that in getting
blackberry bushes for you in the spring, I wish him
to take them from the edge of the wood west of
the new orchard, beginning at the northwest corner, and proceeding about a third of the way. The
berries for that distance are all of the best kind;
beyond and nearer the school-house they are inferior. There is a shrub of the white azalea at the
corner of the road leading from my place in Cummington to Mr. Norton's, which I wish dug up and
transferred this spring to the garden or some other
suitable place.

" I wish also rows of trees to be planted on each
side of the road leading up to Mr. Ellis's place.
It might be well that some of them should be
evergreens.

" Mr. Dawes showed me in Worthington where
a man who has many evergreens on his place had
successfully planted large ones to the north of
his house, screening it from view. I suggested
that he should be employed to plant some large
ones near my house, to be paid liberally for those
that live, and those only. Will you see if anything of this can be done? Please press this
matter. You know I cannot wait for trees to
grow."

From Barcelona, he writes:—

" I have just been to the market here and bought
four oranges for two cents."

From Nice, he writes:—

" I wish you would supply the place of the European chestnut-tree that died near the summer-house, and plant another pine near Captain Post's — the one there is sickly."

From Malaga, he writes : —

"I am glad to hear so good an account as you give of your Sunday-school. Both in that and your district school you are engaged in a great work of good, which I hope you will not desert without mature consideration. As to inconveniences and disagreeable things, there is no situation in life free from them — every condition and occupation having its peculiar troubles, which we must learn to bear and make as light as we can. . . . Julia says she would like you to set out a clematis on the east side of the door, not the wild, strong-growing clematis of our country which is too luxuriant, and would predominate over the honeysuckle. If convenient, she would like the *Clematis flamula.* There was one planted in that spot and it must have died. If this should be inconvenient take any climbing plant from the garden. . . . We are here in Malaga, the country of fine fruits and of the best raisins, and cannot get a grape, though in the seaports to the north we found both that and other fruits most abundant and cheap."

From Marseilles, he writes : —

"Should your mother go to the West this winter, Mrs. Bryant desires that you would get her at our expense, for the journey, a good warm cloak or dress and a warm bonnet, and give them to her from Mrs. Bryant. . . . As for eggs and chickens, my wife says they are yours for the present, — use what you have occasion for, only leaving a stock of hens for us when we come back, — not too many, for they are a nuisance."

From Rome, he writes : —

" There is [at Cummington] a patch of low land or lamb kill, a little to the north of the brook running through it, which I wish Mr. Dawes would extirpate. The Bates's lost a sheep last summer, and I think from eating it. There is also a shrub of white azalea in the middle of the road at the corner between my farm and the new purchase, which I wish to have dug up and transplanted to the garden. You know that it is among the most fragrant of flowers. . . . I would like a row of evergreens — hemlocks, I think the best, — planted north of the new school-house in Cummington so as to shelter it from the winter wind. . . . In sending trees and shrubs to Cummington you will not forget Kohlenterias, which flourish so well about our place, and of which so many have appeared under the large tree. The monthly honeysuckle also would, I am pretty sure, do well there, and the trumpet honeysuckle also, and it would be well to add some of the hardier roses."

From Dresden, he writes : —

" I do not know whether I suggested that you should plant in my plot of ground in the cemetery some of those white violets that grow about the little waterfall that comes out of the pond south of the mill. I think they will do well there. They seem to like a spot partially shaded where the grass is not so thick and the earth a little broken."

From London, he writes: —

"You say that Mrs. Cline has been sewing some sheets together to catch curculios under the plum-trees. I was in hopes that the mixture of sawdust and petroleum under the trees would save this trouble, if spread copiously and wide enough around them. I cannot see how a curculio could well live to get back into the tree after falling among it. At all events, I wish a certain number of trees to be left to that remedy alone, that we may see how it works."

From Cruff, Perthshire, Scotland, he writes: —

"Do not forget the Canada thistles in the field south of Captain Post's. . . . If you were here you would miss many things you have in Roslyn. Garden vegetables are dear and scarce, and some are not to be had. The tomato can be raised only under glass. Yet the winter climate is such that the Portugal laurel flourishes and many other ever-greens too tender to bear the cold on Long Island. The cinnamon rose is just coming into bloom. I see no apple nor pear trees, which abound in the southern counties of the island; indeed, a fruit tree of any sort is an unwonted sight here. Yesterday in going through the grounds of a large landed proprietor I found a walk of an eighth of a mile between plantations of rhododendrons in full flower. The jonquil grows wild here, and is just passing out of bloom."

From Cummington, he writes: —

" The rainy weather has given place to bright and beautiful days. I went to church on Sunday at the east village, and heard a sermon so much poorer than the previous one at the west village, that I think of going back to the west village next Sunday."

From the office of the " Evening Post," he writes: —

" I forgot to say to you that I hoped you would see that the pears do not decay in the front room and the library. . . . You will give, of course, the usual presents to the men. Please get a black alpaca dress for Mrs. Tilfor if she needs it. . . . I send you an advertisement relating to the Japanese flower, the *Lilium auratum*, which is sold cheap. Mr. Nordhoff suggests that if you care to have any of the bulbs, you had better see him before getting them."

From Mount Savage, he writes: —

" I think it will be well to make two or three barrels of cider, but I do not wish to have it made of apples which are half rotten or in any way unsound. I want it made of picked, selected apples, and put in barrels which are perfectly sweet. It will probably be well to attend to this before I return."

From Cummington, he writes: —

" The pears came last evening, Friday, in a pouring rain, the sixth rainy day that we have had in succession. The earth is as full of moisture as a sponge just dipped in water, and is letting it out everywhere. As to the pears, they came in very good order. A few of the Tysons and the Otts were spoiled, and but a few; they were all except the spoiled ones ready for eating. Both the Otts and the Dearborns are much better than those you sent before, and the Cedarmeres which we have left can hardly be eaten after the excellent pears which we got last evening. I think of coming for the plums with my brother next Tuesday."

When in town, his correspondence was, of course more frequent, but wherever he was, whether at home, or in Europe or Asia or Africa or Spanish America, he never seemed to lose sight of nor interest in whatever nature or art were doing. or could be persuaded to do at Roslyn and Cummington. He was a good farmer and an accomplished botanist. There was nothing that drew its life from the soil which was not to him a divine expression of profound and fascinating mysteries, which he was always desiring to penetrate; much of his poetry shows with what success.

Bryant was about five feet ten inches in height, very erect, lithe, and well formed. He never became fleshy, but to the last retained the elasticity and alertness which in the lower animals are tokens of high breeding and careful training. He was among his school-fellows noted for his beauty, and in his old age his appearance was very distinguished. A finer looking head than his at eighty was only to be seen in art galleries. Whoever saw him in his later years would discern a new force and fitness in those lines of Dr. Donne : —

> " No spring nor summer beauty has such grace
> As I have seen in an autumnal face."

The austerity of his life, for he never cultivated any artificial appetites, contributed to keep him comparatively lean in flesh. Hence his endurance even at eighty was remarkable. There were few young men who cared to follow him in his tramps, or who could scale a mountain with less physical inconvenience. He was not fond of riding, and was rarely seen in a carriage for recreation. I never knew of his riding a horse. Walking was his favorite out-of-door exercise. He was a great favorite with ladies and with children, and had the rare art of entertaining them without seeming to descend for the purpose. He never indulged in chaff or persiflage, nor in jokes at others' expense. The severest punishment he visited upon any one whose society was not congenial, and that was severe enough, was to let him do all the talking and to see as little of him as possible.

Bryant had been brought up in the Presbyterian faith and to regard Calvin as its profoundest expositor. "Calvinism" was practically the religion of all New England, where there was any religion at all, at the beginning of this century. While Dr. Bryant was a member of the General Court, Buckminster and Channing were enthralling vast audiences in Boston, both by their eloquence and by a theology which seemed to a certain class of minds more consistent with the deductions of human reason. A Unitarian professor was also appointed at Harvard University. Dr. Bryant listened to the preachers of these new doctrines, subscribed to their publications, and brought the doctrines of the new school back to his family, where they found a ready acceptance.

When he came to New York to live, Bryant frequented the church of Dr. Follen, less because of his varied intellectual resources, which were exceptional, than because of the freedom he found there for the expansion of the religious life in all directions. Dr. Follen was called a Unitarian. Bryant continued until his death, when in town, to attend the churches of this denomination, under the successive pastorates of Dewey, Osgood, and Bellows. At Roslyn, he attended the Presbyterian church, of which Dr. Ely was pastor. Of this church he was a trustee, a constant attendant, and one of the largest contributors to its maintenance. Though habitually an attendant upon the ministrations of the Unitarian clergy when they were accessible, no one ever recognized more completely nor more devoutly the divinity of Christ. To a little volume from the pen of the Rev. Dr. Alden, entitled " Thoughts on the Religious Life," he contributed a preface, in which he says: —

" I cannot but lament the tendency of the time, encouraged by some in the zealous prosecution of

science, to turn its attention from the teachings of
the gospel, from the beautiful example of Christ's
life, and the supremely excellent precepts which
He gave to his disciples, and the people who resorted to hear Him. To those teachings and that
example the world owes its recovery from the
abominations of heathenism. The very men who
in the pride of their investigations into the secrets
of the material world turn a look of scorn upon
the Christian system of belief are not aware how
much of the peace and order of society, how much
of the happiness of their households and the purity of those who are dearest to them, are owing to
the influence of that religion extending beyond
their sphere. There is no character in the whole
range of qualities which distinguish men from
each other so fitted to engage our admiration and
so pregnant with salutary influence on society as
that which is formed on the Christian pattern by
the precepts of the gospel, and a zealous imitation
of the example of the Great Master.

.   .   .   .

"This character, of which Christ was the perfect
model, is in itself so attractive, so 'altogether
lovely,' that I cannot describe in language the admiration with which I regard it; nor can I express
the gratitude I feel for the dispensation which bestowed that example on mankind, for the truths
which He taught, and the sufferings He endured
for our sakes. I tremble to think what the world
would be without Him. Take away the blessing

of the advent of his life and the blessings purchased by his death, in what an abyss of guilt would man have been left? It would seem to be blotting the sun out of the heavens — to leave our system of worlds in chaos, frost, and darkness.

"In my view of the life, the teachings, the labors, and the sufferings of the blessed Jesus, there can be no admiration too profound, no love of which the human heart is capable too warm, no gratitude too earnest and deep, of which He is justly the object. It is with sorrow that my love for Him is so cold, and my gratitude so inadequate. It is with sorrow that I see any attempt to put aside his teachings as a delusion, to turn men's eyes from his example, to meet with doubt and denial the story of his life.

"For my part, if I thought that the religion of skepticism were to gather strength and prevail and become the dominant view of mankind, I should despair of the fate of mankind in the years that are yet to come. . . .

"The religious man finds in his relations to his Maker a support to his virtue which others cannot have. He acts always with a consciousness that he is immediately under the eyes of a Being who looks into his heart and sees his inmost thoughts, and discerns the motives which he is half unwilling to acknowledge even to himself. He feels that he is under the inspection of a Being who is only pleased with right motives and purity of intention, and who is displeased with whatever is otherwise.

He feels that the approbation of that Being is infinitely more to be valued than the applause of all
mankind, and his displeasure more to be feared
and more to be avoided than any disgrace which
he might sustain from his brethren of mankind."

I will here allow myself the liberty of quoting
a few paragraphs from a letter of Miss Bryant
which exhibits some of the aspects of her father's
domestic life of peculiar interest. After inviting
my attention to Dr. Alden's book, she says : —

" This preface must have been one of the last things
written by my father. It speaks more fully than I
have known him to do elsewhere of his religious belief
and of his belief in Christ, and is very touching, I think.
I remember how earnestly he used to enjoin upon me
to study the character and example of Christ and to try
to follow it. He was so reserved even with his children
in speaking of such subjects that he rarely admonished
any one in this way, but when he did it was done with
a simplicity and earnestness that made it something
never to be forgotten.

" My father and mother with Dr. Ely took an active
part in procuring for the village the cemetery at Roslyn,
where they both now are buried, and since Dr. Ely's
death my father was always liberal in subscribing toward the salary of the clergyman sent there. He com-
muned there because Dr. Ely was a liberal man, and
always invited all members of other churches and de-
nominations who might be present to join in the communion service. Every Sunday my father and I prepared flowers which we took to my mother's grave to

lay upon it, and upon those of the Godwin children. When I was out at Roslyn, my father and Mr. Cline went together; and also, on the day of my mother's death, the 26th of July, the graves were covered with flowers. My father was much interested in picking the flowers himself, and nothing ever interfered with this task of love.

" On Sunday mornings he always read prayers and a chapter from the Bible, using Tyndal's translation always when at Roslyn, and Furness's Prayers generally, sometimes Sadler's. In the evenings, in town, after my father had left the parlor, I would sometimes go up to his library, and almost always find him reading the book of prayers or some other religious book. He never spoke of it, but I think it was his invariable custom to read in his room some pages of books of this kind before retiring. Every Sunday morning, from the time I can remember, we had morning prayers, and I suppose it was only on Sundays, because in earlier years my father was obliged to leave home on week days before the family could be assembled for prayers; and when we were in the country he passed most of the week in town. Dr. Bellows remarked upon the regularity of his attendance at morning and evening church; he scarcely ever failed. On Sunday evenings if anything prevented his going to church, and generally in the country where we had no church, he read a sermon aloud, one of Dr. Dewey's or South's, or formerly one of Beecher's (but of late years he did not read his to the family circle), sometimes Phillips Brooks's or James Freeman Clarke's, or Robertson's, for whose works and life he had great admiration. Very few people knew how much my father's time was occupied with religious matters, especially during the last years of his life, and after my mother's death he read more books of that character than any other. He wrote a preface to a book of devotional poems collected by Miss J. Dewey, and published after his death. Miss Dewey was one of the persons to whom my father talked most freely on religious matters, although he was very reserved about his feelings and sentiments."

Bryant used to say that a gentleman should never talk of *his* love affairs or of *his* religion. There was no subject, however, as Miss Bryant states, that, during many of the later years of his life, occupied so large a share of his thoughts as religion itself; none about which he seemed more inclined to listen; but of his own spiritual experiences he was singularly reticent. I do not remember to have heard of his defining his creed upon any of the differentiating questions of theology, or of avowing a single dogma; neither do I believe such an utterance can be found in any of his writings. The preface to Dr. Alden's little book already cited approaches nearest to an exception.

The catholic, unsectarian character of Bryant's religion, his profound conviction of the presence of God wherever He is made welcome, doubtless had its influence in delaying till quite late in life his connection with " the visible church." What, if any, change in his opinions occurred, or what special motive led him to take this step when he did rather than at any earlier period of his life, has never transpired. It was at Naples in 1858,

and in the sixty-fourth year of his age, that he first
determined to make a formal public profession of
the Christian faith and " unite with the church."
of this event, we have the fullest, indeed the only
original, account from the Rev. Mr. Waterston, of
Boston.

"Mrs. Bryant," he tells us, " had been suddenly pros-
trated by serious illness, and he had watched over her
through many anxious weeks. . . . At this time [April
23d] I received from him a note stating that there
was a subject of interest upon which he would like to
converse with me. On the following day, the weather
being delightful, we walked in the Villa Reale, the royal
park or garden overlooking the Bay of Naples. Never
can I forget the beautiful spirit that breathed through
every word he uttered, the reverent love, the confiding trust, the aspiring hope, the rooted faith. Every
thought, every view was generous and comprehensive.
Anxiously watching, as he had been doing, in that twilight boundary between this world and another, over
one more precious to him than life itself, the divine
truths and promises had come home to his mind with
new power. He said that he had never united himself
with the church, which with his present feelings he
would most gladly do. He then asked if it would be
agreeable to me to come to his room on the morrow
and administer the Communion, adding that, as he had
not been baptized, he desired that ordinance at the same
time. The day following was the Sabbath, and a most
heavenly day. In fulfillment of his wishes, in his own
quiet room, a company of seven persons celebrated together the Lord's Supper. With hymns, selections

from the Scripture, and devotional exercises, we went back in thought to the 'large upper room' where Christ first instituted the Holy Supper in the midst of his disciples. Previous to the breaking of bread William Cullen Bryant was baptized. With snow-white head and flowing beard, he stood like one of the ancient Prophets, and perhaps never since the days of the Apostles has a truer disciple professed allegiance to the Divine Master. . . . After the service, while standing at the window looking out with Mr. Bryant over the bay, smooth as glass (the same water over which the Apostle Paul sailed, in the ship from Alexandria, when he brought Christianity into Italy), the graceful outline of the Island of Capri relieved against the sky, with that glorious scene reposing before us, Mr. Bryant repeated the lines of John Leyden, the Oriental scholar and poet, — lines which, he said, had always been special favorites of his, and of which he was often reminded by that holy tranquillity which seems, as with conscious recognition, to characterize the Lord's Day.

> " 'With silent awe, I hail the sacred morn,
>   That scarcely wakes while all the fields are still;
>   A soothing calm on every breeze is borne,
>   A graver murmur echoes from the hill,
>   And softer sings the linnet from the thorn.
>   Hail, light serene!   Hail, sacred Sabbath morn!'"

It was under the spell of the emotions which guided him to the "large upper room" on this occasion that Bryant penned the following lines, which reveal more of his "inner life" than any outside of his household ever learned probably from his lips.

THE CLOUD ON THE WAY.

"See before us, in our journey, broods a mist upon the ground;
Thither leads the path we walk in, blending with that gloomy
    bound.
Never eye hath pierced its shadows to the mystery they screen;
Those who once have passed within it never more on earth are
    seen.
Now it seems to stoop beside us, now at seeming distance lowers,
Leaving banks that tempt us onward with summer green and
    flowers.
Yet it blots the way forever; there our journey ends at last;
Into that dark cloud we enter, and are gathered to the past.
Thou who, in this flinty pathway, leading through a stranger
    land,
Passest down the rocky valley, walking with me hand in hand,
Which of us shall be the soonest folded to that dim unknown?
Which shall leave the other walking in this flinty path alone?
Even now I see thee shudder, and thy cheek is white with fear,
And thou clingest to my side as comes that darkness sweeping
    near.
'Here,' thou sayst, 'the path is rugged, sown with thorns that
    wound the feet.
But the sheltered glens are lovely, and the rivulet's song is
    sweet;
Roses breathe from tangled thickets; lilies bend from ledges
    brown;
Pleasantly between the pelting showers the sunshine gushes
    down;
Dear are those who walk beside us, they whose looks and voices
    make
All this rugged region cheerful, till I love it for their sake.
Far be yet the hour that takes me where that chilly shadow lies,
From the things I know and love and from the sight of loving
    eyes!'
So thou murmurest, fearful one; but see, we tread a rougher
    way;
Fainter glow the gleams of sunshine that upon the dark rocks
    play;
Rude winds strew the faded flowers upon the crags o'er which we
    pass;

Banks of verdure when we reach them hiss with tufts of withered
    grass.
One by one we miss the voices which we loved so well to hear;
One by one the kindly faces in that shadow disappear.
Yet upon the mist before us fix thine eyes with closer view;
See beneath its sullen skirts, the rosy morning glimmers through.
One whose feet the thorns have wounded passed that barrier and
    came back,
With a glory on his footsteps lighting yet the dreary track.
Boldly enter where He entered, all that seems but darkness here
When thou once hast passed beyond it, haply shall be crystal-
    clear.
Viewed from that serener realm, the walks of human life may
    lie,
Like the page of some familiar volume, open to thine eye;
Haply, from the o'erhanging shadow, thou mayst stretch an un-
    seen hand,
To support the wavering steps that print with blood the rugged
    land.
Haply leaning o'er the pilgrim, all unweeting thou art near;
Thou mayst whisper words of warning or of comfort in his ear
Till, beyond the border where that brooding mystery bars the
    sight
Those whom thou hast fondly cherished, stand with thee in peace
    and light.''

Though Bryant's poetry is mainly devoted to
the illustration of some pious thought, or to the
translation of some of the spiritual sentiments
which he found concealed in nature's mystic ver-
nacular, no one could infer from any poem he ever
wrote the denomination of Christians with which
he was most in sympathy. Any one of them
might have claimed him, as all claim Moses and
the Prophets.

Dr. Bellows, his pastor during the later years of
his life, has spoken with authority of his religious

character in the discourse pronounced at his funeral.
"A devoted lover of religious liberty, he was an
equal lover of religion itself — not in any precise
dogmatic form, but in its righteousness, reverence,
and charity. What his theology was, you may
safely infer from his regular and long attendance
in this place of Christian worship. Still he was
not a dogmatist, but preferred practical piety and
working virtue to all modes of faith. What was
obvious in him for twenty years past was an
increasing respect and devotion to religious institutions, and a more decided Christian quality in his
faith. I think he had never been a communicant
in any church until he joined ours, fifteen years
ago. From that time, nobody so regular in his
attendance on public worship, in wet and dry,
cold and heat, morning and evening, until the very
last month of his life. The increasing sweetness
and beneficence of his character, meanwhile, must
have struck his familiar friends. His last years
were his devoutest and most humane years. He became beneficent as he grew able to be so, and his
hand was open to all just need and to many un-
reasonable claimants."

Bryant showed little taste for metaphysical studies or speculations. He came into the possession
of the most profound and important truths, by
sheltering his judgment from worldly and selfish
influences, and by extirpating all evil and unworthy proclivities. By making his soul a fitting
dwelling-place, wisdom sought its hospitality. But

he trusted himself rarely to the open sea of speculation. His mind was perfectly inaccessible to crotchets. When he went to war he always equipped himself with proved weapons. Yet he was always open to new ideas, and the farthest in the world from believing that man had reached the limits of knowledge in any direction. No man ever had a profounder sense of responsibility for what he taught; and while he listened patiently when necessary to the dreams and speculations of enthusiasts, he never asked any such indulgence from his readers. He never professed to be wiser than everybody else, nor to see farther. He never shocked the most simple-minded of his readers by startling novelties in thought or expression. He never plucked truths before they were ripe. , He never confounded the chemist's laboratory with the kitchen, nor served his readers' table with the products of the crucible, or the retort.

Bryant shrank from ostentation of any kind, and especially from any ostentation of charity, which in its gospel acceptation is the highest practical consummation of the religious life. His charity was like his own

> . . . "clear spring that midst its herbs
> Wells softly forth and wandering steeps the roots
> Of half the mighty forest, tells no tale
> Of all the good it does."

There was no phariseeism of any description in Bryant's make-up. He treated every neighbor as if he were an angel in disguise sent to test his loyalty to the golden rule. For sixteen years, and until his death, he was the principal contributor to a Christmas treat for the inmates of the North Hempstead poor-house. Mr. Cline was instructed by him to distribute the surplus of his garden among his neighbors, and he informs me that he has sometimes given as many as eighty chickens to the poor of the village on Thanksgiving Day under Mr. Bryant's directions.

Mr. Cline one day expressed a desire to Bryant that some one would prepare a good book of prayers for schools. Bryant had one which, with a few changes, he thought would answer. Finding it acceptable to Mr. Cline, he ordered sixty copies for the village school at his own expense. In the holidays he always contributed liberally for the expenses of an entertainment to the school children. The winter before the family went to Europe in 1857, they remained in Roslyn until February. On one of the coldest nights of the season, towards midnight, Bryant was awakened by a noise under his window. On opening it he found there the son of one of his neighbors, intoxicated and noisy. Bryant went down to him and urged him to go home. To this he seemed indisposed. Finally, by dint of some management and many entreaties, and by bearing him company, Bryant succeeded in getting the young man to his own door, half a mile or more distant. No one knew that he had this failing; and rather than expose him to the gossip of the servants and neighborhood, Bryant passed a couple of hours of a fearfully inclement night, at the risk of his own life, in trying to save the life as well as character of this young man, who was in danger of freezing to death if left to himself.

He was not in the habit of giving presents, even to his family. He gave when and what seemed to him to be needed. Neither did he care for presents himself, except a box of candy now and then, which always pleased him, and with which he was always sure to be well provided on holiday occasions.

As he prospered in his basket and his store, his heart seemed proportionately to swell with sensibility for the well-being of others, which he testified in a thousand ways, of which no account has ever been made except in the Book of Life. He learned to regard his worldly possessions as a trust to be consecrated to holy uses. When they abounded he gave bountifully, while in his hand-to-hand struggles with poverty during the first forty or fifty years of his life he sent no one empty away. Two costly institutions founded by him, one at Roslyn and the other at Cummington, will remain, for generations to come, monuments of his judicious munificence.[1]

He had no great faith, however, in the charity that limits itself to the relief of physical suffering and material wants, except in so far as it might affect the benefactor. Knowing that sorrow and privation had their own proper uses in the divine economy,

[1] A fine library and reading-room in each of these places were built, and liberally stocked with books, entirely at his expense.

and that we have only to change ourselves to change
our environment, he regarded it as a less profitable
employment of time and money to spend them in
relieving cases of individual distress than, by his
example and pen, to enlighten and purify whole
communities by demonstrating and commending
sounder principles of thought and conduct.

Bolingbroke says in one of his letters from La
Source, " I have a friend in this country who has
been devoted these five and twenty years to judicial
astrology. I begin to believe, for I know not
whether I should wish it or no, that he will have
the mortification, before he dies, of finding out
that a quarter of an hour well employed in examining principles would have saved him a quarter of a
century spent about consequences."

Bryant had much the same notion of the efficacy of
the charities of the purse which essay to change the
environment and not the individual, as compared
with the charity which changes the environment by
first changing the individual. In a letter to Miss
Dewey, he discloses this view pretty clearly in some
comments upon the career of an eminent contemporary.

" I have read every word of Canon Kingsley's
' Life and Letters,' and thought better of him for
reading it. He was very decided in his opinions,
but very modest in his notion of his own merits;
and though conservative in regard to the Anglican
church, tolerant and kind to those who did not
agree with him. He was a friend to the humbler

classes, and a most faithful and sympathetic pastor, wearing out his life for his flock; yet I cannot see that he contemplated doing them any good, save by personal effort and kind attentions. I do not find in any part of the memoir that he sought to improve the institutions under which the working class in England had been kept poor and degraded."

Bryant's notion was that as an hour's sun would accomplish more than all the fires in all the fireplaces in the land to warm and light it, so any effort of a man of genius like Kingsley to correct public abuses, to define and to smooth the paths of duty to all classes, to remove restrictions, and to adjust the burdens of government more equitably among them, might have reached and ameliorated the conditions of millions, to whom his name was and still is as completely unknown as that of the woman who washed the feet of Jesus with her tears and wiped them with her hair.

With friends whom he knew, or with people whom he respected, Bryant was genial, chatty, and entertaining, but never familiar. Even with his family, whom he always treated with the utmost tenderness and consideration, he was reserved; while expressing what he thought, rarely revealing what he felt. Like Milton, he was frugal though not grudging of praise; and one might have known him for years without receiving from him any special evidence of the regard which he really entertained. He had no objection to lend his presence where it would serve a useful purpose, and he rarely refused an

application from any charitable or religious organization; but he had a more than ordinary aversion
to being made a spectacle of to gratify any one's
vanity or ambition, his own least of all. These
lines of Shakespeare seem to have been always in
his mind, if not on his lips : —

> " I love the people
> But do not like to stage me to their eyes.
> Though it do, well, I do not relish well
> Their loud applause and aves vehement;
> Nor do I think the man of safe discretion
> That does affect it."

Neither was he a " respecter of persons." He
sought no one's acquaintance or society because of
his wealth, or rank, or prominence. His most intimate friends were among quiet not to say obscure
and unpretending people. There was no social
ladder leading to or from his house. It was what
they were, not who they were, that determined him
in his choice of friends.

" I remember," observes Mr. Godwin, " when
Charles Dickens was here, Mr. Bryant was invited
by a prominent citizen to meet him at dinner, but
declined. ' That man,' he said, ' has known me
for years without asking me to his house, and I am
not going to be made a stool-pigeon to attract birds
of passage that may be flying about."

To Dana, who had given some one a letter of introduction to him, he said : " I shall be glad to be
useful to him in any way; but how can you who
know me ask me to get acquainted with anybody.

I do not know that I ever got acquainted with any-body, of set purpose, in my life. The three things most irksome to me in my transactions with the world are, to owe money, to ask a favor, and to seek an acquaintance. The few excellent friends I have I acquired I scarcely know how — certainly by no assiduity of my own."

Bryant had a marvelous memory. His familiarity with the English poets was such that when at sea, where he was always too ill to read much, he would beguile the time by reciting to himself page after page from favorite poems. He assured me that he had never made a voyage long enough to exhaust his resources. I once proposed to send for a copy of a magazine in which a new poem of his was announced to appear. "You need not send for it," said he, "I can give it to you." "Then you have a copy with you," said I. "No," he replied, "but I can recall it," and thereupon proceeded immediately to write it out. I congratulated him upon having such a faithful memory. "If allowed a little time," he replied, "I could recall every line of poetry I have ever written."

He rated his memory at its true value, however, and never abused it. It was a blooded steed which he never degraded to the uses of a pack-horse. Hence he was fastidious about his reading as about his company, believing there was no worse thief than a bad book ; but he never tired of writers who have best stood the test of time. He had little taste for historical reading. Indeed, the habits of his mind were not at all in sympathy with the inductive method of reaching new truths or propagating them. He often deplored the increasing neglect of the old English classics, which our modern facilities for printing were displacing. Johnson's " Lives of the Poets " was one of his favorite books. Pope, who has educated more poets in the art of verse-making than any other modern author, was, from early youth, his pocket companion. I think he had studied him more carefully than any other English writer, and was specially impressed by his wit.

One day, as I was looking over the books on the shelves of his library at Roslyn, he called my attention to his position. " There," said he, " I have fallen quite accidentally into the precise attitude in which Pope is commonly represented, with his forehead resting on his fingers." He then got up to look for an illustration among his books. He did not find what he sought, but he brought two other editions, each representing Pope with an abundance of hair on his head, one an old folio containing a collection of Pope's verses, written before he was twenty-five years of age.

I asked him if he had seen the new edition of Pope's works which Elwin was editing. He said he had not, nor heard of it. I then told him that Elwin left Pope scarcely a single estimable personal quality, and had stripped him of a good share of the literary laurels which he had hitherto worn in peace. He promptly said that he did not care to see it; that he was not disposed to trust such a judgment, however ingeniously defended, and quoted Young's lines on Pope, "Sweet as his own Homer, his life melodious as his verse." That, said he, is the judgment of a contemporary. He then read some lines from other poets in farther defense of his favorite. He was unwilling to have his idea of Pope disturbed, and when I suggested that he should get Elwin, he said, "No, I want no better edition than Warburton's, the edition that was in my father's library, and which I read when a boy." Bryant's admiration of Pope is the more remarkable, as two characters more unlike could not be readily imagined.

Bryant took but little note of any but moral distinctions among men. Mere worldly rank impressed him as little as any man I ever knew, though he appreciated, and no one more justly, the qualities that merited such distinction. I was once his guest at Roslyn with a member of the English peerage, who at the close of the first repast after our arrival presumed upon the privilege accorded to persons of his rank at home to rise first and dismiss the table. Mr. Bryant joined me on our way to the parlor, and with an expression of undisguised astonishment asked me, "Did you see that?" I replied that I did, and, with a view of extenuating the gentleman's offense as much as I could, said that he evidently thought he was only exercising one of the recognized prerogatives of his order. "Well," he said, "he will have no opportunity of repeating it here ; " and he was as good as his word, for during the remainder of our sojourn, no one was left in doubt whose prerogative it was in that house to dismiss the table. Some weeks later he alluded to this incident, and quoted from a conversation he had once held with Fenimore Cooper his strictures upon this exasperating assumption of the titled classes in some communities of the Old World. He was willing that others should adopt any standard that pleased them best by which to rate their fellows, himself included, but he would not accept directly or indirectly for himself any other standard than that which, so far as he knew, his Maker would apply.

Bryant was a man of the most unassailable dignity. It was impossible even for his familiars to take any liberties with him. His influence upon all who entered his presence was akin to that attributed by Cowley to the daughter of Saul.

> "Merab with spacious beauty filled the sight
> But too much awe chastened the bold delight
> Like a calm sea which to the enlarged view,
> Gives pleasure but gives fear and reverence too."

"While preparing for college occurred an event," says Bryant, " which I remember with regret. My grandfather Snell had always been substantially kind to me and ready to forward any plan for my education, but when I did what in his judgment was wrong, he reprimanded me with a harshness which was not so well judged as it was probably deserved. I had committed some foolish blunder, and he was chiding with even more than his usual severity; I turned and looked at him with a steady gaze. 'What are you staring at?' he asked, 'did you never see me before?' 'Yes,' I answered, 'I have seen you many times before.' He had never before heard a disrespectful word from my lips. He turned and moved away, and never reproved me again in that manner, but never afterward seemed to interest himself so much as before in any matter that concerned me." It is harder to forgive a person we have wronged than one who has wronged us. That is probably the explanation of the change in the grandfather's manner and deportment towards his refractory grandchild. The heavy armor of puritanical Philistinism was no proof against the sling and pebbles of this stripling, conscious of deserving and brave enough to insist upon better treatment.

CHAPTER XII.

LAST DAYS.

THE man who knew so well as Bryant how to live must have known as well how to die. It is commonly but too true that "*un mourant a bien peu de chose à dire quand il ne parle ni par faiblesse ni par vanité*," but when Bryant was summoned to take "his chamber in the silent halls of death," he took with him all his noble faculties, and neither feebleness nor vanity were among them.

"In years he seemed but not impaired by years."

It would have been, therefore, in the highest degree interesting and instructive to have watched him in the process of putting the last enemy under his feet, and to have marked the impression which the immediate prospect of shedding his mortality and of putting on immortality would produce on such a rare personality. But this was a privilege which Providence did not see fit to accord. To his closing days there was to be no twilight. He had accepted an invitation to deliver an address at the unveiling of a statue to Mazzini, the Italian patriot, in Central Park, on Wednes-

day, the 29th of May, 1878.   He had not been
feeling well for several days, which, however, did
not prevent his spending the morning at his office
in the discharge of customary duties.   After a
light luncheon he was driven to Central Park.
The day was warm.   The sun shone so brightly
that a friend insisted, though with but partial success, upon sheltering his head with an umbrella.
When he had finished his discourse he appeared
quite exhausted, and should have returned immediately to his home.   He was too amiable to decline an invitation from Mr. James Grant Wilson
to accompany him across the Park to his house, and
on foot.   They ascended the steps together.   What
then occurred has been thus circumstantially reported by Mr. Wilson.

"As we approached my house, about four o'clock,
Mr. Bryant was recalling the scenes of the previous year
on the occasion of the President's visit as such to New
York, and he was still, I think, cheerfully conversing on
that subject as we walked up arm in arm, and entered
the vestibule.   Disengaging my arm, I took a step in
advance to open the inner door, and during the few seconds, without the slightest warning of any kind, the venerable poet, while my back was turned, dropped my
daughter's hand and fell suddenly backward through the
open outer door, striking his head on the stone platform
of the front steps, with one half of his body still lying
in the vestibule.   I turned just in time to see the sick-
ening sight of the silvered head striking the stone, and
springing to his side hastily raised him up.   He was
unconscious, and I supposed that he was dead.   Ice

water was immediately applied to the head, and, with the assistance of a neighbor's son and the servants, he was carried into the parlor. A soft pillow was placed at one end for his head, as he lay unconscious at full length on the sofa. He was restless, and in a few min-utes sat up, and drank the contents of a goblet filled with iced sherry, which partially restored him, and he asked with a bewildered look, 'Where am I? I do not feel at all well. Oh, my head! my head!' accom-panying the words by raising his right hand to his fore-head. He now recognized me, and looked curiously around the room, still with a dazed and uncertain ex-pression: 'Was it not here that President Hayes was received?' again exclaiming, 'How strangely I feel; I don't know what is the matter with me this afternoon. My head! my head!' Still with a bewildered manner, as if he were struggling for the recovery of his reason, he fixed his eyes keenly on me, and apparently with an idea that something had happened to him, and with a view to relieving our terrible anxiety concerning him, he attempted to make some pleasant remarks. 'Where did you say you were building?' 'Is that not one of Audubon's pictures?' 'How many children have you?' 'Where are you going with your family this summer?' are a few of the questions that he asked. The gentleman, as was remarked of Sir Walter Scott, may be said to have survived the genius. Declining to retire to a sleeping-room and to permit us to send for our own or his physician, he expressed a wish to be taken home. He objected to going in a carriage, saying he preferred a street car. Although still not quite him-self, he expressed his wishes in a most emphatic man-ner, and about 4.30 said he would like to start. We

accordingly walked together to the corner and entered a
Madison Avenue car, and whenever the car stopped to
take on or let off a passenger he would ask, ' Where
are we now? ' and manifested much impatience to reach
his residence. For some time he held a few pieces of
silver in his hand, but when I quietly asked him to replace the money in his pocket he did so. Once on our
way down he added my name to the usual inquiry
of ' Where are we now? ' Calling a carriage, we
stepped into it from the car at Seventeenth Street, the
conductor showing us every attention, and drove rapidly
to his house. Once only on our way did he speak, and
then to remark, ' I am a very sick man.' On our arrival his mind again wandered, and looking up he said,
' Whose house is this? What street are we in? Why
did you bring me here? ' Without replying, I sooth-
ingly said, We will step in since we are here, and rest for
a few minutes, and so gently led him up the steps.
Reaching the inner door he mechanically took out his
pass-key, opened it, and returned the key to his pocket,
when he passed into the parlor, and through to the din-
ing-room, where he sat down in a large easy-chair. At
the request of his niece, Miss Fairchild, I assisted him
upstairs to the library, where he lay down on the lounge,
and then went for Dr. John F. Gray, who returned with
me immediately, and on examining the patient said the
fall was produced by syncope, and had caused concus-
sion of the brain, but not necessarily fatal. This was
before six o'clock. At seven he came again, accompanied by Dr. Carnochan, the eminent surgeon, whose
views, I understood, coincided with those of Mr. Bryant's physician. Mr. and Mrs. Graham and other intimate family friends arrived, and I then took my leave
a little before eight o'clock."

In Dr. Gray's report of the case, he said : —

" Mr. Bryant during the first few days would get up
and walk about the library or sit in his favorite chair.
He would occasionally say something about diet and air.
When his daughter Julia arrived from Atlantic City,
where she had been for her health, she thought her
father recognized her, but it is uncertain how far he
recognized her or any of his friends. The family were
hopeful and made the most of every sign of consciousness or recognition. On the eighth day after the fall,
hæmorrhage took place in the brain, resulting in paraly-
sis, technically called hemiplegia, which extended down
the right side of the body. After this he was most of
the time comatose. He was unable to speak, and when
he attempted to swallow, his food lodged in his larynx
and choked him. He was greatly troubled with phlegm
and could not clear his throat. There was only that one
attack of hæmorrhage of the brain, and that was due to
what is called traumatic inflammation."

For fourteen sad and tedious days, Bryant thus
lingered while life was ebbing

> . . . "unmarked and silent
> "As the slow neap-tide leaves yon stranded galley.
> Late she rocked merrily at the least impulse
> That wind or wave could give; but now her keel
> Is settling on the sand; her mast has ta'en
> An angle with the sky from which it shifts not.
> Each wave receding shakes her less and less
> Till bedded on the strand she shall remain
> Useless and motionless." . . .

At half-past five on the morning of the 12th of
June, that heart which for eighty-four years had
never rested from its labors ceased to beat.

The news of Bryant's death produced an impression only to be expected from the death of one who had long been regarded as the first citizen of the republic. His genius and his virtues were the theme of every periodical, of every pulpit, and of every literary society in the land. For a time, little was to be seen or heard but these swirling eddies which marked the place where the ship went down. The flags of the city where he died and of the shipping were raised at half-mast, his portrait was displayed in all the shop windows, and his writings were in special demand at every bookstore and library.

"There is probably no eminent man in the country," wrote Mr. George William Curtis in "Harper's Monthly," "upon whose life and genius and career the verdict of his fellow-citizens would be more immediate and unanimous. His character and life had a simplicity and austerity of outline that had become universally familiar, like a neighboring mountain or the sea. His convictions were very strong, and his temper uncompromising; he was independent beyond most Americans. He was an editor and a partisan; but he held politics and all other things subordinate to the truth and the common welfare, and his earnestness and sincerity and freedom from selfish ends took the sting of personality from his opposition, and constantly placated all who, like him, sought lofty and virtuous objects. Those who watched the character of his influence upon public affairs, and who saw him daily moving among us a venerable citizen noiselessly going his way, as they marked the hot and bitter strife of politics, could not but recall the picture by the French painter Couture, of the ' Decadence of Rome,' in which the grave figure of the older Roman stands softly contemplating the riotous license and luxury of a later day. Bryant carried with him the mien and the atmosphere of antique public virtue. He seemed a living embodiment of that simplicity and severity and dignity which we associate with the old republics. A wise stranger would have called him a man nurtured in republican air upon republican traditions."

The late Dr. Holland, commenting upon the loss the world had sustained in the death of Bryant in " Scribner's Monthly," of which he was the editor, wrote : —

" By reason of his venerable age, his unquestioned genius, his pure and lofty character, his noble achievments in letters, his great influence as a public journalist, and his position as a pioneer in American literature, William Cullen Bryant had become, without a suspicion of the fact in his own modest thought, the principal citizen of the great republic. By all who knew him and by millions who never saw him he was held in the most affectionate reverence. When he died, therefore, and was buried from sight, he left a sense of personal loss in all worthy American hearts.

" He never sought notoriety, and was never notorious. The genuine fame that came to him came apparently unsought. It grew with his growth and strengthened with his strength, and at the last it became a shadow of the man that lengthened momently across the earth as his sun descended. Nothing can be purer, nothing more natural, nothing more enduring than his reputation ; for it was based in real genius, genuine character, and legitimate achievement. He never postured himself before the public; he shrank from all thought of producing a sensation; he had the humblest opinion of himself; and his fame was simply one of the things that he would not help and could not hinder. He was a man of character, a man of business and affairs, and a poet — or perhaps he was first of all a poet, and afterward all that made up a complete manhood. These are the aspects of the man which seem most worth talking about.

"Mr. Bryant was a poet who could take care of himself and get a living. He could not only do this, but he could do a wise and manly part in guiding the politics of the country. He could not only manage his own private and family affairs in a prosperous way, but he could discharge his duties as a citizen and a member of society. In his own personal character and history he associated probity with genius, purity with art, and the sweetest Christianity with the highest culture. He has proved to all the younger generation of poets that hysterics are not inspiration, that improvidence is not an unerring sign of genius, that Christian conviction and Christian character are not indications of weakness, but are rather a measure of strength, and that a man may be a poet and a poet a man. So much of a certain sort of eccentricity has been associated with the poetic temperament and with poetic pursuits, that, in some minds the possession of practical gifts and homely virtues is supposed to invalidate all claims to genius. If Mr. Bryant's life had accomplished nothing more than to prove the falsity of this wretched notion, it would have been a fruitful one."

It was to multitudes a disappointment that respect for his often expressed wishes compelled the family to decline the *supervacuos honores* of an ostentatious public funeral. On the 14th, his remains were taken to All Saints Church, where the poet had worshiped for many years. The occasion attracted a vast throng from every rank of life, and far exceeding the seating capacities of the church. After the customary devotional exercises, the pastor, Dr. Bellows, delivered a feeling and impressive discourse, from which I allow myself to make a single extract : —

"It is the glory of this man that his character outshone even his great talent and his large fame. Distinguished equally for his native gifts and his consummate culture, his poetic inspiration and his exquisite art, he is honored and loved to-day even more for his stainless purity of life, his unswerving rectitude of will, his devotion to the higher interests of his race, his unfeigned patriotism, and his broad humanity. It is remarkable that with none of the arts of popularity a man so little dependent on others' appreciation, so self-subsistent and so retiring, who never sought or accepted office, who had little taste for coöperation, and no bustling zeal in ordinary philanthropy, should have drawn to himself the confidence, the honor, and reverence of a great metropolis, and become, perhaps it is not too much to say, our first citizen. It was in spite of a constitutional reserve, a natural distaste for crowds and public occasions, and a somewhat chilled bearing towards his kind, that he achieved by the force of his great merit and solid worth this triumph over the heart of his generation. The purity of the snow that enveloped him was more

observed than its coldness, and his fellow-citizens believed that a fire of zeal for truth, justice, and human
rights burned steadily at the heart of this lofty personality, though it never flamed or smoked. And they
were right! Beyond all thirst for fame or poetic honor
lay in Bryant the ambition of virtue. Reputation he
did not despise, but virtue he revered and sought with
all his heart. He had an intense self-reverence that
made his own good opinion of his own motives and
actions absolutely essential. And though little tempted
by covetousness, envy, worldliness, or love of power, he
had his own conscious difficulties to contend with, a
temper not without turbulence, a susceptibility to in-
juries, a contempt for the moral weaknesses of others.
But he labored incessantly at self-knowledge and self-
control, and attained equanimity and gentleness to a
marked degree. Let none suppose that the persistent
force of his will, his incessant industry, his perfect consistency and coherency of life and character were not
backed by strong passions. With a less consecrated
purpose, a less reverent love of truth and goodness, he
might easily have become acrid, vindictive, or selfishly
ambitious. But he kept his body under and, a far more
difficult task for him, his spirit in subjection. God had
given him a wonderful balance of faculties in a marvelously harmonious frame. His spirit wore a light and
lithe vesture of clay that never burdened him. His
senses were perfect at fourscore. His eyes needed no
glasses, his hearing was exquisitely fine. His alertness
was the wonder of his contemporaries. He outwalked
men of middle age. His tastes were so simple as to be
almost ascetic. Milk and cereals and fruits were his
chosen diet. He had no vices and no approach to

them, and he avoided any and every thing that could
ever threaten him with the tyranny of the senses or of
habit. Regular in all his habits he retained his youth
almost to the last. His power of work never abated,
and the herculean translation of Homer, which was the
amusement of the last lustre of his long and busy life,
showed not only no senility or decline in artistic skill,
but no decrease of intellectual or physical endurance."

These ceremonies over at the church, the remains were immediately taken to Roslyn for inter-
ment in the cemetery which Bryant had himself
been largely instrumental in having consecrated
to the public use, attended by the surviving members of his family and a few of his more intimate
friends, where they were laid beside those of the
wife and mother at whose grave he had shed the
tears of a husband and father twelve years before.[1]

Dr. Bellows availed himself of a pause in the
preparations to commend to the villagers and other
persons assembled some of the lessons of Bryant's
life by reading selections from his poems which had
been made for the occasion by Mr. John C. Bryant, the poet's brother. He then read some ex-

[1] It was a gratification to Bryant's friends that, in the time of
his death, one of his long cherished wishes had been realized.
In one of his sweetest poems, written as early as 1825, he expressed the hope

> " That when *he* came to lie
>   At rest within the ground
> 'T were pleasant ; that in the flowery June
> When brooks send up a cheerful tune
>   And groves a joyous sound
> The Sexton's hand *his* grave to make,
> The rich, green mountain turf should break."

tracts from the Scriptures, made a brief prayer, and the coffin was lowered to the place prepared for it.

There was probably no time in Bryant's life on earth when he occupied so large a space in the heart of the nation or so much of its attention as in the remaining months of the year succeeding his death. It was not till he no longer walked among men, till his tongue was still, and the press had ceased to be freighted with his strengthening messages of wisdom and patriotic faith, that his countrymen began to realize the magnitude of the loss they had sustained, and the high rank he would take among those for whom, by a noble climax, Virgil reserved the Elysian Fields.

> "Patriots were there in freedom's battle slain,
>   Priests whose long lives were closed without a stain,
>   Bards worthy him who breathed the poet's mind,
>   Founders of arts that dignify mankind,
>   And lovers of our race, whose labors gave
>   Their names a memory that defies the grave." [1]

He had left this world with no wish or ambition unsatisfied. Life to him had been in no sense a disappointment. He had never allowed himself to desire what it did not please the Master to send to him, nor to repine for anything that was denied him. "Thy will be done," had been the daily prayer, not only of his lips but of his heart and life.

[1] As rendered into English by Bryant himself.

For months, commemorative addresses followed each other in convenient succession. That which was delivered before the New York Historical Society by George William Curtis is entitled to a permanent place in our literature.

The Century Association, which Bryant had helped to found, and of which at the time of his death he was the president, testified their respect for his memory in a special meeting held on the 12th of November following the poet's death, at which poems from the pens of Bayard Taylor, then Minister of the United States at Berlin, Richard H. Stoddard, and E. C. Stedman were read, and an address was delivered by the writer of these pages.

Bryant left two children: the elder, the wife of Mr. Parke Godwin, for many years associated with him in the editorship of the " Evening Post," and Miss Julia Sands Bryant, each of whom has been the inspiration of several of their father's sweetest poems.

Mr. Bryant was possessed of a very handsome estate, which he devised mainly to his two children by a will executed on the 6th of December, 1872,[1] but he was to a large extent his own executor, having alienated most of his real estate before his death in accordance with the provisions of his will. The " Evening Post," of which he was the half proprietor, was sold two or three years after his death for about $900,000.

[1] Appendix B.

In the foregoing pages I have attempted to portray the more prominent features of the most symmetrical man I have ever known. I may be suspected of having indited a eulogy instead of a biography; of trying to produce a picture that shall be all light and no shadow; of exhibiting to the world a monster of perfections. If I am laying myself open to such suspicions, I do not know what I can change to avoid them, without injustice to my theme. I have not sought to conceal anything about Mr. Bryant of good or bad that was known to me. I have represented his life as it was revealed to me and as I appreciated it.

Bryant was born to the same sinful inheritance as the rest of us; but I can say of him with perfect truth, that with his faults he was always at war. No one better than he knew the enemies with which the human heart is always besieged, — the enemies of his own household; and few men ever fought them more valiantly, more persistently, or more successfully. Those who knew him only in his later years would scarcely believe that he had been endowed by nature with a very quick and passionate temper. He never entirely overcame it, but he held every impulse of his nature to such a rigorous accountability, that few have ever suspected the struggles with which he purchased the self-control which constituted one of the conspicuous graces of his character. Bryant had his faults, but he made of them agents of purification. He learned from them humility and faith, a wise distrust of himself, and an unfaltering trust in Him through whose aid he was strengthened to keep them in abeyance. By God's help he converted the tears of his angels into pearls.

It was this constant and successful warfare upon every unworthy and degrading propensity that sought an asylum in his heart that made him such a moral force in the country, that invested any occasion to which he lent his presence with an especial dignity, that gave to his personal example a peculiar power and authority, that made his career a model which no one can contemplate without being edified, which no one can study closely without an inclination to imitate, and which no one can imitate without strengthening some good impulses and weakening the hold upon him of every bad one.

APPENDIX A.

REMINISCENCES OF THE "EVENING POST."

BY WILLIAM CULLEN BRYANT.

Extracted from the Evening Post of November 15, 1851, with additions and corrections by the writer.

On the 15th inst. closed the first half century of the *Evening Post*. It may not be without entertainment to our readers, and, perhaps, not entirely without instruction, if we now take a brief survey of its past history; in other words, if we write the Life of the *Evening Post*.

The first number of the *Evening Post* appeared on the 16th of November, 1801, printed on a sheet a little more than a quarter of the present size of the journal. It was established by William Coleman, a barrister from Massachusetts, then in the prime of manhood, who had won the good will of the distinguished federalists of that day — Hamilton, King, Jay, and many others, worthy by their talents and personal character to be the associates of these eminent men. They saw in Mr. Coleman a combination of qualities which seemed to fit him for the conductor of a daily political paper in those times of fervid and acrimonious controversy, and several of the most public-spirited of them furnished him the means of entering upon the undertaking.

Mr. Coleman was a man of robust make, of great appearance of physical strength, and of that temperament which some physiologists call the sanguine. He was fond of pleasure, but capable of exertion when the occasion required it, and, as he was not disinclined to controversy, the occasion often arose. His temper was generous and sincere, his manners kind and courteous; he was always ready to meet more than half way the advances of an enemy; a kind or appealing word disarmed his resentment at once, and a pitiful story, even though a little improbable, always moved his compassion. He delighted in athletic exercises before his health failed, and while yet residing in Massachusetts is said, in Buckingham's Reminiscences, to have skated in an evening from Greenfield to Northampton, a distance of twenty miles. He was naturally courageous, and having entered into a dispute, he never sought to decline any of its consequences. His reading lay much in the lighter literature of our language, and a certain elegance of scholarship which he had the reputation of possessing was reckoned among his qualifications as a journalist.

The original prospectus of the *Evening Post*, though somewhat measured in its style, was well written. The editor, while avowing his attachment to the federal party, acknowledges that " in each party are honest and virtuous men," and expresses his persuasion that the people need only to be well informed to decide public questions rightly. He seems to contemplate a wider sphere of objects than most secular newspapers of the present day, and speaks of his design " to inculcate just principles in religion," as well as in " morals and politics." Some attempt was made to carry out this intention. In one of the earlier numbers is a communication in reply to a heresy avowed by the *American Citizen*, a democratic daily paper of that time, in which it had been maintained that the soul was material, and that death was a sleep of the mind as well as the body. Still later, in an editorial article, appeared a somewhat elaborate discussion of the design of the Revelation of St. John.

New York, at that time, contained a little more than sixty thousand inhabitants, and scarcely extended north of the City Hall and its Park. Beyond, along Broadway, were then country houses and green fields. That vast system of foreign and internal intercourse, those facilities of communication by sail, by steamers, by railways, the advertisements of which now fill column after column in our largest daily newspapers, was not then dreamed of; and the few ships and sloops soliciting freight and passengers did not furnish advertisements enough to fill a single column in the small sheet of the *Evening Post*. Yet, the names which appear in the advertisements of its very first number indicate a certain permanence in the mercantile community. The very first advertisers in the first number of the paper are Hoffman & Seaton. In the same sheet appear the names of N. L. & G. Griswold, names which, extending over a space of fifty years, connect the commencement of the nineteenth century, on which we have now entered, with the last half of the eighteenth. Here, too, appear the advertisements of Frederick Depeyster, of William Neilson, Richard & John Thorne, Bethune & Smith, Gouverneur & Kemble, Archibald Gracie, and John Murray. At a later period, in the first year of the paper, came in the names of Minturn & Champlin, of Aspinwall, McVicar, and Oakey.

T. & J. Swords, whose names are familiar to all readers of American publications, then had their bookstore at 99 Pearl Street; J. Mesier sold books at 107 Pearl Street; Brown & Stansbury, at 114 Water Street; George F. Hopkins and D. Longworth, familiar names, were then following the same vocation, and J. W. Fenn was offering the American Ladies' Pocket Book for 1802, just published at Philadelphia, in a long and elaborate advertisement, describing the elegant engravings with which it was embellished.

Among the advertisements in the early numbers of the paper are some which show that the domestic slave trade was then in existence in the State of New York. In one, "a young negro woman, twenty-one years of age," "capable of all kinds of work, and an excellent cook," was offered for sale, "for want of employment." A black woman, "twenty-six years of age, and a good cook," was offered for sale " on reasonable terms." The advertisers seem to have been willing to avoid publicity in this matter, for no names are given; but in the first of these cases, the purchaser is referred to the printer, and in the other, the name of the street and number of the house at which application is to be made are given.

In the outset, Mr. Coleman made an effort to avoid those personal controversies, which at the time were so common among conductors of party papers, and with which their columns were so much occupied. In the leading article of his first number, signed with his initials, he expresses his abhorrence of "personal virulence, low sarcasm, and verbal contentions with printers and editors," and his determination not to be diverted from "the line of temperate discussion." He found this resolution difficult to keep.

At that time, besides the *American Citizen*, published at New York, a democratic daily print was issued in Philadelphia, called the *Aurora*, with both of which the *Evening Post* soon found itself involved in unpleasant disputes. James Cheetham was the editor of the *American Citizen*. He is called by Bronson, conductor of the Philadelphia *United States Gazette*, in an affidavit, "an Englishman and a hatter," and appears to have been a man of coarse mind and manners, and not easily abashed. The occasional replies to his attacks in the *Evening Post* indicate that he kept up a pretty constant fire of small personalities. In the fourth number of the paper, the *Evening Post* answers an insinuation that a letter published in its columns was not authentic. The editor cautions "Mr. Cheetham" to beware of wantonly repeating the insinuation, protesting that he will not allow any impeachment of his veracity, and that he will not engage in a contest of abusive epithets. The editor of the *Aurora* was William Duane, a native of Ireland, whom the *Evening Post* stigmatized as "a low-bred foreigner." In all its contentions with these journals, as the organ of their party, the squabble is always with Mr. Cheetham and Mr. Duane, most commonly without any mention of their respective papers, and these men in return seem to have conducted the warfare in the same spirit, and to have thought that if they could but bring Mr. Coleman into personal discredit, they should have demolished the federal party.

The *Evening Post* of the 24th of November records the death of Philip Hamilton, eldest son of General Alexander Hamilton, in the twentieth year of his age — "murdered," says the editor, "in a duel." The practice of dueling is then denounced as a "horrid custom," the remedy for which must be "strong and pointed legislative interference," inasmuch " as fashion has placed it on a footing which nothing short of that can control." The editor himself belonged to the class with which fashion had placed it upon that footing, and was destined himself to be drawn by her power into the practice he so strongly deprecated.

The quarrel with Cheetham went on. On the next day, in a discussion occasioned by the duel in which young Hamilton fell, he mentioned Cheetham, and spoke of "the insolent vulgarity of that base wretch." At a subsequent period, the *Evening Post* went so far as, in an article reflecting severely upon Cheetham and Duane, to admit the following squib into its columns : —

> "Lie on Duane, lie on for pay,
> And Cheetham, lie thou too;
> More against truth you cannot say,
> Than truth can say 'gainst you."

These wranglings were continued a few years, until the *Citizen* made a personal attack upon Mr. Coleman of so outrageous a nature that he determined to notice it in another manner. Cheetham was challenged. He was ready enough in a war of words, but he had no inclination to pursue it to such a result. The friends of the parties interfered ; a sort of truce was patched up, and the *Citizen* consented to become more reserved in its future assaults.

A subsequent affair, of a similar nature, in which Mr. Coleman was engaged, was attended with a fatal termination. A Mr. Thompson had a difference with him which ended in a challenge. The parties met in Love Lane, now Twenty-first Street, and Thompson fell. He was brought, mortally wounded, to his sister's house in town ; he was laid at the door, the bell was rung, the family came out, and found him bleeding and near his death. He refused to name his antagonist, or give any account of the affair, declaring that everything which had been done was honorably done, and desired that no attempt should be made to seek out or molest his adversary. Mr. Coleman returned to New York and continued to occupy himself with his paper as before.

Such is the tradition which yet survives concerning the event of a combat to which the parties, who bore no previous malice to each other, were forced by the compulsion of that "fashion" against which one of them, on the threshold of his career as a journalist, had protested, even while indirectly recognizing its supremacy. The quarrel arose out of political differences, Mr. Coleman being in the opposition, and Mr. Thompson a friend of the administration.

When the *Evening Post* was established, William Dunlap, author of a History of the Arts of Design, and a History of the American Stage, whose books are in the hands of many of our readers, and whose paintings, after he returned to his original profession of an artist, many of them have seen, was manager of the Park Theatre. At that time the fashionable part of the New York population were much more frequent in their attendance at the theatre than now, and the *Evening Post* contained frequent theatrical criticisms, written with no little care, and dwelling at considerable length on the merits and faults of the performers. Public concerts were also criticised with some minuteness. Still lighter subjects sometimes engaged the attention of the editor. In 1802 the style of the ladies' dresses was such as to call forth, in certain quarters, remarks similar to those which are now often made on the Bloomer costume. On the 18th of May, 1802, the *Evening Post*, answering a female correspondent who asks why it has not, like the other newspapers, censured the prevailing mode, says: —

"Female dress, of the modern Parisian cut, however deficient in point of the ornament vulgarly called clothing, must at least be allowed to be not entirely without its advantages. If there is danger of its making the gentlemen too prompt to advance, let it not be unobserved that it fits the lady to escape. Unlike the dull drapery of petticoats worn some years since, but now banished to the nursery or kitchen, the present light substitute gives an air of celerity which seems to say — Catch me if you can."

We are not sufficiently skilled in the history of the modes of former days to inform our readers what was the substitute for petticoats which is here alluded to.

In the *Evening Post*, during the first twenty years of its existence, there is much less discussion of public questions by the editors than is now common in all classes of newspapers. The editorial articles were mostly brief, with but occasional exceptions, nor does it seem to have been regarded, as it now is, necessary for a daily paper to pronounce a prompt judgment on every question of a public nature the moment it arises. The annual message sent by Mr. Jefferson to Congress in 1801 was published in the *Evening Post* of the 12th of December, without a word of remark. On the 17th a writer who takes the signature of Lucius Crassus begins to examine it. The examination is continued through the whole winter, and finally, after having extended to eighteen numbers, is concluded on the 8th of April. The resolutions of General Smith, for the abrogation of discriminating duties, laid before Congress in the same winter, were published without comment, but a few days afterwards they were made the subject of a carefully written animadversion, continued through several numbers of that paper.

Mr. Coleman had no skill as a manager of property; he took little thought for the morrow; when he happened to have any money, it was spent freely, or given away, or somebody who would never return it contrived to borrow it. In a short time the finances of the *Evening Post* became greatly confused and embarrassed. From its first appearance, the journal bore, in a card at the bottom of its final column, the name of Michael Burnham, as the printer and publisher; he had, however, no property in the paper. Mr. Burnham was a young printer from Hartford, in Connecticut, a man of sense, probity, and decision, industrious and frugal, with an excellent capacity for business; in short, he was just such a man as every newspaper ought to have among its proprietors, in order to insure its prosperity. The friends of Mr. Coleman saw the importance of associating Mr. Burnham with him in the ownership of the paper, and negotiations were opened for the purpose. The result was, that the entire control of the finances of the *Evening Post* was placed in Mr. Burnham's hands, under such regulations as were prescribed in the articles of copartnership. From that time the affairs of the journal became prosperous; it began to yield a respectable revenue; Mr. Coleman was relieved from his pecuniary embarrassments, and Mr. Burnham began to grow rich. He died in the beginning of 1836, worth two hundred thousand dollars, acquired partly by his prudent management of the concerns of the paper, and partly by the rise in the value of real estate. Mr.

Coleman died in 1829, worth, perhaps, a quarter of that sum.

The *Evening Post*, until the close of the second war with Great Britain, was a prominent and leading journal of the federal party. It took its share in the heated discussions of the non-intercourse law, the embargo, and, finally, the justice of our war with Great Britain, and the wisdom with which it was managed. On the question of coöperating with the government in that war, the New York federalists differed with those of New England; they held that when the country was once engaged in a war, the citizen could not rightfully take any step to obstruct its prosecution, but must give the common cause his cheerful aid and support till peace should be made. When the New England States held their Convention at Hartford, the New York federalists refused to send delegates, and their refusal was sustained by the *Evening Post*. Mr. Coleman, however, went to Hartford on that occasion, as an observer. We recollect that, some years afterwards, in his journal, he taunted Theodore Dwight, then editor of the *Daily Advertiser*, in this city, with having been the Secretary of the Hartford Convention. Mr. Dwight replied that his accuser was also a participator in the doings of that body, and spoke of his presence there as the representative of the New York federalists. Against this imputation, Mr. Coleman defended himself with warmth, and in his usual frank and sincere manner stated very minutely the object and circumstances of his visit. From this narrative, his ingenious adversary, who would otherwise have had little to say, contrived, by a skillful selection of expressions and circumstances, to make out a plausible though by no means a fair case against him.

About the year 1819, the health of Mr. Coleman was seriously affected by a paralytic attack. Until then he had found no occasion for a coadjutor in his labors as an editor. Several slighter shocks followed; his lower limbs became gradually weak and unmanageable, until he was wholly unable to walk without support. Different assistants were called in from time to time, but they were again dismissed as soon as Mr. Coleman was able to be in his chair. It was while he was in this condition that an affair took place which was thought by his friends to have greatly impaired his health. A person named Hagerman, holding a public office, had been guilty of some improper conduct at one or two hotels in the interior of the State. The story was a nauseous one, but Mr. Coleman, thinking that such behavior deserved public exposure, gave it with all its particulars in his sheet. Hagerman was furiously enraged, and having no other answer to make, watched his opportunity, while Mr. Coleman was driving to his office in a little wagon, fell upon him with a cane, and beat him so severely that he was obliged to keep his room for a considerable time.

About this time it was said that a remedy had been discovered for the hydrophobia in the herb called skull-cap, a species of *scutellaria*, so named from the peculiar shape of its seed vessels, resembling a plain close-fitting cap for the head. The *Evening Post* took great pains to bring the subject before the public, collected examples of the virtues of the plant, and insisted on its efficacy so frequently and with such warmth as to occasion some jokes at its expense.

This period of the existence of the *Evening Post* was illuminated by the appearance of the poems of Halleck and Drake in its columns, under the signatures of Croaker, and Croaker & Co., in which the fashions and follies, and sometimes the politicians of the day, were made the subjects of a graceful and good-natured ridicule. The numbers containing these poems were eagerly sought for; the town laughed, the subjects of the satire laughed in chorus, and all thought them the best things of the kind that were ever written; nor were they far wrong. At a subsequent period within the last twenty-five years another poem, which, though under a different signature, might be called the epilogue to the Croakers, was contributed by Mr. Halleck to the paper. It was addressed to the Honorable Richard Riker, Recorder, better known as Dick Riker. This poem, with the marks of a riper intellect, is as witty as the best of the Croakers.

In the fusion of parties which took place after the second war with Great Britain, the *Evening Post* lost somewhat of its decided federal character. When a successor to Mr. Monroe was to be elected to the Presidency of the United States, the *Evening Post* supported the claims of Mr. Crawford. No choice, as our readers know, was made by the people, and the election devolved upon the House of Representatives, who conferred the office upon Mr. Adams.

It was in the year 1826, a quarter of a century from the first issue of the *Evening Post*, that William C. Bryant, now one of its conductors, began to write for its columns. At that time the population of New York had grown from sixty thousand, its enumeration in 1801, to a hundred and eighty thousand. The space covered with houses had extended a little beyond Canal Street, and on each side of Broadway a line of dwellings, with occasional vacant spaces, had crept up as far as Fourth Street. Preparations were making to take up the monuments in the Potter's field, now the site of Washington Square, and fill it up to the level of Fourth Street. Workmen were employed in opening the street now called St. Mark's Place, and a dusty avenue had just been made through the beautiful farm of the old Governor Stuyvesant, then possessed by his descendants. The sheet of the *Evening Post* had been somewhat enlarged, the number of its advertisements had been doubled since its first appearance, they were more densely printed, and two columns of them were steamboat advertisements. But the eye, in running over a sheet of the *Evening Post* printed at that time, misses the throng of announcements of public amusements, lectures, concerts, and galleries of pictures, that now solicit the reader's attention; the elaborately displayed advertisements of the rival booksellers, of whom there are now several houses, any one of which publishes yearly a greater number of works than all the booksellers of New York then did; the long lists of commercial agencies and expresses, and the perpendicular rows of cuts of ships, steamboats, and railway engines which now darken the pages of our daily sheet.

The *Evening Post* at that time was much occupied with matters of local interest, the sanitary condition of the city, the state of its streets, its police, its regulations of various kinds, in all which its conductors took great interest. There was little of personal controversy at that time in its columns.

The personal appearance of Mr. Coleman at that period of his life was remarkable. He was of a full make, with a broad chest, muscular arms, which he wielded lightly and easily, and a deep-toned voice; but his legs dangled like strings. He expressed himself in conversation with fluency, energy, and decision, particularly when any subject was started in which he had taken an interest in former years. When, however, he came at that period of his life to write for the press, he had the habit of altering his first draught in a manner to diminish its force, by expletives and qualifying expressions. He never altered to condense and strengthen, but almost always to dilute and weaken.

Immediately after Mr. Bryant became connected with the *Evening Post*, it began to agitate the question of free trade. The next year he became one of the proprietors of the paper. Mr. Coleman and Mr. Burnham, who desired to avail themselves of the activity and energy of younger minds, offered at the same time a share in the paper to Robert C. Sands, a man of wit and learning, whose memory is still tenderly cherished by numbers who had the good fortune to know him personally. He entertained it favorably at first, but finally declined it. A majority of both Houses of Congress were in favor of protective duties, and the *Evening Post*, at that time, was the only journal north of the Potomac which attempted to controvert them. In the northern part of the Union, it was only in certain towns on the seacoast that a few friends of a freer commercial system were found; the people of the interior of the Atlantic States and the entire population of the West seemed to acquiesce, without a scruple, in the policy of high duties. The question of modifying the tariff, so as to make it more highly protective, was brought up before Congress in the winter of 1828, and on the 19th of May following, a bill prepared for that purpose became a law. It was warmly opposed in the *Evening Post*, and the course of Mr. Webster, who had formerly spoken with great ability against protection, but who had now taken his place among its supporters, was animadverted upon with some severity. That gentleman, in a letter to Mr. Coleman, justified his conduct by saying that the protective system was now the established policy of the country, and that taking things as they were, he had only endeavored to make this system as perfect and as equally beneficial to every quarter of the Union as was possible.

In contending against the doctrine of protection, the *Evening Post* gradually fell into a position of hostility to the administration of Mr. Adams, by which that doctrine was zealously maintained. In the election of 1828, it took the field in favor of the nomination of General Jackson, who had declared himself in favor of a "judicious tariff," by which his friends understood a mitigation of the existing duties. Mr. Coleman lived to see the triumph of his party, and to hear the cheers of the exulting multitude at his door. In the summer following, the summer of 1829, he was cut off by an apoplectic stroke. William Leggett, who had earned a reputation for talent and industry by his conduct of the *Critic*, a weekly journal, several of the last numbers of which were written entirely by himself, put in type with his own hand, and delivered by himself to the subscribers, was immediately employed as an assistant editor. He only stipulated that he should not be asked to write articles on political subjects, on which he had no settled opinions, and for which he had no taste — a dispensation which was readily granted. Before this year was out, however, he found himself a zealous democrat, and an ardent friend of free trade, and in the year 1830 became one of the proprietors of the paper.

Mr. Leggett was a man of middle stature, but compact frame, great power of endurance, and a constitution naturally strong, though somewhat impaired by an attack of the yellow fever while on board the United States squadron in the West Indies. He was fond of study, and delighted to trace principles to their remotest consequences, whither he was always willing to follow them. The quality of courage existed in him almost to excess, and he took a sort of pleasure in bearding public opinion. He wrote with surprising fluency, and often with eloquence, took broad views of the questions that came before him, and possessed the faculty of rapidly arranging the arguments which occurred to him in clear order, and stating them persuasively.

The acts of General Jackson's administration brought up the question of the power of the federal government to make public roads within the limits of the different States, and the question of renewing the charter of the United States Bank. With what zeal he was supported by the *Evening Post*, in his disapproval of the works of " internal improvement," as they were called, sanctioned by Congress, and in his steady refusal to sign the bills presented to him for continuing the United States Bank in existence, many of our readers doubtless remember. The question of national roads, after some sharp controversy, was disposed of finally, perhaps, and forever ; the contest for the existence of the National Bank was longer and more stubborn, but the popular voice decided it, at last, in favor of the President.

The first sign of a disposition in the country to relax

the protective policy was given in General Jackson's administration, when the law of 1832, sometimes called the compromise tariff, was passed, providing for the gradual reduction of the duties, on all imported goods, to the rate of twenty per cent. on their value.   Mr. McLane, the Secretary of the Treasury, had proposed a somewhat reduced tariff, in his annual report, and Mr. Verplanck, in the House of Representatives, had introduced a bill on a still more liberal basis.   The compromise swept them both away ; but the compromise was welcomed by the friends of free trade in the Union, as indicative of a great revolution in public opinion, and as a virtual abandonment of the protective policy.   Since that time, the doctrines of commercial liberty, so early espoused by the *Evening Post,* have been making gradual progress, till they are professed by large majorities in many parts of the North, and have pervadad almost the entire West.

Those who recollect what occurred when General Jackson withdrew the funds of the government from the Bank of the United States, a measure known by the name of the removal of the deposits, cannot have forgotten to what a pitch party hatred was then carried. It was a sort of fury; nothing like it had been known in this community for twenty years. and there has been nothing like it since.   Men of different parties could hardly look at each other without gnashing their teeth ; deputations were sent to Congress to remonstrate with General Jackson, and some even talked — of course it was mere talk, but it showed the height of passion to which men were transported — of marching in arms to the seat of government and putting down the administration.   A brief panic took possession of the money market; many worthy men really believed that the business and trade of the country were in danger of coming to an end, and looked for a universal ruin. In this tempest the *Evening Post* stood its ground, vindicated the administration in its change of agents, on the ground that the United States Bank was unsafe and unworthy, and derided both the threats and the fears of the whigs.

In June, 1834, Mr. Bryant sailed for Europe, leaving Mr. Leggett sole conductor of the *Evening Post.* Mr. Burnham had previously withdrawn as a proprietor, substituting his son in his place. The battle between the friends and enemies of the Bank proceeded with little diminution of virulence, but the panic had passed away. The *Evening Post* was led by the discussion of the Bank question to inquire into the propriety of allowing the state banks to exist as monopolies, with peculiar powers and prerogatives not enjoyed by individuals. It demanded a general banking law, which should place on an equal footing every person desirous of engaging in the business of banking. It attacked the patronage of the federal executive, and insisted that the postmasters should be chosen by the people in the neighborhoods to which they ministered. A system of oppressive inspection laws had gradually grown up in the State, — tobacco was inspected, flour was inspected, beef and pork were inspected, and a swarm of creatures of the state government was called into being, who subsisted by fees exacted from those who bought and sold. Nobody was allowed to purchase an uninspected and untaxed barrel of flour, or an uninspected and untaxed plug of tobacco. The *Evening Post* renewed its attacks on the abuse, which had previously been denounced in its columns, and called for the entire abrogation of the whole code of inspection laws. The call was answered some years afterwards, when the subject was taken up in earnest by the legislature, and the system broken up.

Meantime, another question had arisen. The Washington *Telegraph* had procured printed reports of the Abolition Society, in New York, then a small body, and little known to the public, and extracting the most offensive passages, held them up to the people of the South as proofs of a deliberate design on the part of the North to deprive the planters of their slaves, without their consent and without remuneration. Other extracts followed from day to day, with similar inflammatory comments, till at length the Southern blood took fire, and the Southern merchants began to talk of ceasing to trade with New York. The New York commercial community disclaimed all sympathy with the abolitionists, and to prove its sincerity, began to disturb their meetings. From slight disturbances the transition was easy to frightful riots, and several of these, in which the genteel mob figured conspicuously, occurred in the year 1835, at different places within the State. The meetings of the abolitionists were broken up, their houses were mobbed, and Arthur Tappan was obliged, for a while, to leave the city, where his person was not safe. The *Evening Post* at first condemned the riots, and vindicated the right of assembling, and the right of speech. As the mob grew more lawless, it took bolder ground, and insisted that the evil and the wrong of slavery were so great that the abolitionists were worthy of praise and sympathy in striving for its extinction. It rang this doctrine from day to day in the ears of the rioters and their abettors, and confronted and defied their utmost malice. No offer was made, in the midst of all this excitement, to mob the office of this paper.

During Mr. Bryant's absence in Europe, the interest of the younger Burnham was purchased for his two associates, who thus became the sole proprietors.

In October, 1835, Mr. Leggett became seriously ill; he returned to his labors after a short interval; but a relapse came on, and confined him to a sick room for months. Mr. Bryant returned in the spring of 1836 from Europe, and found him still an invalid, the editorial chair being ably filled, for the time, by Charles Mason, since distinguished as a lawyer in Iowa. He resumed his labors, and engaged in the controversy respecting the state banks, which was then at its height, and which continued to agitate the community till the adoption of a general banking law by the State, and of the independent treasury scheme by the federal government.

In the month of June, 1836, an attempt was made in different parts of the State to compel journeymen to refrain from entering into any understanding with each other in regard to the wages they would demand of their employers. Twelve journeymen tailors were indicted in this city for the crime of refusing to work, except for a certain compensation, and a knot of journeymen shoemakers at Hudson. In this city, Judge Edwards, — Ogden Edwards, — and at Hudson, Judge Savage, laid down the law against the accused, pronouncing their conduct a criminal conspiracy, worthy of condign punishment. The *Evening Post* took up the charge of Judge Edwards almost as soon as it fell from his lips, and showed its inconsistency with the plainest principles of personal freedom, with the spirit of all our institutions and laws, and with the rule by which we allow all employers and purchasers to regulate their transactions. The other journals of the city took a different view of the question, but the doctrine maintained by the *Evening Post* commended itself to the public mind, and is now the prevailing and universal one.

In October of the same year, Mr. Leggett, after a sojourn of some months in the country, returned to his office with his health in part restored. His return led to an examination of the finances of the *Evening Post*, which had suffered very much during his illness. Its circulation, though lessened, was still respectable, but its advertising list was greatly diminished, and its income was not more than a quarter of what it had been. Some of its friends had been alienated by the vehemence with which the journal had attacked slavery and its defenders. The proprietors of steamboats and ships, and those who had houses to let, had withdrawn their advertisements, because no cuts, designed to attract the attention of the reader, were allowed a place in its columns. Mr. Leggett, with an idea of improving the appearance of his daily sheet, had rigidly excluded them.

This examination ended in the retirement of Mr. Leggett from the paper. He established a weekly sheet, the *Plaindealer*, which he conducted for about a year with great ability, and which, but for the failure of his publisher, would have been highly successful, as was evident from the rapid increase of its circulation so long as it was published.

About the close of the year, two passenger ships from Europe, the Mexico and the Bristol, were wrecked at the mouth of the New York harbor, covering the shore

with corpses. The *Evening Post* showed that this disaster arose from the negligence of the New York pilots,
who were unwisely allowed a monopoly of the business,
and joined with the mercantile community in demand-
ing such a change as should subject them to the wholesome influence of competition. The change was made
in the same winter.

We have mentioned the short panic of 1834. It was
followed by a season of extravagant confidence, and of
delirious speculation, encouraged by all the banks, —
that of Mr. Biddle and the deposit banks coöperating
in a mad rivalry, — a season such as the country had
never seen before. It might sound like a vain boast
of superior discernment to say that the *Evening Post*
insisted, all along, that the apparent prosperity of the
country was but temporary, that its end was close at
hand, and that it would be followed by a general collapse and by universal distress — but it is nevertheless
true, and as we are writing the history of our journal,
it must be said. The crash came quite as soon as the most
far-sighted had anticipated, and thousands were ruined ;
the banks stopped payment, and the Legislature of New
York, in a fright, passed a sort of stop law in their favor,
absolving them from the engagement to pay their notes
in specie.

It was shortly before this collapse, in the year 1837,
that Nathaniel P. Tallmadge, a senator in Congress,
from this State, gave the country his famous speech on
the credit system, the object of which was to justify the
practices of the banks at that time, and of those to
whom the banks furnished the means for their speculations. His eulogy of the credit system was attacked in
the *Evening Post ;* he replied in the tone of a man who

had been wronged ; he was answered ; his friends got up
a letter, signed by several hundred democrats, certify-
ing to the political orthodoxy of Mr. Tallmadge and his
credit system ; the *Evening Post* attacked both the letter
and its signers.   Mr. Tallmadge struggled a little while
longer to maintain his place in the democratic party,
and then sought a temporary refuge among the whigs.
At that time, the *Times*, a democratic morning paper,
in the interest of Mr. Tallmadge and his friends, was
published in the city.   The *Evening Post* had occasion
to allude to the men who made the *Times* their instrument.   The editor of the paper, one Dr. Holland, since
dead, who had some skill in turning a paragraph, wrote
a note to Mr. Bryant, informing him that he was the
proprietor of the newspaper, and that it spoke his opinions, and those of no one else, and demanded that justice should be done him in this respect.   He received
a reply with which he was not satisfied, and failing to
obtain any other, he sent a challenge to Mr. Bryant, by
a friend, who was authorized to make the due arrangements for the meeting.

It has already been seen how great, in the first years
of this journal, was the force of custom among a certain
class of the New York population in keeping up the
practice of dueling.   In the thirty years which had
since elapsed, it had grown obsolete, and even ridiculous.
Only very hare-brained young men, and sometimes offi-
cers of the navy, ever sent or accepted a challenge to
the field, and it no longer required any firmness to decline one.   Mr. Bryant treated the matter very lightly ;
he put the challenge in his pocket, and told the bearer
that everything must take its proper turn, that Dr.
Holland, having already been called a scoundrel by Mr.

APPENDIX. 335

Leggett, must give that affair the precedence, and that
for his own part, he should pay no further attention to
the matter in hand till that was settled. The affair
passed off without other consequences.

Meantime, no means were left untried to bring back
the paper to its former prosperous condition. William
G. Boggs, a practical printer, and a man of much activity, was taken into the concern, first with a contingent
interest, and, in 1837, as a proprietor. The figures of
steamboats, ships, and houses were restored to its columns, and nothing omitted which it was thought would
attract advertisers. They came with some shyness at
first, but at last readily and in great numbers. It required some time to arrest the decline of the paper, and
still more to make it move in the desired direction, but
when once it felt the impulse, it advanced rapidly to its
former prosperity.

The book press of the country, about this time, had
begun to pour forth cheap reprints of European publications with astonishing fertility. Few works but those
of English authors were read, inasmuch as the publisher, having nothing to pay for copyright to the foreign
author, could afford to sell an English work far cheaper
than an American one written with the same degree of
talent and attractiveness. The *Evening Post* was early
on the side of those who demanded that some remedy
should be applied to this unequal operation of our copyright laws, which had the effect of expelling the American author from the book market. It placed no stress,
however, on the scheme of an international copyright
law, as it has been called, but consistently with its course
on all commercial questions insisted that if literary property is to be recognized by our laws, it ought to be

recognized in all cities alike, without regard to the legislation of other countries; that the author who is not naturalized deserves to be protected in its enjoyment equally with the citizen of our republic, and that to possess ourselves of his books simply because he is a stranger is as gross an inhospitality as if we denied his right to his baggage, or the wares which he might bring from abroad to dispose of in our market.

The public mind, in the course of a short time, seemed to be perfectly prepared for a change in the copyright laws, abolishing any unequal distinctions in the right of property, founded on birth or citizenship. The publishers and booksellers, who had at first been unfavorable to the measure, were at length brought to give it their assent, but the members of Congress were not ready. They did not understand the question, nor did nine in ten of them care to understand it. No party purpose was to be served by studying it, or supporting any measure connected with it; no disadvantage was likely to arise to either party from neglecting it; and for this reason, more we believe than any other, the subject has been untouched by our legislators to this day. It is observed that politicians by profession are very apt to yawn whenever it is mentioned.

The dispute between the friends of the credit system, as they called themselves, and their adversaries continued till the scheme of making the government the keeper of its own funds, instead of placing them in the banks, to be made the basis of discounts, was adopted by Congress. For this measure, which is now very generally acknowledged by men of all parties to have been one of the wisest ever taken by the federal government, and perhaps more wholesome in its effect on the money market than any other adopted before or since, the country is indebted to Mr. Van Buren's administration, and to those who sustained it against the credit party. The *Evening Post* was one of the very earliest in the field among the champions of that scheme, and lent such aid as it was able in the controversy.

In 1840 it was engaged in the unsuccessful attempt to reëlect Mr. Van Buren. In the four years of that gentleman's administration, nearly all the disastrous consequences of the reaction from the speculations of the four previous years were concentrated. He and his friends applied what is now acknowledged to be the wisest remedy, the independent treasury scheme; but a sufficient time had not elapsed to experience its effects, and the friends of the credit system everywhere treated it as the most pernicious quackery. The administration of Mr. Van Buren was made responsible for consequences which 'it had no agency in producing, and General Harrison was elected to the Presidency.

We have now arrived at a period the history of which, we may presume, is so fresh in the memory of our readers that we need give no very circumstantial narrative of the part borne in the controversies of the time by the *Evening Post*. In this year, Parke Godwin, who for some time had been employed as an assistant on the paper, became one of its proprietors, and continued so until the year 1844, when the interest he held was transferred to Timothy A. Howe, a practical printer, who has ever since been one of the owners of the concern.

In the year 1841 the proprietors began to issue a *Weekly Evening Post*, the circulation of which has been regularly increasing to the present moment. A Semi-

Weekly had been issued from the earliest establishment
of the journal, and it is remarkable that the popularity
of the Weekly has seemed, of late, to attract subscrip-
tions to the Semi-Weekly also.

In 1841 the subject of abolishing the punishment of
death was brought up in the New York Legislature, by
Mr. O'Sullivan, who for that purpose had sought an
election to the House of Assembly as a delegate from
this city, and who prepared an excellent report giving a
full statement of the argument for its abolition.   In the
following winter he had several able coadjutors in this
cause, among whom was Major Auguste Davezac, who
had studied the question under the teachings of Edward
Livingston, and who, though a native of a French col-
ony, was one of the finest declaimers in English of his
time.   The *Evening Post* took a decided part in favor
of this change in the criminal law of the state, a change
which it has never since ceased on proper occasions to
urge, on the ground that in the present age there is no
longer any necessity to inflict the penalty of death, and
that experience has shown it to be less effectual in re-
straining the repetition of crimes than other modes of
punishment.   The legislature, at times, seemed half persuaded to try the effect of putting an end to the practice
of taking life by sentence of law, but it finally shrunk
from the responsibility of so important a step.

During the time that the Executive chair was filled
by Mr. Tyler — for General Harrison passed so soon
from his inauguration to his grave that his name will
scarcely be noticed in history — several of the questions
which formerly divided parties were revived.   The question of the independent treasury had to be debated over
again ; the measure was repealed.   The question of a

national bank came up again in Congress, and we had to fight the battle a second time; the bill for creating an institution of this kind presented to Mr. Tyler was refused his signature and defeated. Mr. Tyler, however, had a dream of a peculiar national bank of his own; this also was to be combatted. The compromise of 1832, in regard to duties on imported goods, was set aside by Congress, without ceremony, and a scheme of high duties was proposed which resulted in the tariff of 1842. Here, also, was matter for controversy. The question of admitting Texas into the Union, which had several times before been discussed in the *Evening Post*, was brought before Congress. It was warmly opposed in this journal, which contended that if Texas was to be admitted at all, a negotiation should first be opened with Mexico. This was not done, but the result has shown that such a course would have been far the wisest. The eager haste to snatch Texas into the Union brought with it the war with Mexico, the shedding of much blood, large conquests, California, and those dreadful quarrels about slavery and its extension which have shaken the Union.

It is unnecessary, we believe, to refer to the part taken by the *Evening Post* in behalf of the economical policy which in 1842 retrieved the credit of the State of New York, impaired by the large expenditures for public works; nor to its exertions in favor of such an alteration of the constitution, as should incorporate in the constitution of the State an effectual check upon further extravagances. That was soon done by the convention of 1848.

In 1848 Mr. Boggs parted with his interest in the *Evening Post* to John Bigelow; and William J. Tenney,

who had been for some time past the able and useful
assistant of Mr. Bryant, withdrew. The controversies
which have since arisen are yet the controversies of the
day ; they still occupy all minds, and there is no occasion to speak of their nature nor of the part we have
taken in them.

We have now brought our narrative down to the present moment. It does not become us to close without
some expression of the kindly feeling we entertain towards those subscribers — for there are still a few of
them — who read the *Evening Post* in 1801, and who
yet read it, nor to those — and there are many such —
in whose families it is looked upon as a sort of heir-
loom, and who have received a partiality for it as an inheritance from their parents. When these examples
occur to our minds, we are consoled for the occasional
displeasure and estrangement of those we had deemed
our friends ; and we think of our journal as of something
solid, permanent, enduring.

This impression is strengthened when we reflect that
in the mechanical department of the paper are men who
came to it in their childhood, before any of the present
proprietors of the paper had set foot within the office,
and are employed here still, — worthy, industrious, and
intelligent men.

An experience of a quarter of a century in the conduct of a newspaper should suffice to give one a pretty
complete idea of the effect of journalism upon the character. It is a vocation which gives an insight into
men's motives, and reveals by what influences masses of
men are moved, but it shows the dark rather than the
bright side of human nature, and one who is not disposed to make due allowances for the peculiar circum-

stances in which he is placed is apt to be led by it into the mistake that the large majority of mankind are knaves. It brings one perpetually in sight, at least, of men of various classes, who make public zeal a cover for private interest, and desire to avail themselves of the influence of the press for the prosecution of their own selfish projects. It fills the mind with a variety of knowledge relating to the events of the day, but that knowledge is apt to be superficial, since the necessity of attending to many subjects prevents the journalist from thoroughly investigating any. In this way it begets desultory habits of thought, disposing the mind to be satisfied with mere glances at difficult questions, and to dwell only upon plausible commonplaces. The style gains by it in clearness and fluency, but it is apt to become, in consequence of much and hasty writing, loose, diffuse, and stuffed with local barbarisms and the cant phrases of the day. Its worst effect is the strong temptation which it sets before men, to betray the cause of truth to public opinion, and to fall in with what are supposed to be the views held by a contemporaneous majority, which are sometimes perfectly right and some-times grossly wrong.

To such temptations we hope the *Evening Post*, whatever may have been its course in other respects, has not often yielded. Its success and the limits to its success may both, perhaps, be owing to this unaccom-modating and insubservient quality. It is often called upon, by a sense of duty, to oppose itself to the general feeling of those from whom a commercial paper always must receive its support; it never hesitates to do so. It sometimes finds a powerful member of that community occupied with projects which it deems mischievous; it puts itself in his way, and frustrates his designs, if possible. In this way it makes bitter enemies, who would break it down if they could; it makes also warm friends, by whom it is cordially supported. Its proprietors are satisfied with its success and its expectations. For the last quarter of a century it has been the only democratic paper which could subsist in New York. Others have come and departed like shadows. It is now well appointed in all its departments, and has as fair a prospect of surviving to another century as it had at any time during the last fifty years of subsisting to this day.

APPENDIX B.

I, WILLIAM CULLEN BRYANT, of Roslyn, in Queens County, Long Island, do make this my last will and testament.

1. I give to my daughter Fanny Bryant Godwin the house and land in Roslyn east of the highway where she now lives with her family, with all the houses and other buildings thereon.

2. Also a strip of land west of the said highway two rods in width, to be taken from the land now occupied by me at said Roslyn, and to extend from the highway to the water of Roslyn harbor as far as I own.

3. Also all the land and buildings adjoining the premises now occupied by my said daughter Fanny bought by me of Stephen Smith. Also all the Mudge Farm owned by me, including the land and buildings now occupied under a lease by Amy Mudge and her two nieces.

4. Also all my lands and buildings in Roslyn west of the highway and south of the fence, which forms the southern boundary of the premises now occupied by W. D. Wilson and of the road leading to his house.

5. Also the little piece of land east of said highway and the last mentioned lands and buildings bought by me of Isaac Henderson.

6. I also give her one half of all my government

bonds and government securities of whatever nature, subject, however, to charges hereinafter mentioned.

I also except from the Mudge Farm bequeathed to the said Fanny four acres hereinafter mentioned on the northeast corner of said farm.

7. Moreover I give to my said daughter Fanny the Snell Farm in Cummington, purchased by me of a Mr. Ellis, with all the buildings thereon and a right of way thereto by a road now made, but reserving from this bequest the use of certain springs on the northeast corner of the farm now used by me on the Bryant Homestead.

1. I give to my second daughter Julia Sands Bryant all my real estate in Roslyn not devised to the other daughter, including the dwelling-houses, and buildings now occupied by George B. Cline and W. D. Wilson — a tract of land extending from the highway near the shore to the highway passing by the Roslyn Cemetery.

2. I give also to my said daughter Julia all my books, pictures, engravings, furniture, and other movables, animals, carriages, farming implements, and my crops gathered or on the fields on whatsoever part of my real estate at Roslyn they may be.

3. I also give her all my real estate in the city of New York.

4. Also all my real estate in the State of Illinois.

5. Also the farm and buildings in Cummington called the Bryant Homestead, with the use of the springs in the northeastern corner of the Snell Farm as said springs are now used.

6. Also all my furniture, books, pictures, and other movables of every kind at the Bryant Homestead afore-

said, and at Number 24 West Sixteenth Street in the city of New York.

7. Also one half of my government bonds and government securities of whatever nature, subject to charges hereinafter mentioned.

1. I give to my two daughters already named all my right, title, and interest in the *Evening Post* newspaper establishment and job printing office, and all the personal property appertaining, and debts due to the same, to be possessed by them in such a manner that each shall have, together with what interest therein she may possess before my death, an equal share with the other. And this they are to take subject to any indebtedness which may appear against me on the books of the *Evening Post*, and subject also to any charges hereinafter mentioned.

2. I also give my said two daughters jointly all my property in the copyright of any of my published writings.

1. I give to George B. Cline, of Roslyn aforesaid, four acres of land in the northeastern corner of the Mudge Farm in one quadrangular parcel at the intersection of the two highways, to be set off to him in such a manner that the width of two acres shall be on each highway.

2. I also bequeath to the said Cline eight thousand dollars, to be paid out of the profits of the *Evening Post* if any be due me on the books, and if not, then out of the government bonds and securities aforementioned.

1. I bequeath to William Bryant Cline, son of the said George B. Cline, two hundred dollars, to be paid out of the same funds.

If either of my daughters should die without children, I direct that whatever she is to receive by this instrument shall go to her surviving sister. I direct further that the property given to my daughters shall be settled upon them in such a manner as to be free from any intermeddling or control of the husband of either of them.

In case that I should survive both of my daughters and their children and direct descendants, I direct that my estate, after paying the legacies to other persons, shall be divided among my nephews and nieces and the nephews and nieces of my late wife Fanny Fairchild Bryant, each of them to receive an equal share with the exception that Mrs. Ellen T. Mitchell, daughter of my sister Sarah, and Mrs. Hannah H. Culver, daughter of my wife's sister Esther Henderson, and Anna R. Fairchild, daughter of my wife's brother Egbert N. Fairchild, shall receive each a share twice as large as the shares of the others.

Should I die possessed of any property not herein specified, I direct it to be equally divided between my two daughters, or if that cannot be done, then I direct that it follow the disposition of the other property made by this will.

I give to each of my grandchildren living at my death a copy of my poems of such edition as they may choose.

I empower my executors to convey my real estate by deed whenever it shall become necessary or expedient.

I constitute my friends John A. Graham, John Bigelow, John H. Platt, George B. Cline, and my daughter Julia S. Bryant executors of this my last will and testament.

I revoke all my previous wills and codicils.

In testimony whereof I have hereunto set my hand and seal this sixth day of December in the year one thousand eight hundred and seventy-two.

WM. CULLEN BRYANT.

Signed, sealed, and published by the testator, etc., etc.

ISAAC HENDERSON, 18 West 54th St , N. Y.
ALBERT H. KING, 563 Willoughby Ave., Br.
ISAAC HENDERSON, JR., 18 West 54th St., N. Y.

INDEX.

A noted writer and diplomat, JOHN BIGELOW (1817-1911) was also a close friend and colleague of Bryant's. From 1848 to 1861 he was co-editor and co-owner with Bryant of the *New York Evening Post*. Bigelow then went abroad to serve first as U.S. consul general at Paris and later as U.S. minister to France. In addition to writing Bryant's biography, he edited Benjamin Franklin's *Autobiography* and authored studies of Franklin and Samuel J. Tilden.

JOHN HOLLANDER is Professor of English at Yale University. He is the author of several books of poetry, most recently *Blue Wine* and *Spectral Emanations*, and of a forthcoming critical study, *The Figure of Echo*.